CW00447729

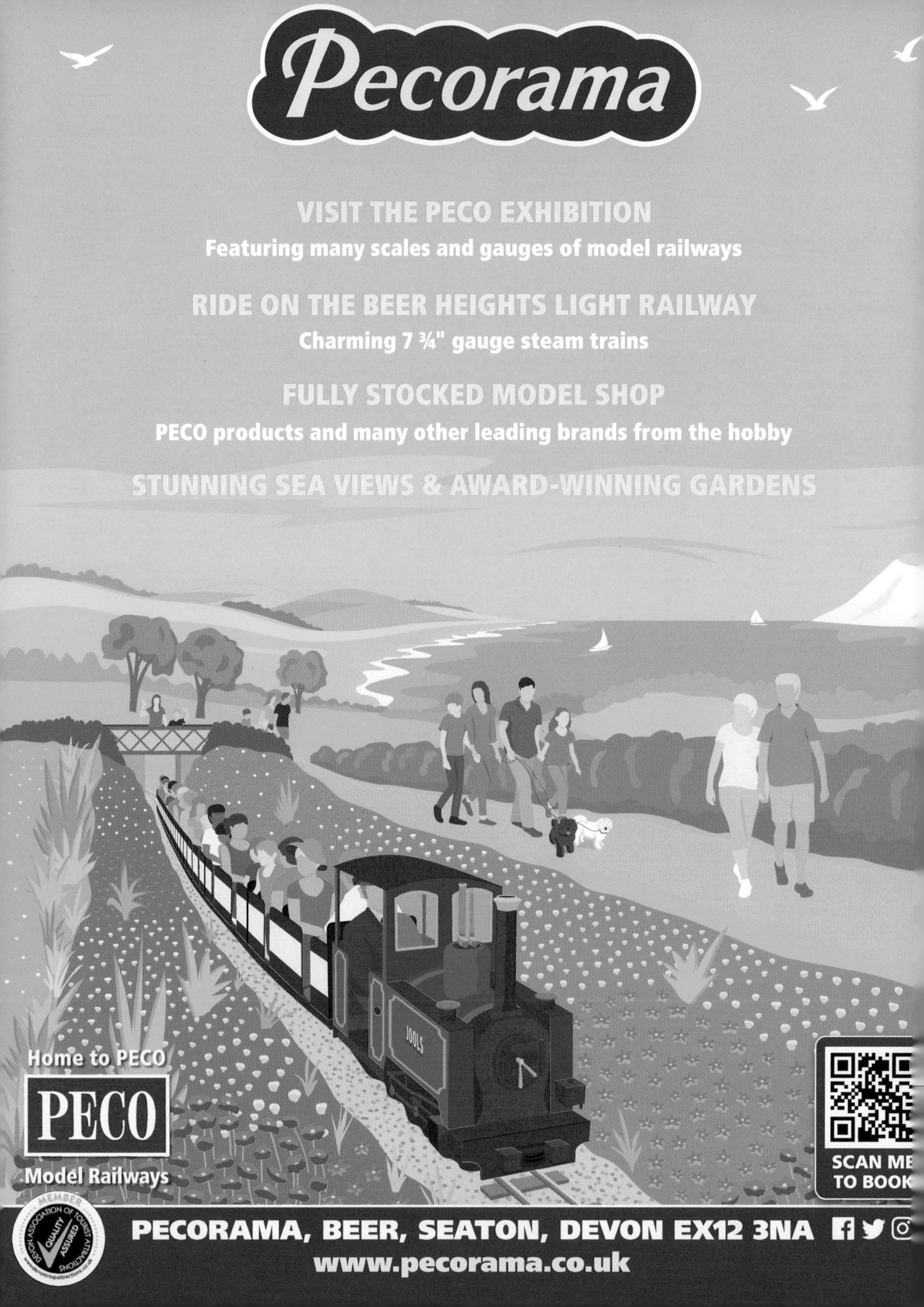
Pecorama
VISIT THE PECO EXHIBITION
Featuring many scales and gauges of model railways
RIDE ON THE BEER HEIGHTS LIGHT RAILWAY
Charming 7 ¾" gauge steam trains
FULLY STOCKED MODEL SHOP
PECO products and many other leading brands from the hobby
STUNNING SEA VIEWS & AWARD-WINNING GARDENS
JOOLS
Home to PECO
PECO
Model Railways
SCAN ME
TO BOOK
MEMBER
DEVON ASSOCIATION OF TOURIST ATTRACTIONS
QUALITY ASSURED
PECORAMA, BEER, SEATON, DEVON EX12 3NA
www.pecorama.co.uk

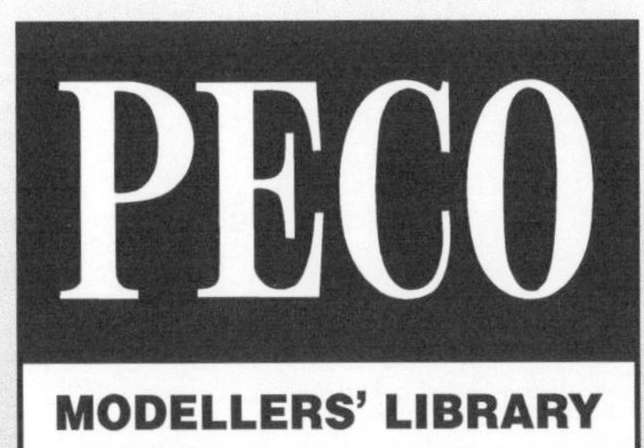

Your Guide to RAILWAY MODELLING & LAYOUT CONSTRUCTION

Welcome to the wonderful hobby of railway modelling: a creative leisure activity that can, and does for many, last an entire lifetime. I first came into the hobby in the late 1960s, having been amazed by a model railway description published in RAILWAY MODELLER. The article described a miniature replica of a long closed branch line terminus set amidst finely detailed model scenery and buildings. It was called Coalport, described by R J Harvey, who had built it as a true historical represen-tation of an actual LNWR station, showing how passenger and goods trains looked and operated in Edwardian times.

Prior to this discovery, my contact with railway layouts, and model making in general, had been through childhood trainsets and the Airfix range of plastic assembly kits; all interesting and fun in their own right, but none had the captivating appeal of that authentic model of Coalport which had the power to transport me back in time to the heyday of Britain's steam railways.

Since then I have become thoroughly engrossed in a hobby which is absorbing, interesting and fulfilling in many ways: it's a pastime I would recommend to anyone seeking to be creative with their hands and find an outlet for artistic or practical talents.

Moreover, in becoming involved yourself, you can take an easy and relaxing pathway, or one as complex and intensive as you wish: indeed as you take your first steps, you will soon find that there is a monumental diversity of amazing model railway products from which to choose.

It can be all very bewildering in the beginning, and lots of questions will be thrown up; which scale and gauge should I use? Branch terminus or main line? What control system should I adopt? Is a static grass applicator easy to use?

This book is designed to help you answer some of those questions, and allow you to discover a pathway through the hobby which most suits your personal skills and aspirations. It is divided into three sections; Introduction, Practical Guidance and Skills Workshop. The Introduction gives a brief overview of the hobby today, and explains some of the key choices you will need to make before you begin. The second section demonstrates some of the many tried and trusted methods in which the various elements of a model railway layout are constructed; it considers initial planning and design of a layout, base-board construction, track laying, controllers and layout wiring, scenery construction and backscenes. The third section is all about acquiring some of the practical skills you will need to help you build your railway, examining some of the modelling materials, tools and methods estab-lished railway modellers use everyday; such as working with cardboard, plasticard, metal, etc., or how to build plastic kits.

Although not an encyclopaedic treatise covering absolutely everything there is to know about model railways in the 21st century, it will give you an excellent 'apprenticeship' in the hobby: one from which you can move onto more advanced projects and techniques when you are ready.

So yes, welcome to this most wonderful hobby; one in which you can develop many practical and artistic skills and in turn, create fine models with your own hands. An activity which I believe is a refreshing and fulfilling antidote from the trappings of the modern world: instead of having all our creative output stored as digital files some-where on virtual 'cloud', we can get out into the real world and build something of which each and everyone of us can be justly proud.

Let's go railway modelling!

Steve Flint
Editor

Below
The Great Western Railway is a popular choice for many railway modellers, and there's ample trade support. *Hadley Road* was built in 7mm scale by Paul Jones.

Contents

Your guide to building a model railway

Planning

Scales and gauges

Track types

Baseboards

Baseboard types

Baseboard building

Scenery

Basic landscaping

Scenic top layer

Controls

Speed controllers

Two-rail wiring

Tutorials

Working with card

Working with plastic

How to use this book

To help you navigate this book our contents page has been arranged under construction topic headings, rather than in a chapter by chapter format. This way you can dip in and out of its pages as you progress with your layout building project.

Trackwork

Some recent developments in the hobby

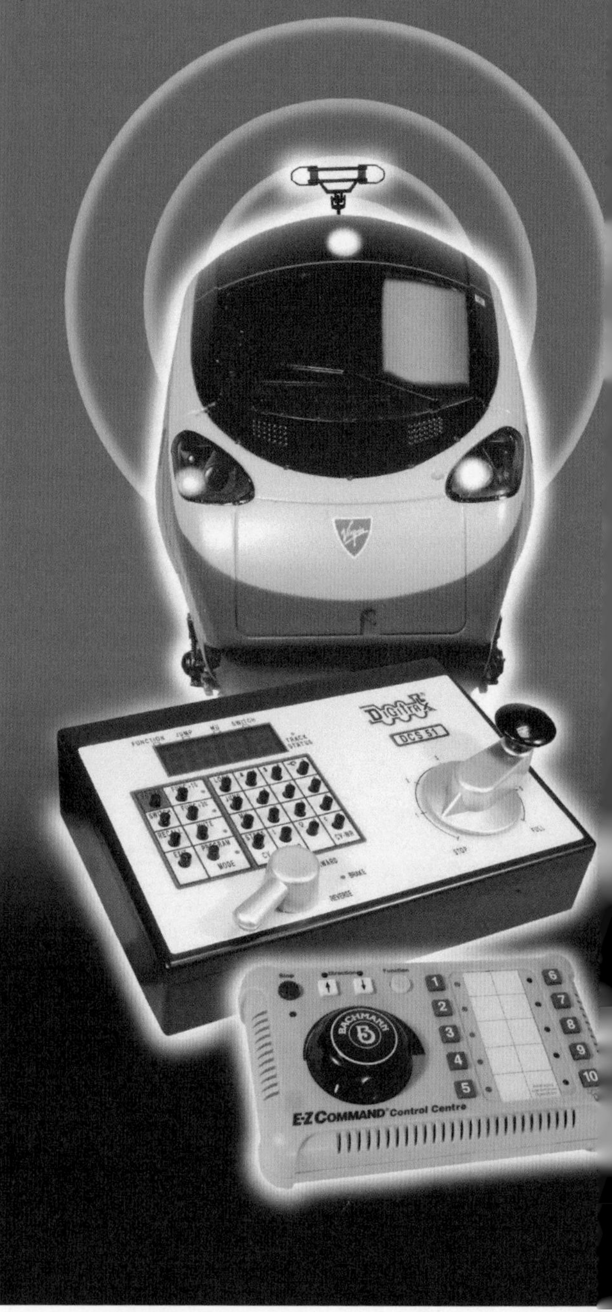

Many who recently return to the fold, after firstly discovering railway modelling in their teens, only to leave it aside whilst developing a career, getting married and bringing up a family, find that there has been some radical and significant, but truly exciting, developments in the hobby since they were last involved many years ago.

Perhaps the most fundamental change is in the way we operate our railways. It used to be that layouts were powered by large chunky speed control units which provided a variable voltage to the tracks: the higher the voltage the faster the locos ran, and if you wanted to operate more than one train on your set up, you had to divide the track up into individual electrical sections each controlled by a separate switch. Not any more. Over the last 15 or so years, model railway control, like everything else has gone digital. DCC (Digital Command Control) is now embraced by about half of the enthusiast fraternity, and offers many new dimensions to the model railway control experience. Firstly it brings sound and lighting effects to the layout, but more significantly it can simplify layout wiring and enable the user to link-up his or her railway to a computer or mobile device, and programme and control locomotives through touch-screen technology. All this is streets away from how our parents and grandparents ran their model railways, and although it is seen as the way forward for many, traditional 12V dc control systems are still available for those who find the marvels of digital control just a little bit complicated and intimidating. So, by all means marvel at the opportunities DCC can offer the layout builder, but don't be put off by others telling you that it is the only way forward: it isn't, modellers still have a choice

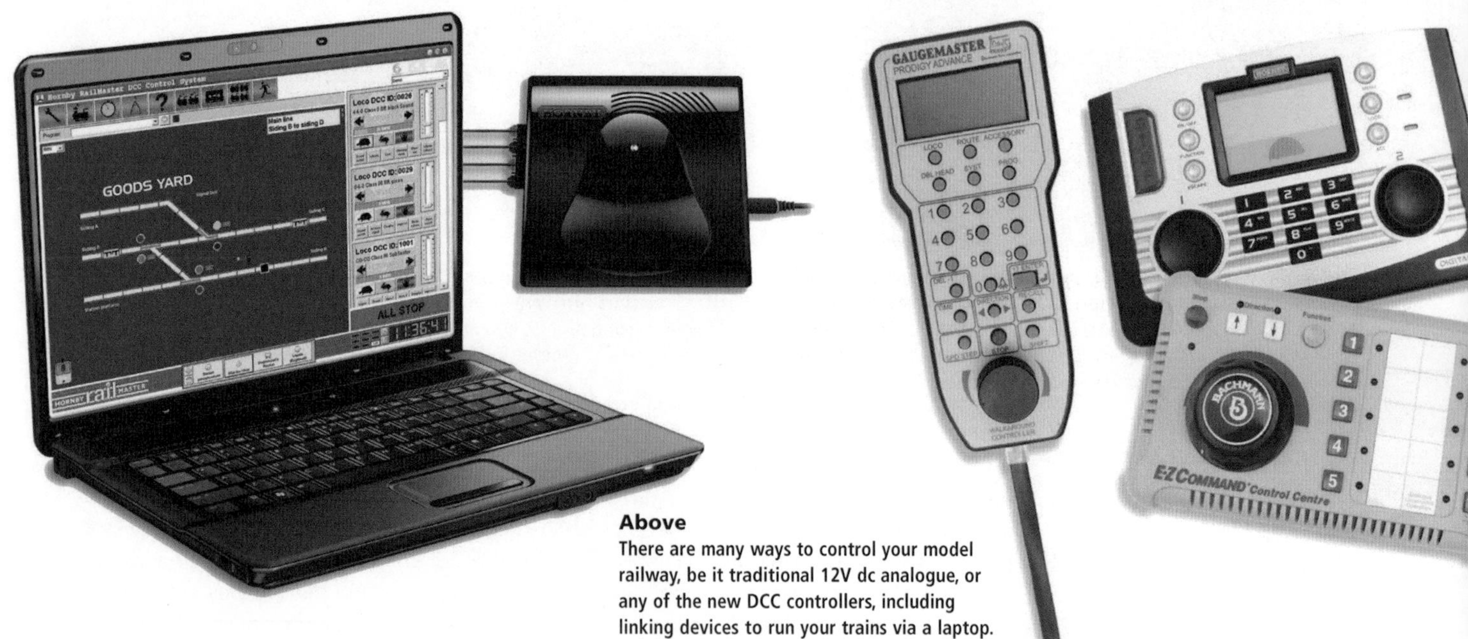

Above
There are many ways to control your model railway, be it traditional 12V dc analogue, or any of the new DCC controllers, including linking devices to run your trains via a laptop.

in how they control their trains, and you will find on page 10 some guidance notes on the topic to help you to decide for yourself.

The second major development in the hobby in recent times has been the rapid rise in the availability of highly detailed ready-to-run models, mostly in OO gauge and N gauge, but more recently in 7mm O gauge and OO9 narrow gauge. This has been down to many diverse factors, though it is probably improvements in manufacturing techniques that has had the most profound effect, bringing us intricate moulded details, finer standard wheels, vastly improved drive mechanisms and much more. New technology in manufacturing has also enabled the development of many new products as short-runs, such as cast resin buildings, laser cut kits in card, plastic or wood, and 3D 'printed' scenic items and loco parts. Enthusiasts, to quote a former Prime Minister, have never had it so good! And yet, there are still modellers who like to make as much as they can themselves, true scratch-builders who use traditional materials and techniques to create their own individual and unique models.

Getting involved in the hobby is now more than ever about choice: choosing the scale in which to model, which control system to adopt, whether to buy everything off the shelf or learn some new skills and make a lot yourself. As we mentioned previously, the aim of this book is to help you make those choices yourself and find your own route through the bewildering array that today is railway modelling.

Above
In just 20 years or so, models have gone from 'pancake' motors, traction tyres on deep-flange wheels and obtrusive couplers to fine detail, all-wheel drive, easy DCC compatibility and more. 'Westerns' in OO from Dapol (front) and Lima.

Above
Modern production techniques allow the most elaborate of pre-Grouping liveries to be applied to a model efficiently and economically. Who would have thought that a humble 0-6-0 goods engine, such as this SECR C Class model by Bachmann, could look so good?

Choosing the models which are right for you

If you have joined the ranks of this hobby through visiting a model railway exhibition, or reading a magazine such as Railway Modeller, or you are rediscovering the hobby after a long period of absence, you will probably be a little bowled over at the enormous diversity that you have discovered – or rediscovered – and wondering where to start. Individuals have all sorts of different needs and expectations from the hobby, and seek different outcomes too, so prescribing a specific starting point, and a specific pathway to follow, is not obvious for the writers of this guidebook.

Now you could read this book cover to cover, from front to back, in the old fashioned way, but as it has been assembled in the form of a reference book, you may prefer to dip into it from time to time, to find help on a specific topic. Accordingly, as well as a conventional index at the back of the book, the contents section on pages 12 and 13 are laid out in a flow chart format which will, depending on what you want to achieve, or what skill you want to learn, guide you to the specific topic about which you are seeking information.

Firstly however, let's consider the key choices you will need to make at the initial stages.

Scale and gauge

Model trains come in a variety of physical sizes, and virtually all are built to what we call 'scale'. In other words a scale model is one constructed to a size which is at a constant ratio to the real thing.

For instance, OO gauge models in the UK are built to a ratio of 1:76 – they are $^1/_{76}$th the size of the real thing –

Left
BR 'Deltic' locomotives showing comparison of gauges, from left; N (Graham Farish), OO (Bachmann) and O (Heljan).

The popular gauges

British N gauge

Built to a scale of 2 1/16mm:1ft, N gauge uses a track gauge of 9mm and a scale ratio of 1:148. Bachmann and Dapol offer extensive ranges of ready-to-run stock and can be used in conjunction with the extensive track range manufactured by Peco.

Broadly speaking, N gauge models are priced similar to (and sometimes slightly more than) OO gauge equivalents and therefore the advantage of N is primarily the ability to fit more in an available space; it is half the scale which means the same model occupies only a quarter of the space.

OO gauge

Built to a scale of 4mm:1ft, OO gauge uses a track gauge of 16.5mm and a scale ratio of 1:76. It has long been established as the most popular gauge for those modelling British outline subjects.
OO gauge has been very well supported by the trade throughout its existence. Current major manufacturers offering a range of British outline models include Hornby, Bachmann, Heljan and Dapol. Peco offers an extensive range of trackwork components.

In terms of lineside accessories and kits, there is a huge choice of products available for 4mm scale, making it perhaps the most accessible for new modellers.

O gauge

Built to a scale of 7mm:1ft, O gauge uses a track gauge of 32mm and a scale ratio of 1:43.5. Historically, O gauge pre-dates OO and N and its height of popularity occurred in the first half of the 20th century.

In recent years however, British O has seen something of a revival as a result of a wave of ready-to-run models that have been produced. Only a few years ago, O gauge was the preserve of the kitbuilder or scratchbuilder with almost nothing available in ready-to-run form. Although the ranges of models currently available 'off the shelf' are not as extensive as those for OO and N, the market is well served by the likes of Heljan, Lionheart Trains, Tower Brass and Dapol, with a range of R-T-R models, which is being added to all the time.

Together with a suitable track system available from Peco, there is little reason why O gauge should not be considered on an equal footing to OO and N. Although prices of individual models can be expensive, a small layout only needs a couple of locomotives and a few items of rolling stock, and therefore the overall cost could be no more – if not less – than a more extensive N or OO gauge system occupying the same amount of space

N

Peco code 55 track and R-T-R stock (from Dapol and Bachmann) are used on Simon Addelsee's *Polpendra* layout. The layout featured in the December 2011 RM.

OO

Roger Nicholls' *Millfield Road* utilises items from the Peco code 100 flexible track range. The layout was featured in the May 2012 RM.

O

A Lionheart R-T-R 54xx 0-6-0PT operates a push-pull working on Paul Jones' *Hadley Road*. An article on this layout was published in the December 2010 RM.

likewise N gauge models are built to a ratio of 1:148 ($^{1}/_{148}$th the size of the real thing) and O gauge to a nominal ratio of 1:43 ($^{1}/_{43}$rd the size of the prototype). In addition to the size ratio, modellers also define scale by equating the full size measurement units to the equivalent model measurement units, such that the OO gauge ratio of 1:76 could be written as $^{79}/_{500}$"=1ft. Normally however, for historical reasons, a mix of metric and imperial units is used; hence 1:76 is much more commonly known by the nominal scale of 4mm=1ft., and so on for all other scales.

All this might sound rather technical, but the size/scale of your chosen models will impinge on the sort of layout space you require in the home and the amount of money you will have to spend to achieve your goals, so it is important at the outset to make the right choice of scale.

Whilst the popular scales in the UK are OO (4mm=1ft), N (2.06mm=1ft) and O (7mm=1ft), there are numerous others; some to the same scale but including different sets of wheel and track gauge standards; and those representing narrow or broad gauge railways. An important factor which will influence your ultimate choice of scale and gauge as a beginner, is likely to be the availability of ready-to-run locos and stock – unless of course you want to build these yourself from kits or scratch at the outset.

Choice of track

In addition to rolling stock, you will also need to choose whether you want to use sectional clip-together track, or flexible track which has to be cut to length to suit, or indeed track which you want to make yourself. Beginners usually select the clip-together systems to get them started, but to help you decide, the adjacent panel 'Setrack or flexible track?' gives an overview on the two main types available commercially.

Below
Black Sheep Lane **by Ian Arkley is a good example of how a combination of sectional and flexible track can result in an attractive model in a small space. The scale is N.**

Setrack or flexible track?

Sectional track

This clip-together rigid track system is ideal for the beginner, or for those who want to lay track instantly, because cutting and bending is not necessary. The Peco OO Setrack range includes five different lengths of straight track, four different radius curves, left-hand and right-hand points, together with a diamond crossing for use when tracks need to cross each other.

Individual track sections and Setrack packs are available, all of which are compatible with the sectional track supplied in train sets manufactured by companies such as Hornby and Bachmann.

For any design of layout the minimum desirable radius will have to be determined. Generally, the larger the radius the better, but this is likely to be a compromise based on fitting everything into the available space. As a rough guide, most OO proprietary stock will negotiate 15" radius curves, whilst in N gauge it is 9".

The key benefits of sectional track are that it can be assembled quickly (preferred by the younger modeller who is eager to run trains!) and the point polarity is switched automatically, so no extra wiring is needed.

Accessories in the Setrack range (such as level crossings) can be installed simply by clipping in place between adjoining sections of track. The Setrack items are also fully complementary to flexible track so if in the future you decide to progress to the latter track type, the investment in Setrack will not be wasted.

Flexible track

Essentially, flexible track allows for a more realistic appearance; in particular the modelling of gentler, flowing curves whilst also facilitating the construction of complex track formations. Points in the Streamline range are supplied ready to use like those in the Setrack range and are usually pre-wired to switch the polarity to the correct direction automatically.

Flexible plain track sections (as per the Peco Streamline ranges) can be laid to varying radii but need to be cut to the exact lengths, which consequently requires a greater level of skill and dexterity than laying sectional track.

For OO, the Setrack range is only available in code 100 form, but Peco flexible track is available in both code 100 (ie matching Setrack rail height) and code 75; the latter has a much finer rail section but is compatible with the majority of modern R-T-R models. Rail section is measured in thousandths of an inch; thus code 75 (0.075") has a finer rail section than code 100 (0.100").

Similarly, for N, Peco offers a flexible track system in both code 80 (as per the Setrack range) and code 55. As with OO, the latter (finer) rail section is suitable for modern N gauge R-T-R models.

If you are a newcomer to the hobby, the required techniques for laying flexible track can be quickly mastered. Laying Streamline flexible track is described in detail on pages 26-25. The methods described are equally suited to flexible track systems in other scales. Tracksetta templates can be used to get the correct radius and ensure the formation of smooth curves. Six-foot way gauges (such as those made by Peco) are useful for laying double track sections accurately to the correct spacing.

Sectional and flexible plain track is offered by Peco for O gauge, along with a selection of Streamline points, crossing and double slip.

A small selection of the items available in the Peco code 100 Setrack range.

Tracksetta templates are useful – but not essential – tools when forming curves with flexible track.

Peco Streamline flexible track enables the forming of realistic, flowing curves, as illustrated here in N, OO and O gauges respectively.

Analogue or digital?

Analogue control

The traditional and long established method of model railway locomotive operation uses a variable 12V dc speed controller. This provides a variable voltage between 0V and 12V to the track, which changes the current passing through the motor and thus alters the speed of the locomotive. The general principle applies to the majority of model railway scales and gauges.

Two-rail wiring comprises an electrical connection to each running rail (a 'feed' and a 'return'). A simple oval can be wired with just these connections, however if the layout is more complex then separate electrical sections in the track are required.

In order to provide a layout with a 0-12V dc control voltage, three items are needed; a transformer to convert domestic mains voltage from 240V ac to 16V ac, a rectifier to change the 16V ac to 12V dc, and a means of varying the dc output voltage.

Proprietary controllers, like those supplied in train sets, are usually fully integral units which come complete with the transformer, rectifier and electronic speed controller all pre-wired and safely enclosed in a sturdy casing. Transformer/rectifier units and separate hand held speed controllers are available from manufacturers such as Gaugemaster.

Analogue control can prove to be more cost effective than DCC, but it does depend on what you want from your model railway: If you intend on modelling a simple setup with only one or two locomotives in operation at any one time, then analogue could be the most suitable approach, especially if various gimmicks of DCC operation (lights, sound and multiple locomotive operation) are outside your interest.

The locomotive and analogue controller from a Hornby OO gauge 'Flying Scotsman' train set.

Choice of control system

Earlier we mentioned the advent of digital control systems for model railways (DCC). This now gives you the choice of adopting it from the start, or selecting traditional 12V dc control (now popularly known as analogue). In theory, all sizes (scales) and types of trains can be controlled by either method, but there are many practical issues to contend with when installing one or the other.

The topic is vast, both systems have their devotees and advocates, and an awful lot of opinion can be found on the internet and elsewhere, so choosing can be difficult. The panel 'Analogue or digital?' gives an overview of the alternative systems to help you reach a decision. Bear in mind however that you can change over at any time, and there's always new and exciting developments taking place with both; such as using a computer, tablet PC, or mobile phone to control your trains, rather than a conventional speed controller.

Left

In order to allow a locomotive to be operated digitally, a decoder must be fitted to the socket with which most modern models' chassis are supplied (termed 'DCC Ready'). Often the manufacturer will sell locomotives factory-fitted with a decoder; look for a box labelled 'DCC On Board'.

Digital Command Control

This alternative control system exploits the benefits of modern digital technology. Different DCC systems and products are offered by a number of manufacturers, but the underlying principle of the technology is common to all of them: all the track on a layout is permanently 'live' with a continuous 14.5v-16v (depending on the manufacturer) supply provided by just the 'feed' and 'return' wires. Each locomotive is then independently controlled by an onboard electronic chip which receives its 'instructions' via digital signals transmitted along the track. Points and signals can also be controlled by the same centralised system. If a layout is built from the outset with DCC operation in mind, the amount of wiring can be reduced, although not eliminated completely.

If you are a young person coming into the hobby, you are likely to have a suitable level of confidence with digital technology to be able to embrace the operating potential that DCC offers. The cost element should be considered carefully though; the capabilities of DCC operation are suited to large systems with a large number of locomotives, the flip side of which is the increased cost of fitting decoders to so many locomotives.

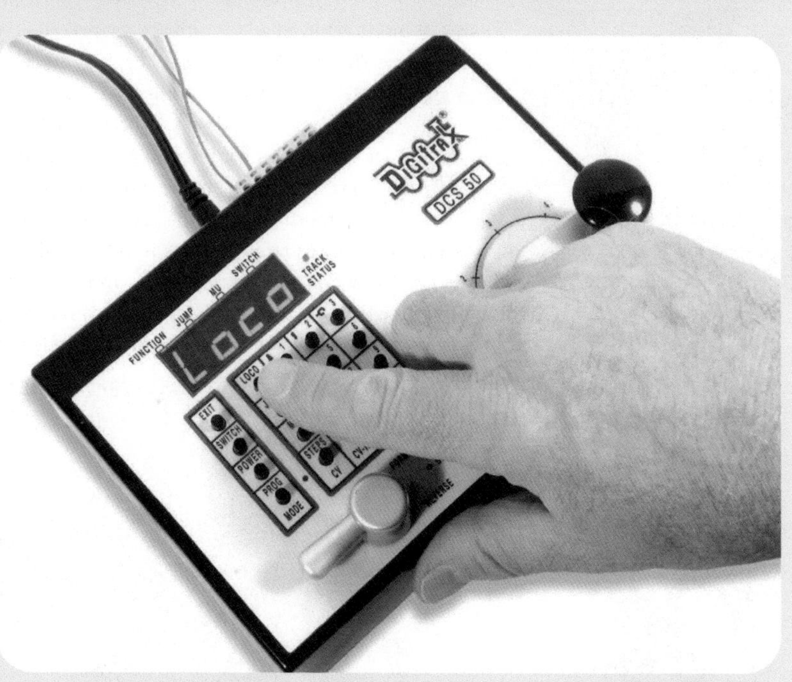

The new look of digital control means that all locomotives, points and other accessories are controlled by keying in specific address numbers for each item.

Multiple choice...

As you can see from the above, there is a lot to contend with, and you may feel a little perplexed. Remember though, most modellers usually come into the hobby through the ready-to-run route, either by choice or default anyway, many having faced much the same issues before moving onto greater things. The attached table details the popular scales and gauges and gives an overview of the sort of commercial support that is available for each. Once you have made your choice, the rest of the book will help you to build your very first layout and set you on the path to a lifetime of creative and fulfilling modelmaking.

		British outline R-T-R		Peco track system		Control system			
Gauge	**Scale**	**Locos**	**Stock**	**Sectional track**	**Flexible track**	**DCC**	**12V dc**	**Indoor/Outdoor**	**Comments**
OO	4mm=1ft	Yes	Yes	Yes	Yes	Yes	Yes	Both	Most popular in the UK
HO	3.5mm=1ft	No	No	Yes	Yes	Yes	Yes	Indoor	Mostly for overseas prototypes
N	2mm=1ft	Yes	Yes	Yes	Yes	Yes	Yes	Indoor	Ideal for smaller locations
O	7mm=1ft	Yes	Yes	Yes	Yes	Yes	Yes	Both	Usually requires a large indoor space
OO9 NG	4mm=1ft	Yes	Yes	Yes	Yes	Limited	Yes	Indoor	British version of HOe
HOe NG	3.5mm=1ft	No	No	No	Yes	Limited	Yes	Indoor	For overseas prototypes
HOm NG	3.5mm=1ft	No	No	No	Yes	Limited	Yes	Indoor	For overseas prototypes
HOn3 NG	3.5mm=1ft	No	No	No	Yes	Limited	Yes	Indoor	Some USA models available
O-16.5 NG	7mm=1ft	No	No	No	Yes	Yes	Yes	Both	Kits and conversions
Gauge 1	10mm=1ft	Limited	Limited	No	Yes	Yes	Yes	Both	Requires a large indoor space
SM-32 NG	16mm=1ft	Limited	Limited	Yes	Yes	Yes	Yes	Both	Usually live steam or battery power
G-45 NG	1:24 nominal	Yes	Yes	Yes	Yes	Yes	Yes	Both	For overseas prototypes
Z	1.38mm=1ft	No	No	No	Yes	Limited	Yes	Indoor	Mostly for overseas prototypes
TT:120	2.54mm=1ft	Limited	Limited	No	Yes	Yes	Yes	Indoor	Ideal for smaller locations
TT	3mm=1ft	No	No	No	Yes	Yes	Yes	Indoor	Kits or old Tri-ang TT R-T-R
EM/P4	4mm=1ft	No	No	No	No	Yes	Yes	Indoor	Conversion kits for OO models
S7	7mm=1ft	No	No	No	No	Yes	Yes	Indoor	Conversion kits for O models
S	3/16"=1ft	No	No	No	No	Yes	Yes	Indoor	Entirely handbuilt

Planning & design

In this first section we will consider how to go about making all the plans for a new model railway project. The key issues here are time, budget, where you will house the layout, and what you want to achieve with it. Making the right choices on these will ensure long-lasting enjoyment and satisfaction. Building a model railway can often take many years, so giving plenty of thought to these initial decisions is very important.

Make a start by considering what you want from the layout, where you can build it, and being realistic about how much time and money you can afford to give it. For instance, main line railway systems with lots of movement, including express passenger and long freight trains, always have huge appeal and are everyone's dream. How practical these dreams are is another matter. This is where you need to think carefully about what size and how complex your railway should be. When you take a good look at the space available it might prove too small for your ambitions. Do not be discouraged, railway modelling is a hobby for you to enjoy. Stay positive and focus on what is possible. The advice and tips in this chapter are to help you do just that.

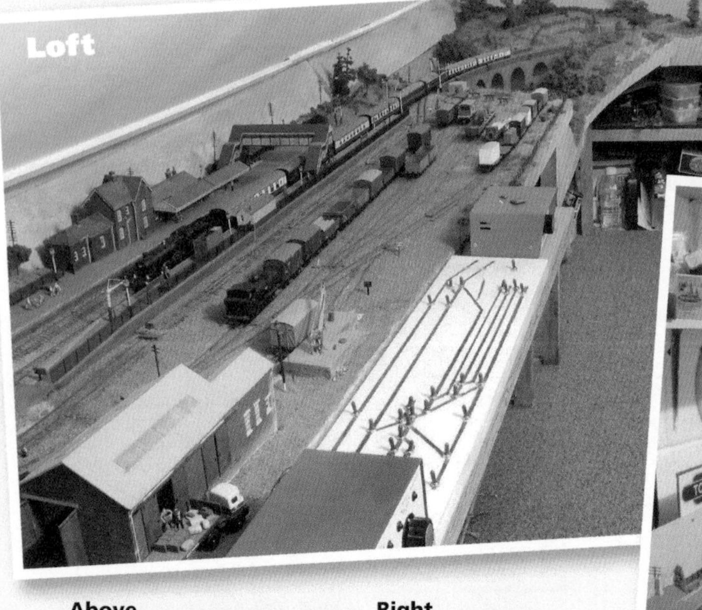

Above
The loft is a traditional location for a layout, as per *Pen-hill*, modelled in OO by Dean Knights (RM January 2010).

Right
Torridge & Westward Ho! in OO by John Bottomley (RM March 2013) lives in the garage.

Garage

Left
Clive Anscott had no choice but to use the kitchen for his model railway, so *Todrighton for Chalmleigh* (RM October 2012) lives under a protective cover when not in use.

Right
The garden has long been a popular layout location for those with the space, as it offers the opportunity to operate large scale models. The *Glenrock Garden Railway* (RM August 2012) by Ian Pethers is a coarse scale O gauge layout.

Left
Wilbury, an N gauge layout in a spare room, was built by Richard Morris to exploit the gauge's potential to provide a lot of railway in a small area. It was featured in the December 2013 RM.

Right & below
Fold-away layouts are handy if your layout has to make way for other domestic arrangements (such as Ken Ballantine's model – situated in a flat, right), or if you wish to make the layout portable for transport to exhibitions. *Moor Lane End Works* was built by Tim Tincknell (RM November 2012), *Burntwood Lane* by members of Bentley MRG (RM April 2013).

So, what space you have available is a major consideration and often, with determination, room can be found somewhere within the home or garden. A spare bedroom, an attic, a garage or garden shed are all popular places for housing the layout. Another option is a portable or fold-away layout that packs up for storage into a corner or cupboard. Once you have determined the space at your disposal, the planning and design stage can begin and the first thing you really need to do is measure it up. With the dimensions to hand, that all-important question can now be asked. "What can I get in this space?"

At this point further matters need to be considered. If you are not entirely sure which scale and gauge you want to model in, now is the time to make the choice. Next to help the planning process, now is the time to make a list of all the things you want to include in your model. Let's start with when and where? Think about the period in which you want to set your model. Present day? The steam age? Early diesel/electric? Next consider whether the scene should be industrial, cityscape, railways with canals, seaside or countryside.

There are plenty of options and often what will appeal will be a result of your own memories, or could be based around models you already own, or even a new one that has appeared on the market. We would suggest that, at this stage you do not waste too much time trying to devise a truly original scheme, for you will find that nearly all worthwhile, practical ideas have already been tried. In any case, all the really outstanding layouts are remarkably similar in structure since they are based on prototype practice. The secret of their success is the attention to detail, their proportions and the degree of authenticity: in other words, does it look right?

Choosing a track plan

When you have decided what you want, made various lists, found a home for the layout and determined the space available, you can now decide on a track plan together with the locations of buildings, platforms, bridges, hidden sidings, etc. This is a creative process and can be both challenging and fun, and costs very little money. You can work from plans which

Garden

Fold-away

Fold-aways

Fig. 1 – suggested minimum planning dimensions – inches (mm)

For standard gauge railways in popular scales

Scale/Gauge	N	OO	Gauge O	Gauge 1
Point length (med. radius)	5½ (140)	8½ (216)	16 (406)	24 (610)
Crossover (long)	11½ (292)	18 (457)	34 (864)	42 (1067)
Minimum track centres	1 (25)	2 (50)	3⅛ (79)	4⅓ (110)
Minimum radius curves	9 (229)	18 (457)	48 (1220)	72 (1829)
Minimum platform width	1¼ (32)	2½ (64)	4¾ (120)	6 (152)
Min. overhead clearance	1½ (38)	3 (76)	6 (152)	9 (229)
Average coach (64')	5½ (140)	10½ (267)	18 (457)	26 (660)
Typical wagon (10' wb.)	2 (50)	3½ (90)	6¼ (158)	9 (229)

Minimum length of loco release = length of loco over buffers + 10%

Suggested minimum length of headshunt = longest loco + three longest wagons

These dimensions are nominal and meant as a guide for use when sketching out ideas. Always check out your plans with trials using paper point templates.

have been already published, or go it alone and develop your own ideas. Either way, choosing a track plan can be split into three stages; initial sketches, a scale drawing, and practical checks.

For the beginner, who may be unaware of real railway practice, it is probably best to start with tried and tested track plans from other modellers, but you do not have to adhere strictly to their plans; sometimes you can combine ideas from several sources. Plans are published every month in Railway Modeller, and there are countless model railway planbooks available that are all good starting points. You will usually not go far wrong with a published plan (especially if you know of a layout built from it). It is important to check that what you see on the page will actually fit in your room before you go out and spend money on baseboard timber and track. There are several ways to check this and this is explained later.

Drawing your own plan

You may prefer to create your own track plan, so it can encompass all the features you may have on your layout 'wish list'. For instance you may be wanting to include long express passenger or goods trains, or a large locomotive depot or freight handling terminal. It is essential therefore to try out your ideas on paper first. Rough sketches are good enough to start with, they can be developed with more detail as you go along. When drawing them it is important to ensure that critical dimensions of items such as points and crossovers, minimum track centres, etc, are adhered to. Otherwise you end with a plan that just isn't workable in practice because you've squeezed in far too many points. As a guide to help anyone considering drawing up their own scheme we have included the accompanying table (Fig. 1) of suggested minimum planning dimensions. They are given in both inches and millimetres. Choosing a suitable scale for your sketches is important. Those using imperial measurements might use, for convenience, one inch to one foot. If you are working in metric you could work at 1:10 or 1:25; graph paper is useful as it is divided into 10 x 10 squares. There is certainly no need for elaborate equipment, just a pencil and a soft rubber to get started on these initial sketches.

As you are aiming for a layout plan that includes all the elements in your list, it will be a trial and error process and it usually takes several sketches, each slightly different, until you arrive at something with which you are happy.

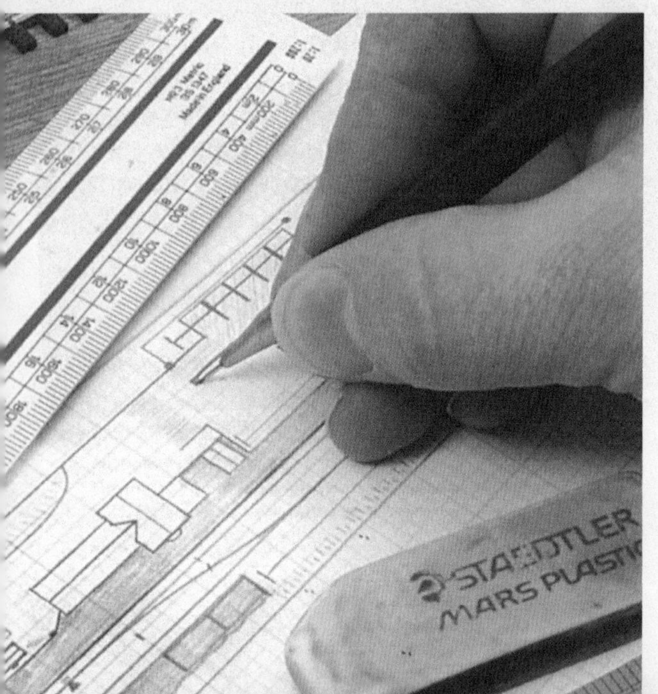

Left
Once you have decided on the type of layout you wish to build, and sketched a few ideas, it's time to make sure everything fits by preparing a scale plan.

Starting the design

How do you design a track plan? What features should be included and what sizes should they be? For a beginner these are important questions and the answer is again to look at other layouts, published plans and the prototype. In all of them you will see some essential track formations. These include run-around loops, headshunts or goods sidings. Knowing the effect each element has on the running of trains will help you identify how you should use them in the layout. Fig. 2 shows the most common elements and includes explanations of their purpose. The most important element is usually a run-around loop, and almost all layouts will require one, especially if you are modelling a terminus station in the steam period.

Right
A continuous run layout, in conjunction with a traverser fiddle yard, is ideal for those wishing to model main lines. They have the advantage of letting locos and stock run-in as per manufacturers' instructions.

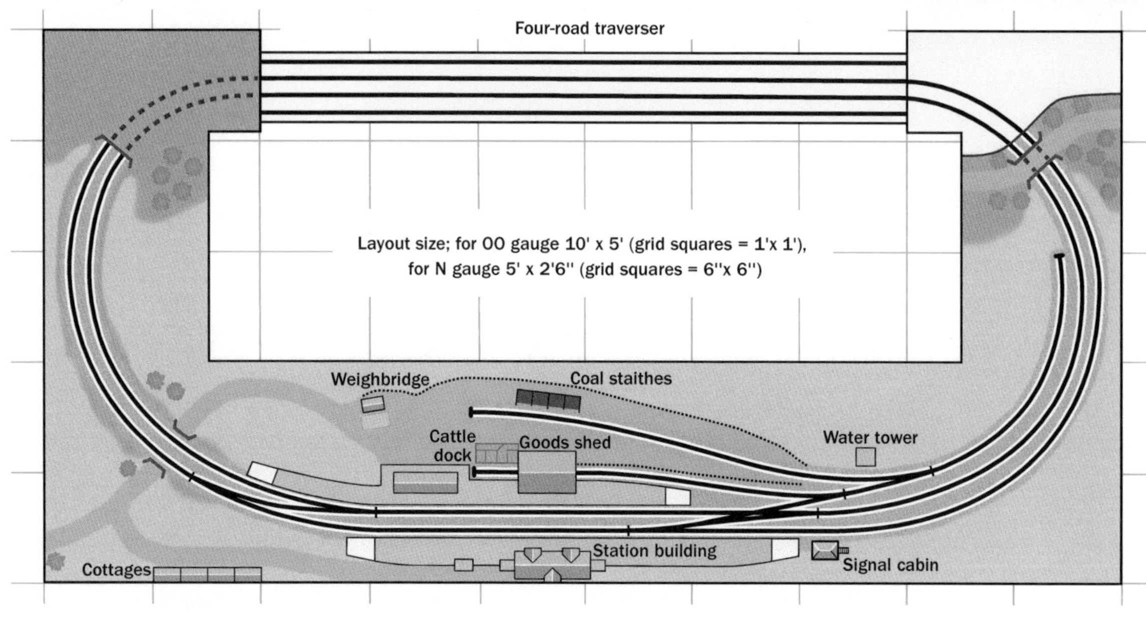

Right
The terminus to fiddle yard layout offers a lot of operation in a small space. The cassette fiddle yard allows easy interchange of trains.

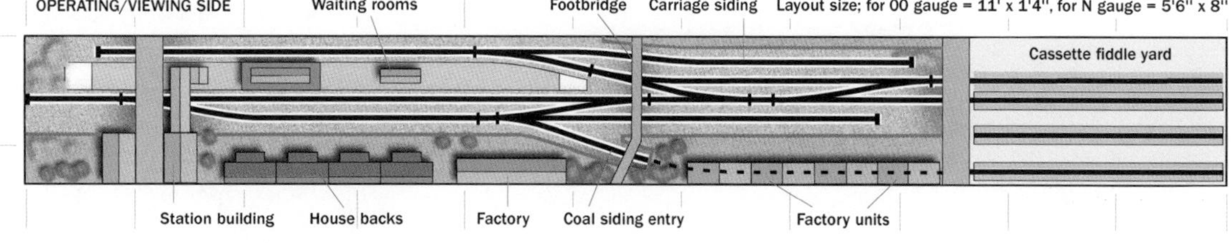

Right
An alternative terminus to fiddle yard layout, employing the popular method of hiding the latter from view by an industry (the viewing side is uppermost).

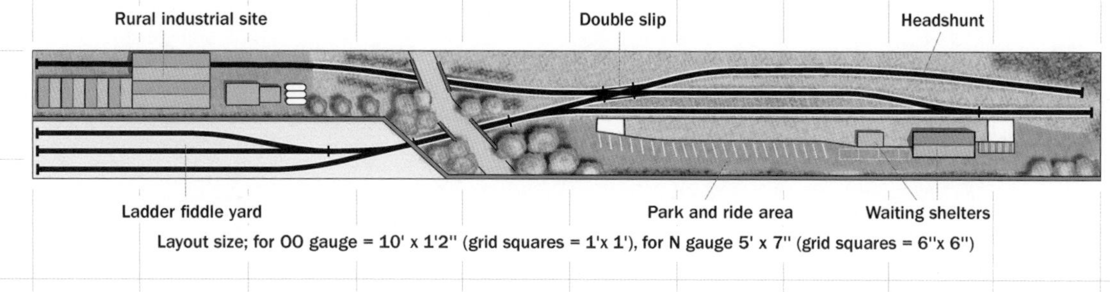

Fig. 2 – the basic elements of track formations

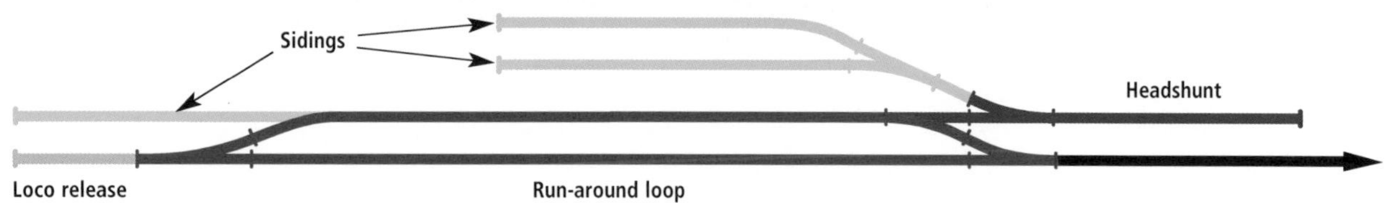

Run-around loop

This allows a locomotive to uncouple from its train, run forward into the loco release, then run around to the other end of the train, usually in order to haul it back in the opposite direction, or to allow freight trains to be shunted. It must be long enough to hold the longest trains you wish to run.

Loco release

An essential part of a run-around loop The length of the loco release track will determine the largest loco you can operate on your layout.

Headshunt

In order to place wagons in the goods sidings, the loco will pull the train into the headshunt and then reverse to push them into the sidings. The length of the headshunt will dictate how long a train can be shunted in one operation.

Sidings

Wagons must always be propelled into these areas otherwise the loco will be trapped by the wagons, and will require another loco to release it.

Fig. 3 – allowing for clearances

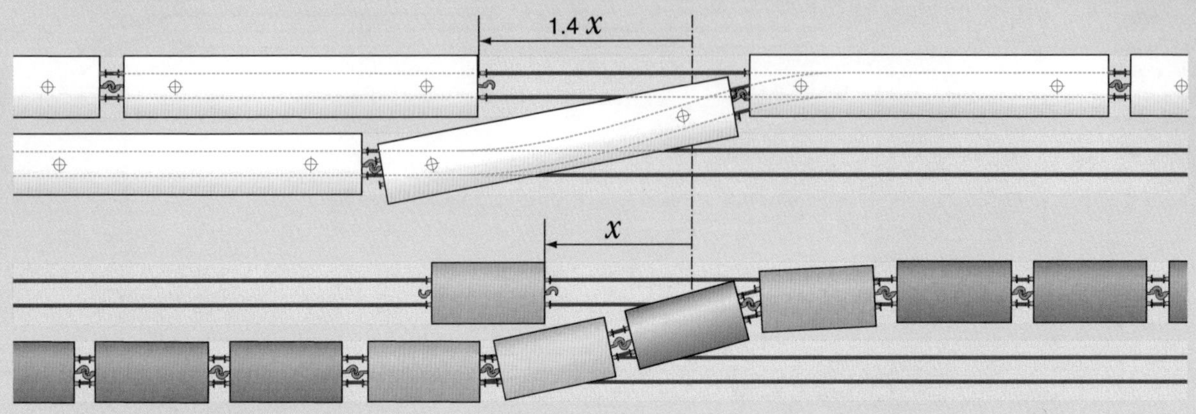

Above
Where a loop is on a running line, you will need to allow about 40% longer for clearances with passenger coaches than for 10' wheelbase wagons in a goods yard. Distance X will be dependent on the radius of the points used in the crossover.

The critical feature of a run-around loop is that it dictates the maximum length of train you can operate. The whole train must fit within the loop so that the locomotive can get to the other end of the train. To run a six-coach passenger train, the length of the loop must be six coaches long plus enough clearance at either end to stop the locomotive fouling the coaches as it passes them, see Fig. 3. Often the size and position of this feature is the starting point from which the rest of the layout design evolves. Use the coach length identified in Fig. 1 to determine the run-around loop length. Sketch that in and then work up from there, adding curves perhaps or some more points feeding goods sidings. If, as you progress, you realise that it just won't fit, then shorten your train length by one coach and start the sketching process again. Eventually you will have a design that includes all or most of the requirements in your original list. At this stage it is a good idea to put it to one side for a day or two, and see if you are still satisfied with it when you come to look at it again. If not, start the process again and when all seems OK, you can now move onto the next stage.

Fig. 4 – radius template

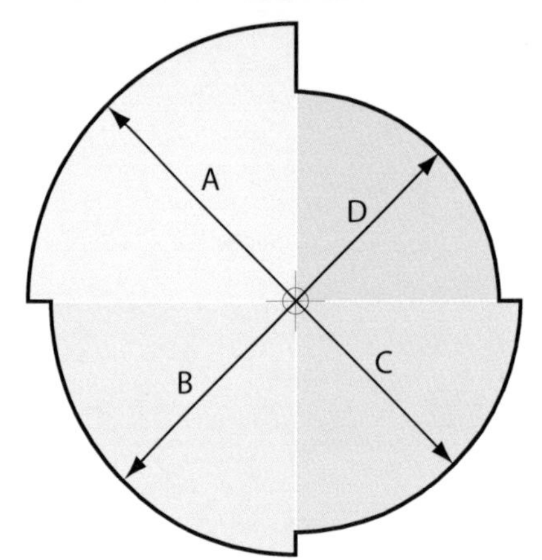

Suggested scale radii in different gauges

	N Gauge	OO Gauge	Gauge O
A	24"(610mm)	36"(914mm)	72"(1829mm)
B	18"(457mm)	24"(610mm)	54"(1371mm)
C	12"(305mm)	21"(533mm)	48"(1220mm)
D	9"(229mm)	18"(457mm)	36"(914mm)

Scale plans

You can now translate your sketch into a full scale working plan. Many modellers like to do this as it helps to check the feasibility of their ideas, but it is not always essential and you can miss out this stage and move straight on to the practical checks section.

If you decide to prepare a scale plan you will not need much equipment, but good quality paper or card is preferable. Some French curves for drawing will be helpful, but you can use a pair of compasses, or even make your own scale curve templates out of stiff card (Fig. 4). Finally a scale rule will be helpful, though a plain rule will suffice. You can of course always make a simple scale ruler for yourself from stiff white card.

Computer drawing packages, such as CorelDraw, are very popular and can be used in place of the good old-fashioned paper and pencil. There are also dedicated track planning packages, such as AnyRail, XtrackCad, and WinRail, all downloadable from the internet. Some have limitations, whilst others can do almost everything and they may well appeal to individual modellers with computer skills.

Practical checks

By this stage, you have identified the space in which you are going to build the layout, taken measurements and prepared either a viable sketch plan or an accurate scale plan. If you feel confident about your plans you can now start building the baseboards. However, it is a good idea to make some practical

Below
Several computer drawing packages are available if you wish to design your track plan this way. This is a screen shot showing the AnyRail software, available via the web.

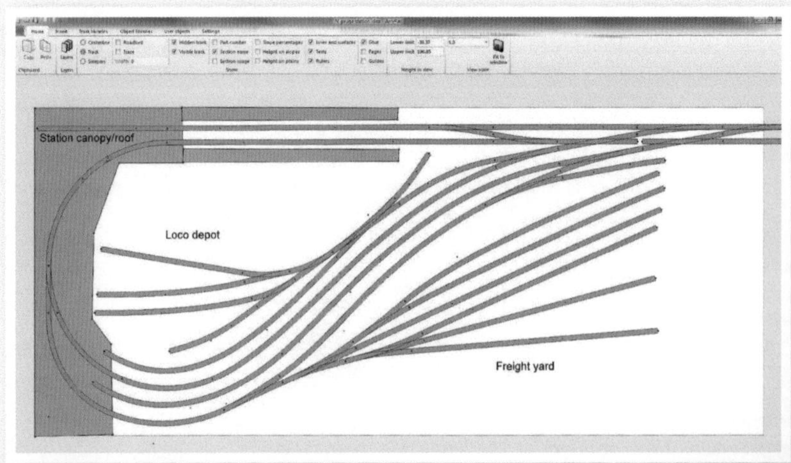

checks at this stage to verify the viability of your plan before you start to spend money. It is well worth going through this final stage of checks even if you are using a published plan. There are a number of ways to do this.

Paper Track Templates

For many years Peco has printed sheets of full-size templates for each of its ranges of Streamline and Setrack points and crossings. They can be cut out from the sheet for positioning or photocopied. You can use them either directly where the layout is going, or by pasting them onto some lining paper cut to the size of the baseboards. With lining paper you can draw in the plain track sections with a pencil. Using paper templates in this way is a reliable and inexpensive way of checking your plans. Templates can now be downloaded as printable pdf files from the Peco website. www.peco-uk.com

Full Size Trials

If, like many modellers, you already possess some items of pointwork, plain track lengths, etc, you can use these as full size 'templates', effectively mocking-up the track plan with actual components. It would be fair to say that this method, if used in conjunction with paper templates, is actually an acceptable substitute for the scale drawing stage: you can go straight from your initial sketch to a full-size trial.

Visualisation mock-ups

The above techniques enable the track configuration to be checked for accuracy. With visualisation mock-ups you can get an idea of how the whole scene will look. Essentially the proposed buildings are assembled quickly in card to the intended size and positioned alongside your trackwork mock-up or templates. Viewed from all sides you can then trim or reposition them until you are satisfied with the composition. Such mock-ups can be created at full size or smaller.

Below
Card mock-ups of the structures you intend to use on the layout can be employed not just to check that clearances for rolling stock are acceptable, but whether they will sit together visually.

Minimum Gradient

Your plan may well incorporate two or more levels on which the trains run, and as such track on a gradient will be required between the various levels if they are to be linked. Obviously if the gradient is too steep the train will not be able to climb up without stalling: the question therefore is what is the recommended minimum gradient that should be incorporated on the layout.

Real railways often have gradients shallower than 1:100, but on occasions these can be steeper, such as the Lickey Incline south of Birmingham at 1:37, and Shap incline in Cumbria at 1:75. On a model railway, it is always wisest to try and attain the shallowest gradient possible, but as a general rule of thumb modellers should aim for a steepest gradient of 1:36 when using either OO and N gauge equipment. This is easily remembered, as it equates to a 1" rise over a 36" length of flexible track.

If you really want to check, then you should consider rigging up a temporary incline to check the performance of your locos, particularly if you are to model in a less common gauge such as 009.

Ready to go!

So that is the planning and design process in a nutshell. You don't have to follow it slavishly, or go through every step, but by adopting these general principles you should ensure success in the long term. You will find that most modellers, whether experienced or not, will use various methods to check their ideas. It could save lots of heartache and expense in the long term! If you have got this far, and your plans all look OK, then it's time to start building the boards and get on with the really enjoyable part — actually doing some modelling.

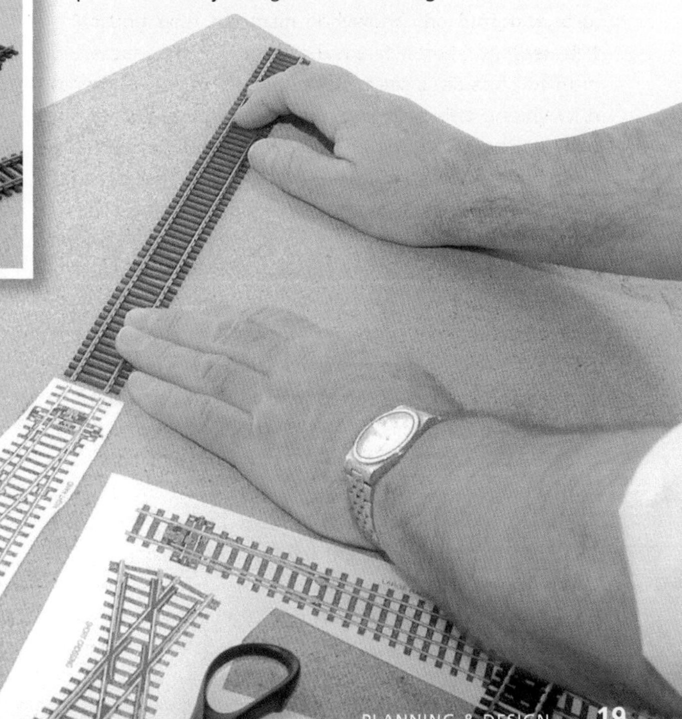

Right
Paper point templates are available from Peco for most items in its ranges, and they can be downloaded from the firm's website. Use them to ensure that the track plan will actually fit the space available.

Baseboards

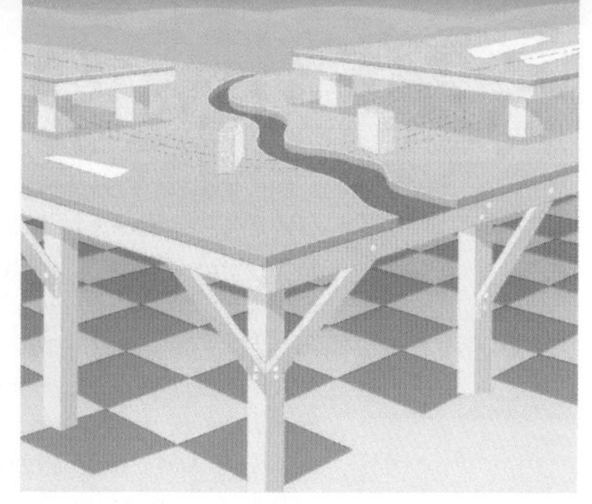

For many enthusiasts building the baseboards is seen as a bit of a chore, but careful thought and planning can see the job done in the quickest possible time. A sturdy baseboard is essential for any model railway – regardless of scale – and helps to ensure optimum running can be achieved. No matter how carefully the trackwork is laid, any warping or sagging of the trackbed will cause problems, so it is important from the outset to get the baseboards right.

Baseboard design is a topic which encompasses a vast choice of materials and construction methods. For most modellers though, there are only two basic designs that need to be considered; the solid top sectional system and the open frame benchwork method, as illustrated in Fig. 1. Both are of traditional timber construction and which of these methods is adopted is generally dictated by the type of layout you are building. The sectional system is by far the most widely used for both permanent and portable layouts, whilst the open frame method is ideal for large, permanently sited layouts incorporating multi-level trackwork and floor to ceiling scenic treatment, such as that illustrated below.

Sectional system

For those starting out on their first layout, the sectional system is recommended because of its flexibility and ease of construction. Board sections can be built to manageable sizes and combined in multiple to produce almost any layout configuration (as shown in Fig. 2 opposite). Each section consists of a strong framework (usually made from planed softwood) fitted with a top surface of suitable sheet timber (see page 22).

Traditionally, a popular section size has been 1220mm x 610mm (4' x 2'), since four pieces of surface board can be cut from a standard 2440mm x 1220mm (8' x 4') sheet without any wastage. However, sections can be built to any size to suit your layout configuration and even sections of different sizes can be combined, though bear in mind if you

Fig. 1 – common baseboard types

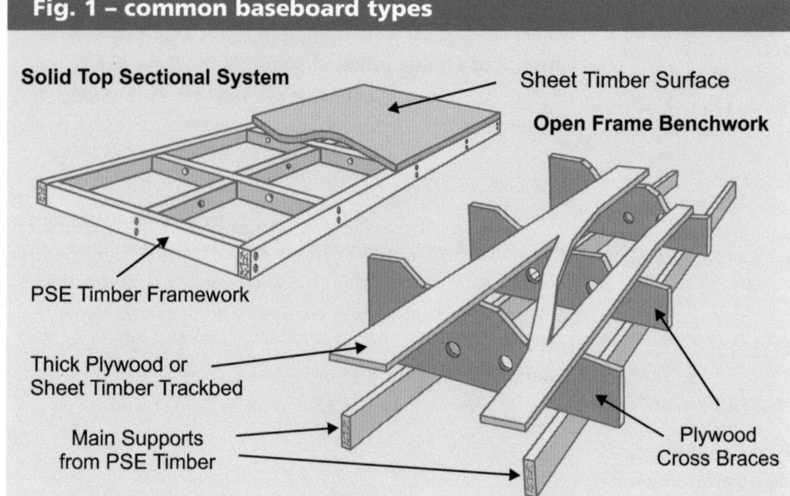

Left
Large, permanently sited layouts which involve multiple levels, are best supported with an open frame baseboard such as this under construction at Pecorama.

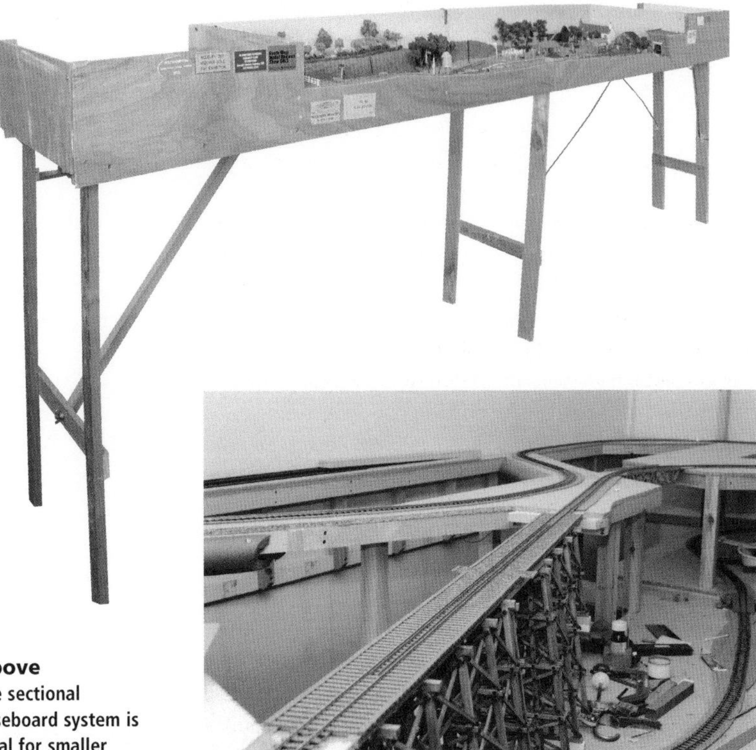

Above
The sectional baseboard system is ideal for smaller portable layouts which have to be transported easily.

Above right
This second image of the Pecorama layout under construction shows how solid top boards have also been incorporated into the open frame design.

Far right
A few typical woodworking tools for baseboard building. Power tools can be very useful, but not essential, as hand saws and hand-drills can do the job just as easily, if only requiring a little more elbow grease!

are building a portable layout for exhibition use, it is often helpful to keep all the sections to a standard size for ease of packing and transportation. Larger sized sections can be built, but may become unwieldy. A classic example is the solid 6ft x 4ft board that many enthusiasts began with in childhood. Whilst they can accommodate a full twin-track oval, they can be awkward to fit into a room and awkward to lift, store and transport.

Tools and materials

Constructing baseboards requires little more than basic woodworking skills and is well within the capabilities of most modellers. Power tools can make certain tasks a lot easier but are by no means essential. At the very least you will need a crosscut or tenon saw, screwdrivers, hand-drill, tape measure, engineers square, bradawl, sanding block and pencil. A woodworker's plane and surform may also come in handy. The only other item that is really essential is a good work bench for cutting and drilling on.

The framework for each sectional board can be built from a variety of timber materials including plywood and MDF sheets cut into appropriately sized strips and glued together on a 'box girder' principle. However the tried and trusted method to begin with is to use good quality planed (pse) softwood for the frame members. The minimum recommended size is 50mm x 25mm, though for extra strength 75mm x 25mm can be used.

Again, for surface materials a number of options are available; plywood, chipboard, MDF, fibre based insulation board such as Sundeala, and even high density polystyrene foams, such as Styrofoam, have all been used. Each have their advantages and disadvantages, plywood for instance is light and strong but has a hard surface and does not accept track pins easily. Both chipboard and MDF are strong, but significantly heavier, and also do not take track pins without predrilling. Sundeala on the other hand is soft and workable (it can be cut with a heavy duty craft knife and straight edge) and accepts pins with relative ease. It is about as heavy as chipboard or MDF, heavier than plywood and is more expensive. Styrofoam is rather specialised and best left for those with more experience. To some extent the top surface material is down to personal choice and circumstances. If you are to glue your track down and want lightweight sections, then 6mm plywood will probably do the job. If you are pinning your track and using foam ballast inlays, then 12mm Sundeala will be the best choice. For a permanent foundation 15mm chipboard

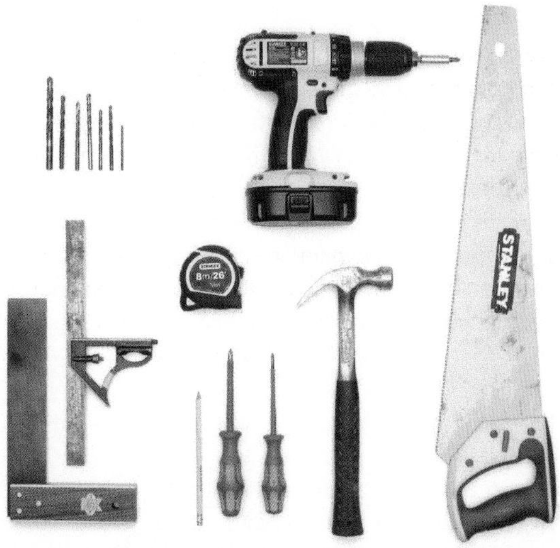
STANLEY

Fig. 2 – layout configurations using sectional baseboards

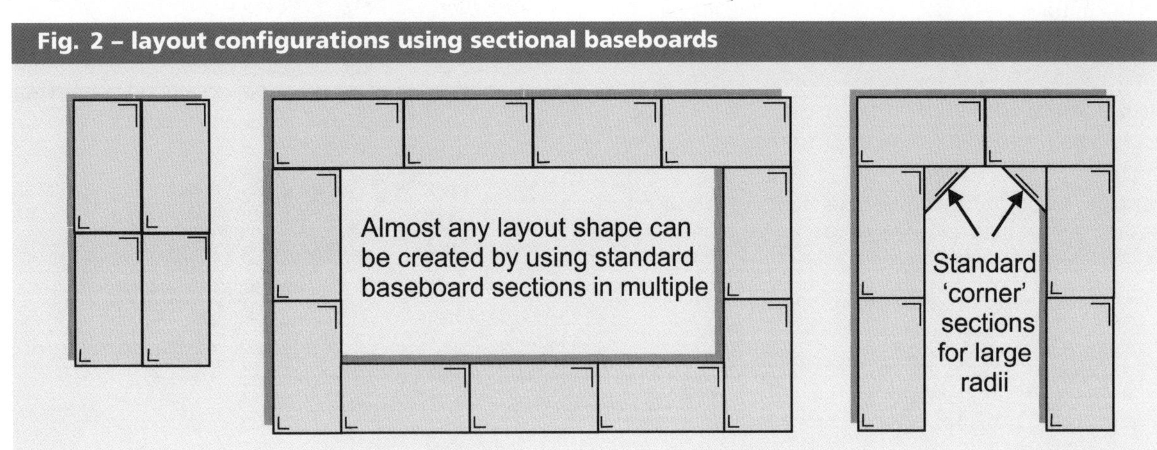
Almost any layout shape can be created by using standard baseboard sections in multiple
Standard 'corner' sections for large radii

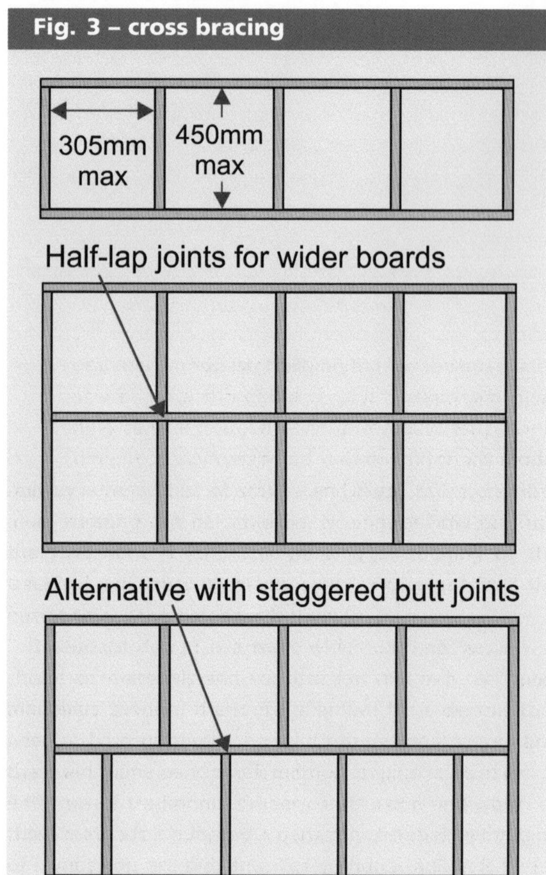

or MDF may prove the cheaper option. Bear in mind also that softer surface materials can be less efficient at transmitting running noise through the board, so Sundeala will usually result in quieter running. Whatever surface material you settle on, all will require sufficient cross bracing fitted within the framework at regular intervals; a maximum spacing of 305mm is generally recommended and sections wider than about 450mm will benefit from longitudinal bracing as well (see Fig. 3).

Planning the sections

Before buying and cutting any timber, you should first plan the baseboard requirements for your layout. To start, you will need a paper copy of your layout plan which can be overlaid with a piece of tracing paper to allow you to sketch on the baseboard section positions and dimensions. Where possible try to keep the sections to a standard size, but also watch out for awkward section joints or frame cross members that may occur under pointwork etc. (especially if the layout is to be portable).

Also, keeping section dimensions to that which makes optimum use of a standard sheet of timber will minimise wastage and help keep your costs down. This planning process is essentially one of trial and error, and you may have to repeat it.

Eventually you will end up with detailed plans and dimensions of the sections from which you can then determine the quantities of plain timber and sheeting you need. Take care when selecting lengths of timber at the merchants store and choose those that are absolutely straight and as free as possible from knots, cracks or splinters.

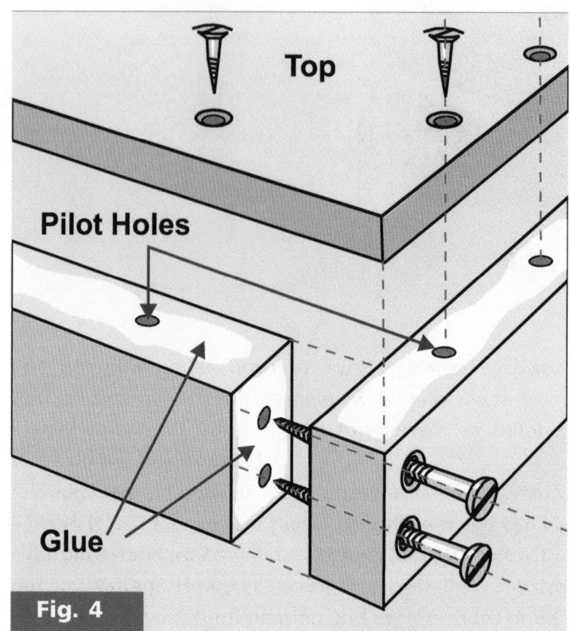

Constructing the sectional boards

When building each board, butt joints that are glued and screwed are perfectly adequate (Fig. 4). PVA woodworking glue and 50mm (2") No.8 countersunk wood screws are recommended. Where cross bracing intersects, either use halflap joints, or use short cross braces and stagger them (Fig. 3). Pilot holes are helpful to prevent splitting even though modern woodscrews can be driven in without using modern power tools.

Supports

For permanent layouts the easiest method of support is to use a batten screwed to the wall at the desired height and fit 50mm x 25mm legs at intervals along the front edge (Fig. 5). Alternatively you could use some self assembly bookcase units, as also shown, but access beneath the boards to wiring, etc, would be restricted.

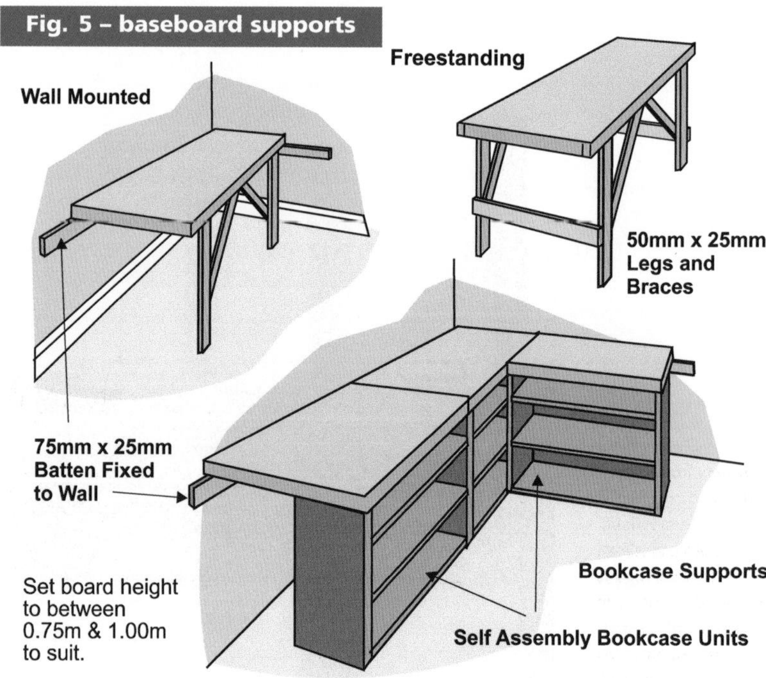

Constructing baseboard sections step-by-step

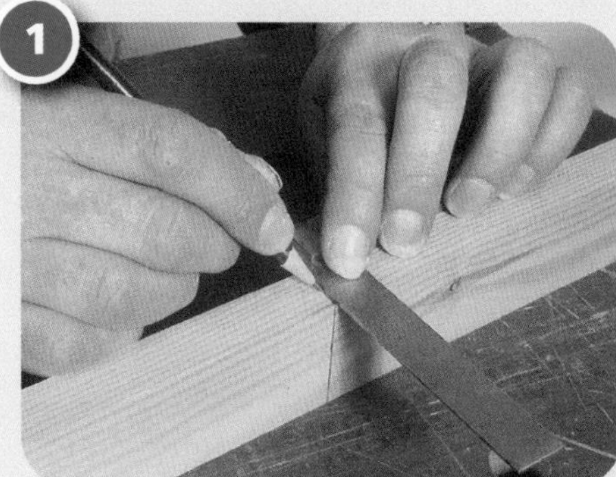

All the plain timber lengths that are required for the sections need to be measured and cut to length. For those less experienced at carpentry, a small engineers square can be used to draw a cutting line around three sides of the timber. This will help you make a true perpendicular cut every time.

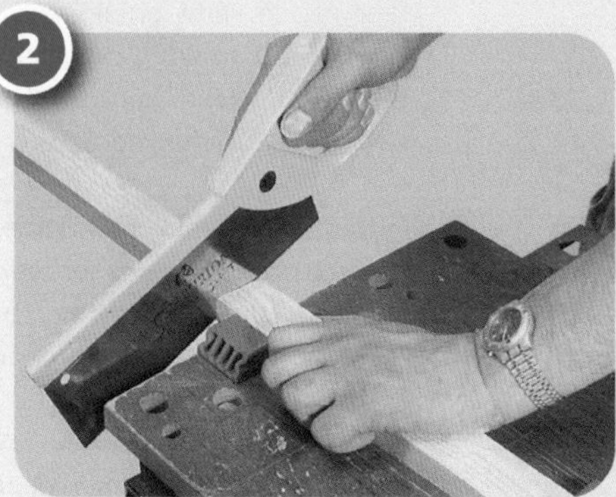

Support the timber against a suitable stop, such as on a workmate type portable workbench, and follow the cutting line around with the saw. It is good practice to sand lightly all the saw cuts to remove burrs and splinters (use medium grade sandpaper and a sanding block).

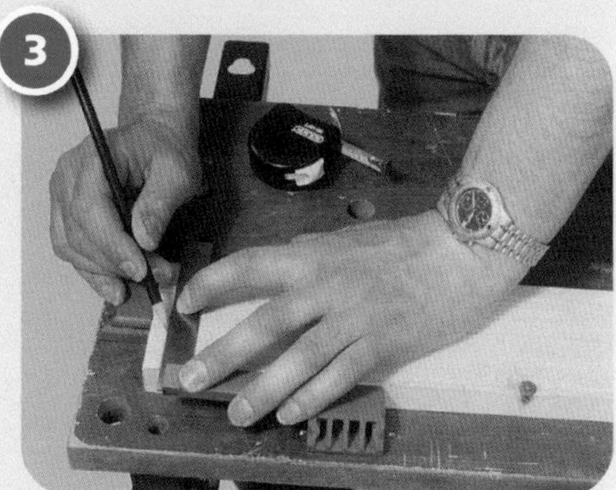

With all the pieces cut to length, mark out the positions for the screw holes in the ends of the longitudinal lengths. Note here how both lengths are set in line with each other so that they can be marked up simultaneously to ensure accuracy, then drill out the screw holes with a 5mm bit and countersink.

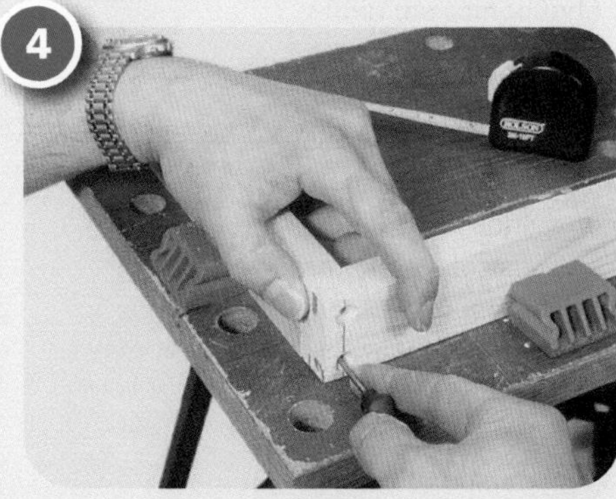

To prepare the cross braces, firstly drill out any holes for wiring (see Fig. 1 on page 20) in the inner cross braces. Prepare pilot holes in the ends of all the cross braces with a bradawl as shown. Then, using a spatula (an offcut of styrene will suffice), spread a little white PVA glue onto the joining surfaces. All the frame parts can now be screwed together.

The top surface can now be fitted. For this example 12mm Sundeala board has been used, pre-cut to size by a DIY merchant.
An off-cut of timber is used to mark the locations of countersink holes in the top surface, drilled to accept 25mm (No.8) screws. Make corresponding pilot holes for the screws around the top edge of the frame.

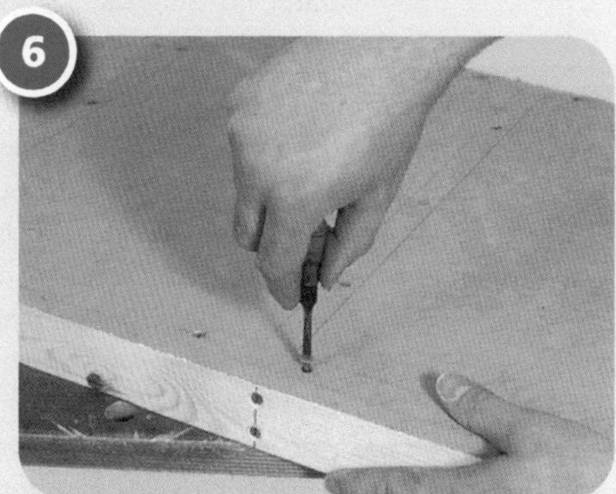

Apply a layer of PVA glue around the top edge of the frame and bring it together with the top surface, checking for correct alignment. Finally, insert the screws and tighten them up to complete the construction of this baseboard section. Repeat this process until you have built all the other sections you require for the layout.

Modern lifestyles often mean that devoting a room solely to a layout can be difficult, especially if it involves disrupting the decorations. So fitting full supports to your layout to make it completely freestanding is a worthwhile option. It may mean a little extra work, but it allows the layout sections to be dismantled and moved to another location should the need arise.

Freestanding supports can be constructed with a leg in each corner and cross and diagonal bracing added as shown in Fig. 5. For small layouts only one section needs four legs, the other sections can be fitted with just two legs and supported piggyback by the four-legged section. Supports can either be secured rigidly with screws or hinged so that they fold up beneath the baseboard. Independent freestanding trestles can also be used and are often seen on exhibition layouts.

Joining sections

There are two widely used methods for joining baseboard sections together. The first is to use coach bolts (of 8mm minimum diameter) through the frames as shown in Fig 6 overleaf. If you intend to use coach bolts to join the sections together then clearance holes for these need to be drilled before adding the top surfaces to the baseboard sections, as once fitted, there may not be room to manoeuvre your drill into the right place. To ensure accurate alignment, clamp together the corresponding end cross members from two sections and drill the clearance holes through both pieces in one go.

Coach bolts are ideal for both permanent and portable layouts, and if the layout is to be dismantled frequently it is also a good idea to incorporate alignment dowels in the mating surfaces. There are several varieties available

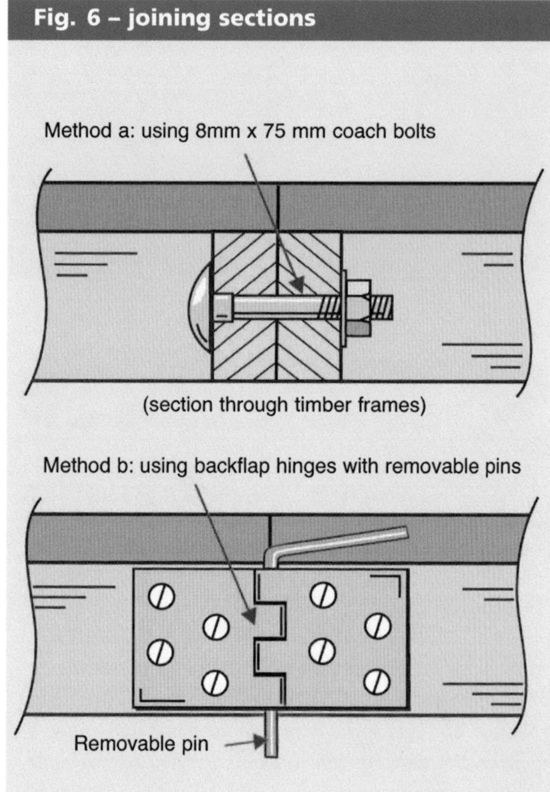

Fig. 6 – joining sections

including the brass dowels. These require separate holes and must be a tight fit. They are best installed at the same time as drilling the clearance holes for the bolts. Another simple method, particularly suited to portable boards, is to use backflap hinges, as also shown in Fig. 6. The hinge pins are knocked out and replaced with longer ones that can be bent over to form handles which can be removed easily. Baseboard joints can often be a potential source of bumps and irregularities in the track, so some enthusiasts reinforce the edges with timber strip and solder the rail to brass screws driven into the wood.

Gradients

If you are to incorporate track at multiple levels on your layout, or want scenic effects below track level then you should aim to build all the rising and falling gradients at the baseboard construction stage. With a solid top board, both rising and falling grades can be made by cutting a tongue in the surface board at the start of the gradient. For a rising grade simply pack up the end of the tongue to the required angle and butt join it to the higher level trackbed, the rest of which is built on top of the main board using supporting blocks and more surface material (Fig. 7). For a falling grade the tongue is pushed downwards and butt joined to the lower level trackbed. This time, since the tracks drop into the framework area, the cross bracing has to be designed to accommodate the route of the lower level trackbed and consequently the carpentry can become quite complex.

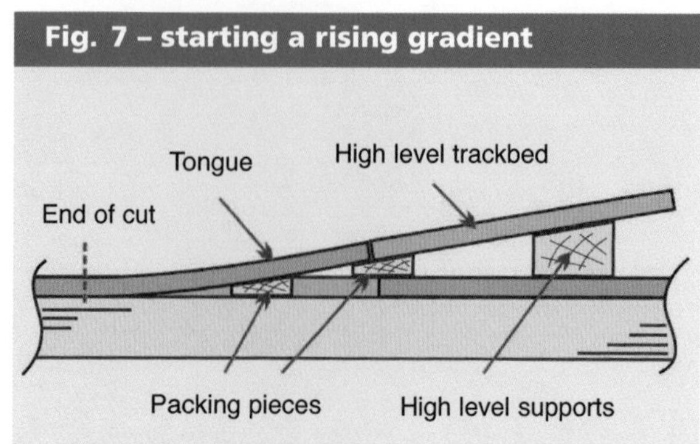

Fig. 7 – starting a rising gradient

Open top sections

To minimise such construction complexities, one option is to build your sections as 'open top' frames and fit the surfacing only where the trackwork is to be laid. The frame tops become the datum for the lowest level trackbed with higher level trackbeds laid on timber supports which rise up from the main frames. This is somewhat similar to the open frame benchwork method described in Fig. 1, but constructed in sections. Depending on your choice of surface, additional cross timbering may have to be installed to support the surface properly, as shown in Fig. 8. This will be the case with thin ply or Sundeala, and even thicker chipboard or MDF may need them, but they can be easily fitted piecemeal as you go along. It is possible, certainly for

Bottom left
The baseboard supports on the 'loft' layout at Pecorama, in the early stages of construction.

Below
Showing the same layout from the opposite corner, with the solid top sections and upper level trackbed sections in position.

Fig. 8 – open top baseboard sections

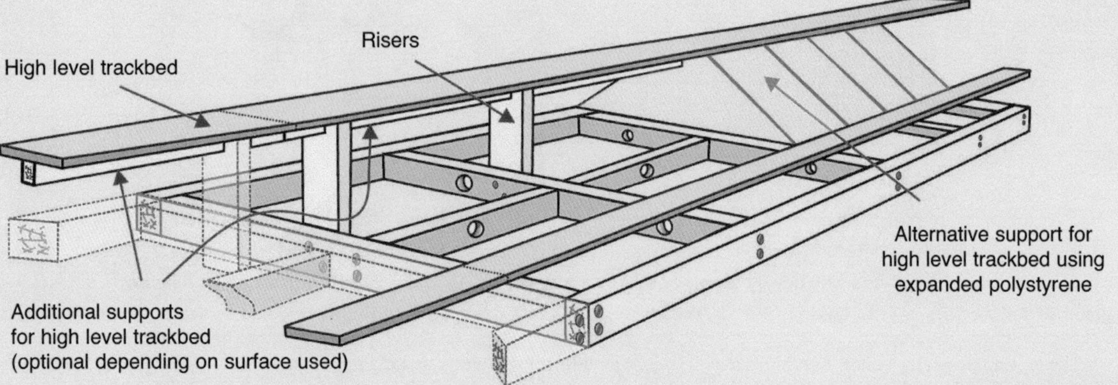

the smaller scales, to use blocks or layers of expanded polystyrene insulation for the extra supports instead of timber as also shown, as this will help to keep the weight down.

Folding sections

When a layout runs around the perimeter of a room, access will be needed at the door. Here a folding section can be installed. This is essentially a separate section built wider than the size of the door opening and is hinged at one end so it can be folded downwards to create the access. For running sessions it is held in place by nothing more than a couple of sliding brass bolts at each side. The folding section can be made to fold upwards if desired, but positioning the hinges is a little more involved.

Right
A folding section on Evan Williams garden shed located layout *Garsdale* in OO gauge.

Below
The 'loft' layout, this time much further on, with all trackwork laid and wired, and a few scenic structures in place. The design of the baseboard is still apparent at this stage.

Laying the track

Once the track plan has been selected, and the baseboards constructed, it is time to start real modelling: and modellers nearly always begin by laying the track. This is one of the most important jobs to do correctly when constructing a model railway, so taking time and care with this stage will reward you with many years of reliable running. Point operation also needs to be considered at this stage too, and tried and trusted methods of remote point operation are described later in this section.

Choosing your track – Sectional or Flexible?

To the beginner, the various different track standards available can be a little confusing. If starting out in OO gauge or N gauge the first consideration is whether to choose 'sectional' unit track or 'flexible' track.

Sectional track (photo A) is a clip-together rigid track system and is ideal for the beginner, or for those who want to lay track instantly, because cutting and bending is not necessary. The Peco OO Setrack range includes five different lengths of straight, four different radius curves, left

Below
Aberddyngwmmu by Steve and Ann Lewis, in 00 gauge. Peco code 100 flexible track was used throughout. This is manufactured to a universal standard and is compatible with many older models fitted with wheels that are not to modern day standards – see paragraph entitled 'Universal or Fine?'.

and right hand points, together with a diamond crossing. Individual track sections and Setrack packs are available, all of which can be connected up to sectional track supplied in train sets manufactured by companies such as Hornby and Bachmann.

The key benefits of sectional track are that it can be assembled quickly (preferred by the younger modeller who is eager to run trains!) and the point frog polarity is switched automatically, so there is no need for any extra wiring. Accessories in the Setrack range (such as level crossings) can be installed simply by clipping in place between adjoining sections of track. The Setrack items are also fully complementary to flexible track so if in the future you decide to progress to the latter track type, the investment in Setrack will not be wasted.

Flexible track (photo B) allows for a more realistic appearance to be achieved; in particular the modelling of smooth curves whilst also facilitating the construction of complex track formations. Points in the Streamline range are supplied ready to use like those in the Setrack range and are usually pre-wired to automatically switch the polarity to the correct direction.

Universal or Fine?

When using Peco Streamline flexible track in OO or N, the second consideration is whether to choose the 'Universal' or 'Fine' track system.

Universal track is designed to ensure that older models with coarser wheel standards will run side by side with today's modern rolling stock. Rail section is measured in thousandths of an inch; thus, for OO gauge, 'Fine' code 75 (0.075") has a shallower rail section than 'Universal' code 100 (0.100"). For N gauge, 'Universal' uses code 80 and 'Universal Fine' has a double foot, so it appears to be code 55 on the outside, but the inside depth is code 80. Whatever scale you are modelling in, if you plan to run older locomotives and rolling stock, then we recommend you use the 'Universal' system.

Marking out

The first step before cutting and laying, is to mark out your chosen track formation to actual size on the baseboard top (photo C). A good way to do this is to use actual points themselves, together with a few lengths of track, or use the full size Peco point and crossing templates (available to download from the Peco website). This enables the integrity of the initial plan to be checked and any modifications made before any track is cut.

When the correct formation is attained, the position of the track itself is marked out on the board using a felt tipped pen, (another method is to paste the paper templates to the board surface to use as a guide later). Sweeping curves can be marked out using a traditional wooden trammel, or alternatively lengths of track can be

curved into the desired radius with a Tracksetta template and then traced around. Also, to obtain the correct spacing for any double track formations that you have in mind, we recommend the use of the Peco 6'-way gauge (ref.SL-36, photo D). This will ensure that the distance between the two tracks will neither be too close nor too far apart.

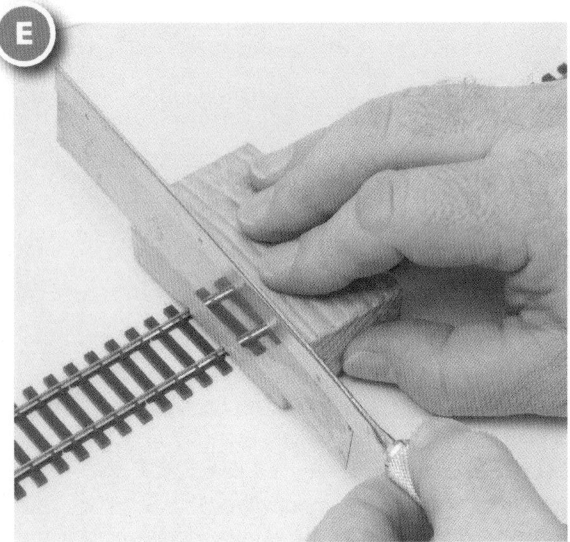

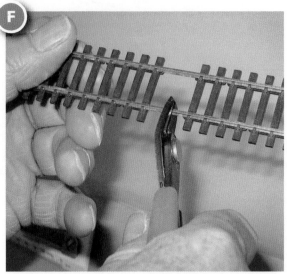

They also allow a little extra for the overhang of scale length bogie coaches used on many layouts.

The method of point operation should also be established at the marking out stage; if points are to be operated from underneath using any sort of mechanical linkage, then holes need to be drilled in the baseboard prior to fixing the track in place (see section on point operation on page 34).

Which ballast?

At this early stage, the track ballasting method you will later use must also be taken into account when marking out. There are two main types of ballast, as seen later; a foam ballast inlay manufactured by Peco which exactly fits the track and point geometry of Setrack, or loose granular ballast such as fine granite chippings. If you intend to use the inlay, the marking out should be done to the width of the inlay – approximately 43mm, if granular ballast is to be used then the sleeper ends can be taken as the line, though if you intend to use a cork sub-base then allow about 8mm each side of the sleeper ends.

Cutting to size

With the marking out completed, the next stage (applicable to flexible track) is to cut and trim all the track parts to length (if you are using Setrack, there is normally no cutting required, so you can move on to the next section). Plain track, supplied in yard lengths, can be cut with a sharp razor saw in conjunction with a cutting block (photo E). It is possible to buy a special track holder, but a piece of wood with two slots cut in the base to hold the rails firmly whilst sawing is just as good.

Special track cutters, such as by Xuron, are also available commercially and useful if a lot of track has to be cut (photo F). Always cut the rail from the top to bottom, not on its side, and aim to do it midway between two sleepers, so that later, when joining to the next piece, no unsightly gap or missing sleeper, occurs.

Cutting inevitably leaves a slight burred end which has to be cleaned with a few strokes of a small file. Remember that when the track is curved, the inner rail will be shorter than the outer rail and thus will have to be trimmed further at the joining stage in order to fit.

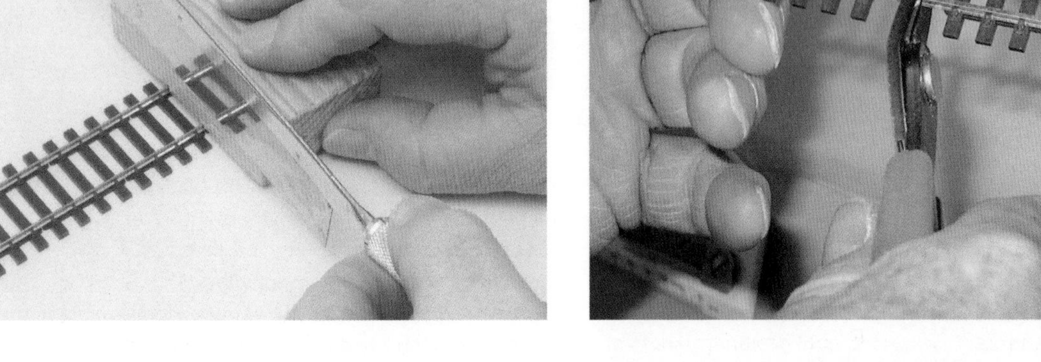

Where plain track is to be joined to points or crossings some of the sleeper ends will have to be trimmed off to ensure an accurate fit (photo G). This is best done by trimming a little sliver off at a time and checking the fit. Further instructions relating to this aspect are included with each point and crossing.

Curved tracks can be joined as shown in the panel on the page opposite.

Joining

At this stage you will now have lots of pieces of track and pointwork that have to be joined together with rail joiners (the equivalent of prototype 'fishplates'). There are two types of rail joiner, an all metal joiner (in nickel silver) which provides continuity of electrical supply, and an insulated nylon joiner, used where electrical continuity is not required (photo H). Thus, before any further track laying work is undertaken, you must now decide the positions of power connections and where any insulated rail joiners will be needed (see the section on Controlling Your Railway on page 54. Note that your choice of Insulfrog or Electrofrog points has a significant effect on this aspect of track laying. If you are unfamiliar with this, we would strongly recommend that you now turn to page 54 and study layout wiring in depth).

To fit rail joiners, the last rail fixings (the equivalent of prototype 'chairs' or 'clips') have to be removed with a sharp blade (photo I). This allows both metal and insulated joiners to be pushed onto the rail ends easily (photo J).

H

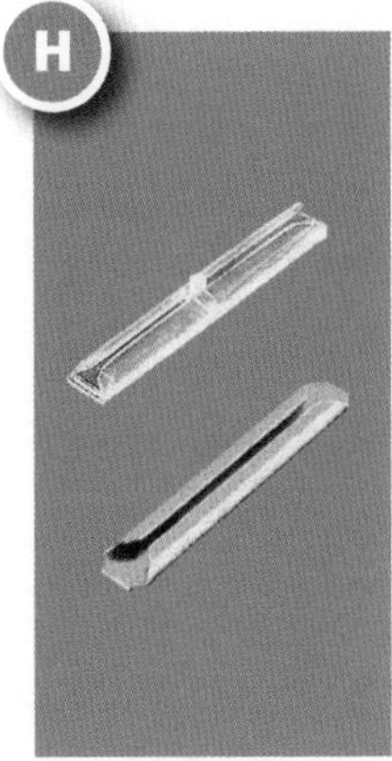

I

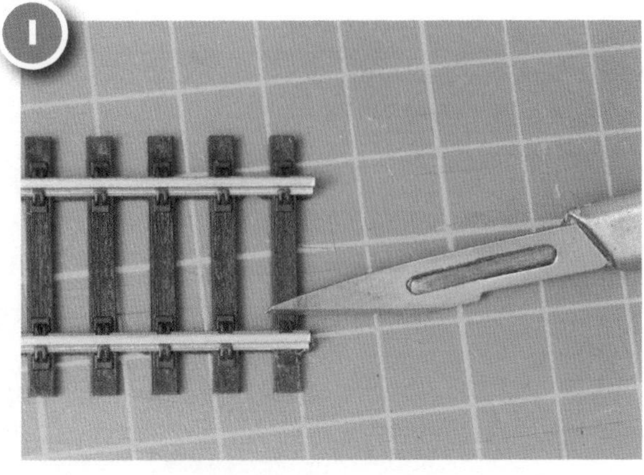

J

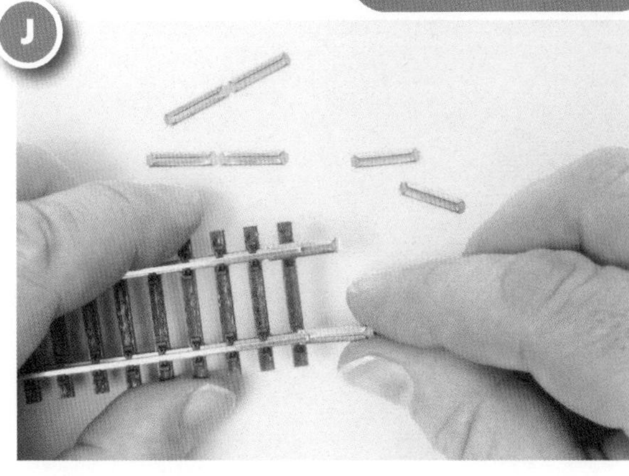

Pre-fixing dry run

With all the appropriate rail joiners in place the whole track formation can now be clipped together and the alignment checked. If any kinks or twists occur in any of the sections you should take them apart and do any further trimming of the rails as required. A final check by running a wagon over the track by hand will show up any other remaining problems. If you intend to fit wire droppers for power connections to the undersides of the rails, or use the Peco Power Feed Joiners, to which the electrical wire droppers are pre-soldered (these are available in the Peco Lectrics range for various scales and gauges; for instance PL-80 is for OO gauge code 100 and O code 124, etc), then now is the time to make the connections and

JOINING CURVED SECTIONS OF STREAMLINE TRACK

1

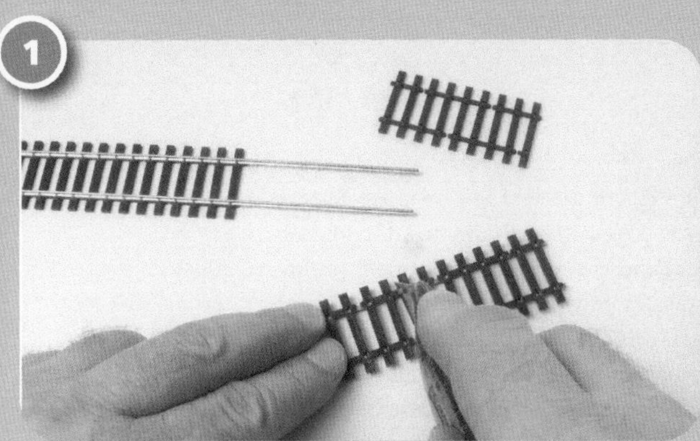

There are several ways to join curved track; this method works well and is suitable for anyone without previous experience. The first 10 or so sleepers from the ends that are to be joined together need to be removed, by cutting through the web. The rail ends are then carefully pre-formed into a curve by hand.

2

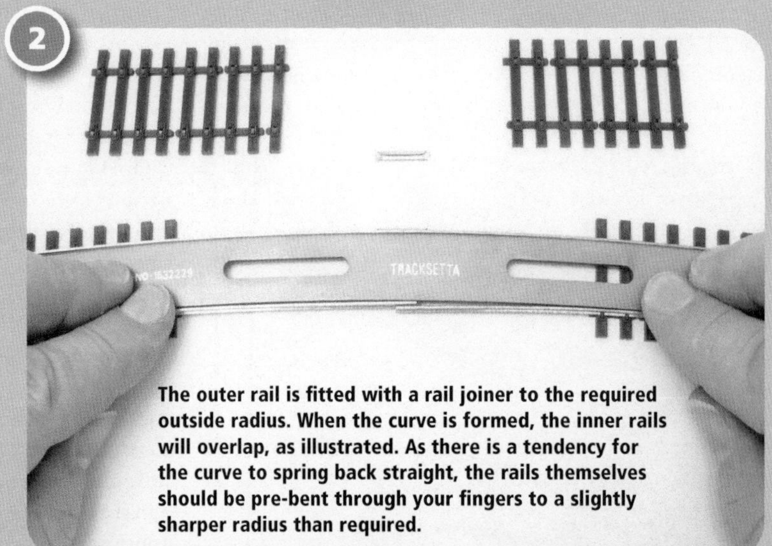

The outer rail is fitted with a rail joiner to the required outside radius. When the curve is formed, the inner rails will overlap, as illustrated. As there is a tendency for the curve to spring back straight, the rails themselves should be pre-bent through your fingers to a slightly sharper radius than required.

3

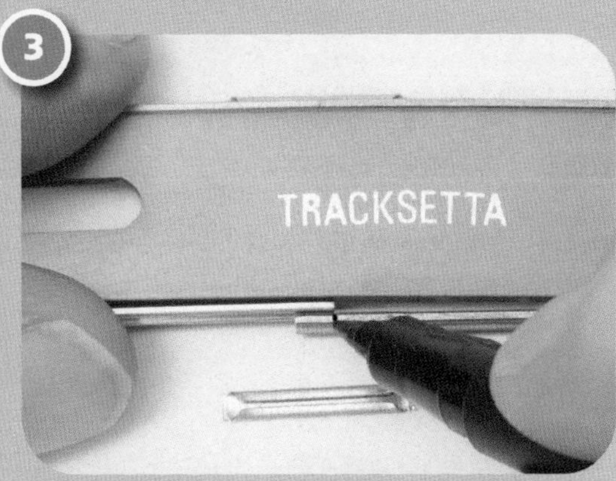

The points at which the rails must be cut are marked with a pen. The use of the Tracksetta template helps to establish the exact amount of overlap, but is by no means essential.

4

The excess rail can be removed by cutting with a razor saw against a wooden block, as demonstrated. Track cutters could be used instead if preferred.

5

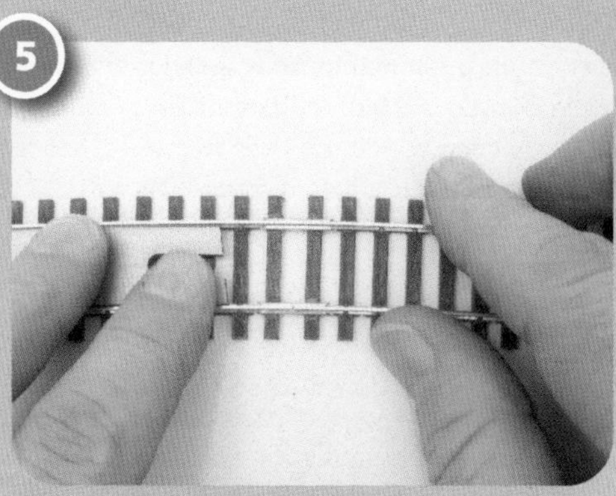

The rail ends are dressed with a file so that the sleeper sections can be threaded back on to the rails and the two sections joined together easily. The Tracksetta template is used to check that the join is smooth and free of any kinks.

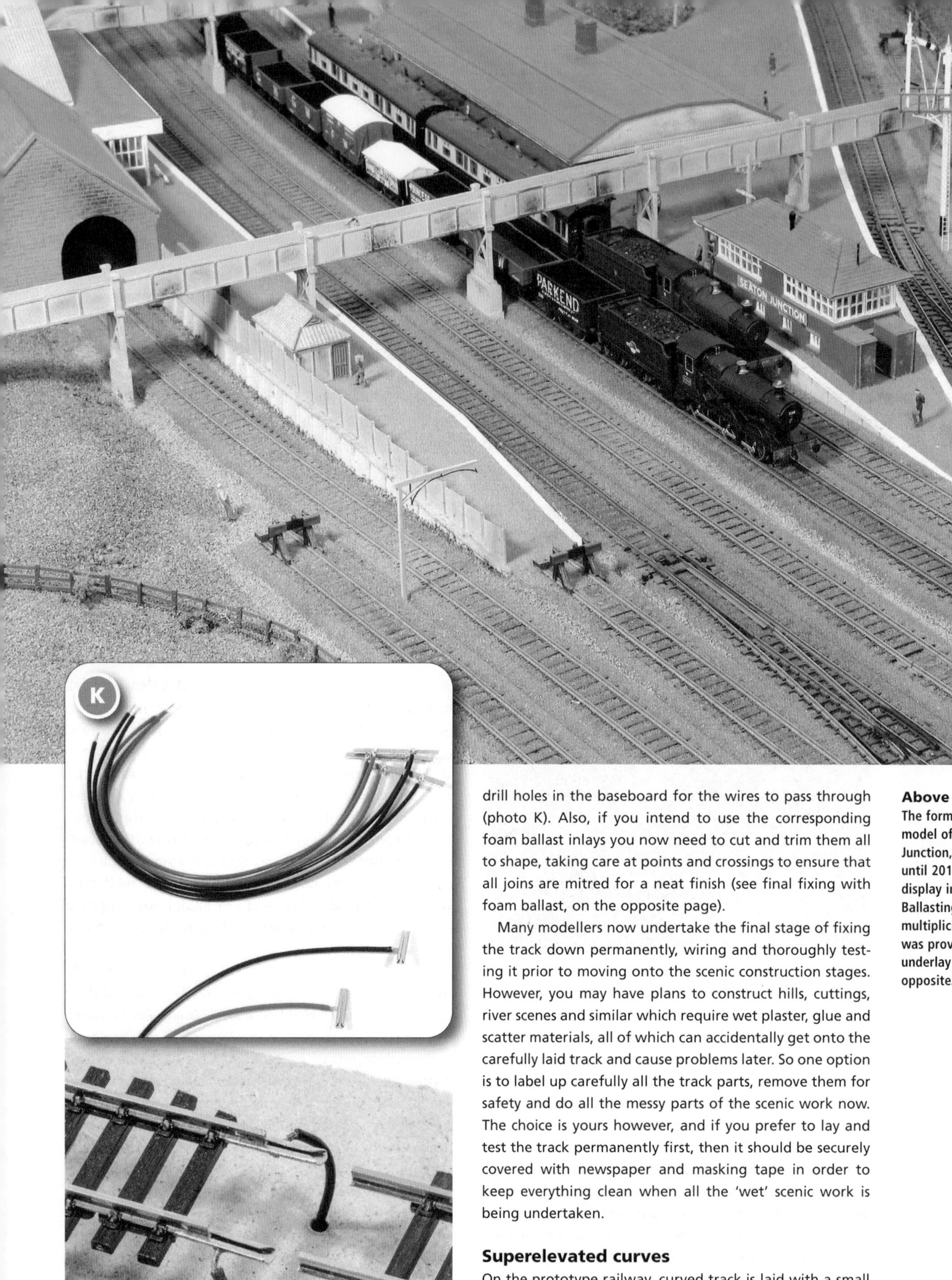

drill holes in the baseboard for the wires to pass through (photo K). Also, if you intend to use the corresponding foam ballast inlays you now need to cut and trim them all to shape, taking care at points and crossings to ensure that all joins are mitred for a neat finish (see final fixing with foam ballast, on the opposite page).

Many modellers now undertake the final stage of fixing the track down permanently, wiring and thoroughly testing it prior to moving onto the scenic construction stages. However, you may have plans to construct hills, cuttings, river scenes and similar which require wet plaster, glue and scatter materials, all of which can accidentally get onto the carefully laid track and cause problems later. So one option is to label up carefully all the track parts, remove them for safety and do all the messy parts of the scenic work now. The choice is yours however, and if you prefer to lay and test the track permanently first, then it should be securely covered with newspaper and masking tape in order to keep everything clean when all the 'wet' scenic work is being undertaken.

Superelevated curves

On the prototype railway, curved track is laid with a small cant down towards the inner rail. This is called superelevation and provides a smoother ride for trains around the curve at high speeds. It also improves running on model railways as well and is easy to achieve. If you are intending to lay curves with super elevation then this must be considered before final fixing of the track; when fixing it down,

Above
The former N gauge model of Seaton Junction, which up until 2013 was on display in Pecorama. Ballasting for the multiplicity of tracks was provided by foam underlay – see section opposite.

HOW TO ATTACH WIRE DROPPERS

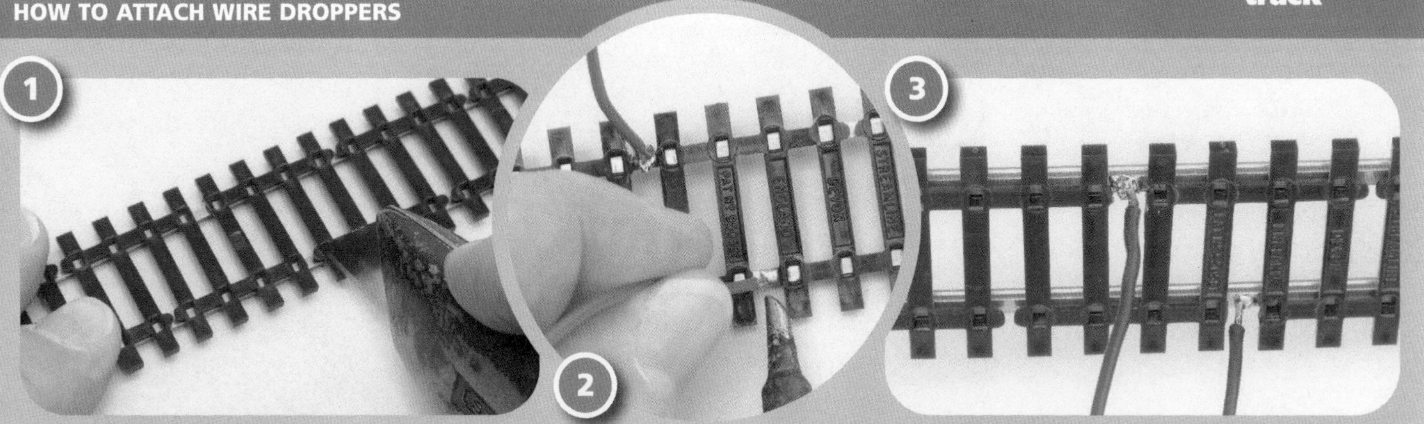
1
2
3

Turn the section of track upside down and cut the required sections of sleeper base away, as demonstrated, to allow wires to be soldered to the underside of each of the rails. Note how the locations are offset on each side so that the sleeper base is not completely severed.

The ends of the wire droppers should be twisted into a neat 'L' shape and tinned with solder. (The subject of soldering is explained in greater detail on p105). The wire is then soldered in place as shown, with care taken to avoid damaging the plastic sleeper base with the tip of the iron.

The wire droppers fixed in place. As explained in the main text, corresponding holes are drilled in the baseboard, or trackbed, to allow these to be passed through and connected to the main layout wiring loom/power bus. Once the track is ballasted the wires are almost invisible.

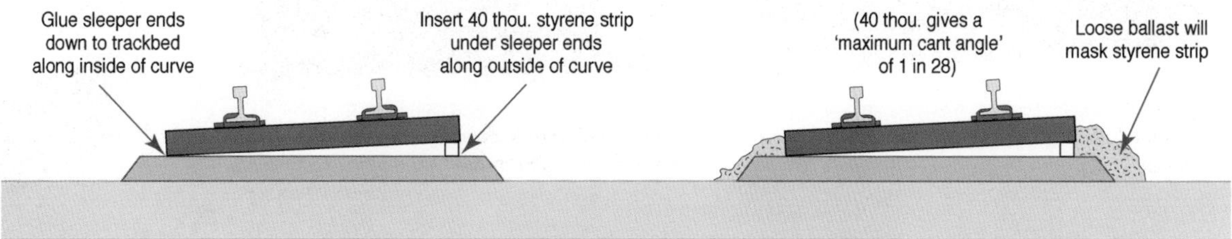
Glue sleeper ends down to trackbed along inside of curve
Insert 40 thou. styrene strip under sleeper ends along outside of curve
(40 thou. gives a 'maximum cant angle' of 1 in 28)
Loose ballast will mask styrene strip

Note: Use 40 thou. strip only on middle section of curve, building up the height gently on either side. Sudden changes will cause derailments. Superelevation works best when combined with some form of transition curve.

initially only glue or pin it along the inner edge. Once the glue has cured, gently lever up the outer edge and insert a 40thou strip of plasticard for OO (use 20thou for N) to lift the outer end of the sleepers. Where there is a transition between the curve and a straight section of track, the fillets of styrene need to be gradually reduced in thickness as the curve eases off; this can be achieved by using progressively thinner sections of styrene such as 20thou and 10thou. See the above diagram.

Ballasting the track

Tracks on prototype railways are almost always laid with ballast which holds it firmly in position and aids drainage. There are two main types of ballast for model railways; pre-moulded foam, or loose chippings. Foam ballast is fitted during the track fixing stage, whilst loose ballast can be secured after the track is fixed.

Final fixing with foam ballast

The Peco Streamline ballast inlays are designed for both plain track and pointwork. They consist of flexible foam strip moulded in a realistic brown/grey colour with matching sleeper indentations into which the track fits exactly. Thus the 'ballast' lies flush with the sleeper tops and the track itself is 'cushioned' with a little up and down movement – exactly like the real thing. Foam also has the advantage of cleanliness, with no loose bits and pieces to get where they shouldn't, and quietens the running. The one disadvantage is that foam ballast has a limited lifespan of six to 10 years before it starts to disintegrate.

Laying track with ballast inlay is simple, and there are two methods to consider. Pinning the track in place is one method, which is useful when track formations may need to be altered in the short term. However, the baseboard top surface material must be one that will readily take pins; Sundeala is a very good surface for pinning track down, but plywood or chipboard surfaces can be too hard.

If you are entirely happy with the track formation and alignment, it can be completely glued to the baseboard for permanence. We suggest that the track itself is first lightly glued to the ballast inlay with impact adhesive run along the bottoms of the sleepers (photo L). When dry this

L

creates a series of 'ballasted units' which are then clipped together and glued to the baseboard with PVA adhesive, positioning it directly onto the previously drawn lines (photo M).

The use on curves of the aforementioned Tracksetta templates can also be really helpful to get a smooth radius before the glue sets. Two or more templates of different radii can be used in conjunction to produce smooth and realistic transition curves. For straight sections, a straight Tracksetta template or steel rule can be used to align the track before the glue dries and the Peco 6'-way gauge again comes in useful here for maintaining the correct spacing on double track sections.

Once aligned to your satisfaction, and before the glue has set, the track, on curves especially, will need to be held in position with some strategically placed pins. Peco fine track pins (ref.SL-14) are most suitable, being lightly driven in and then removed once the glue has set. Alternatively for the smaller gauges, drawing pins are equally useful as they can also be pulled out and repositioned until correct alignment is achieved.

Ballast inlays are available for some plain track, points and crossings in Streamline Z, N (code 80 and some code 55) and OO gauge (code 100 and code 75); they are being phased out. Note that if you are using the Peco PL-10 turnout motors under the track it will be necessary to modify the foam shape either with a craft knife or scissors.

Final fixing with loose granular ballast

An alternative to foam ballast, and for all other gauges not mentioned in the previous paragraph, is to use a loose granular ballast, such as the fine stone chippings in the PecoScene range. Indeed this is the preferred method for countless numbers of experienced modellers.

It is possible to glue the track in place and ballast all at the same time, but for best results it is recommended that a three-stage process is adopted – firstly the track is glued in place; then the electrical connections are installed and thoroughly tested; and only then is ballasting carried out. Streamline track can be glued with waterproof PVA directly to the baseboard surface, though some prefer to incorporate a sub-base made of thin (3mm/4mm) cork sheet, the purpose of which is to quieten the running, especially on plywood baseboards. Also, if another track type is being used, such as hand-made soldered track with copperclad sleepers, the cork helps to provide a prototypical ballast shoulder at each side. If cork is to be used, this must be cut to size using the original marking out as the template, then glued in place with PVA and weighted down until it has set (usually 24hrs).

FIXING STREAMLINE TRACK AND ADDING BALLAST

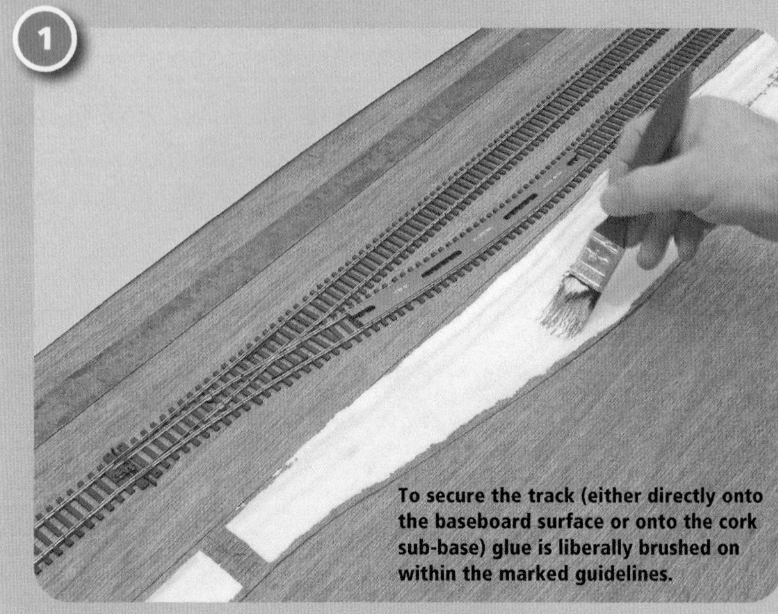

To secure the track (either directly onto the baseboard surface or onto the cork sub-base) glue is liberally brushed on within the marked guidelines.

The pre-cut sections are then repositioned, clipped together and carefully re-aligned in the glue, using Tracksetta templates and 6'-way gauges as necessary. At this stage take extreme care not to get glue into the moving parts of points. When correctly aligned, drawing pins or Peco track pins can be used to hold the track in place until the glue has dried completely.

Methods of point operation

Another aspect that must be considered at the track laying stage is that of point control. As supplied all Peco points are ready to lay and capable of being switched by hand by literally reaching across and pushing the point blades over with your index finger. The moulded spigots on each end of the tiebar are there for this purpose. On a first layout, this method represents the simplest way to get started and there are many modellers who are quite content with this. However it is often desirable to have remote point operation which helps to create a more realistic effect and allows points to be changed from a central control area, rather than having to reach across the layout to change them; a particular problem on large layouts and where points are located in hidden or difficult to reach areas.

After wiring and testing, the ballasting can begin. Patience and care are a requisite here though you will be rewarded in the final outcome. The granules are applied loose and spread carefully between the sleepers with a small brush tackling about 6" (150mm) at a time.

4

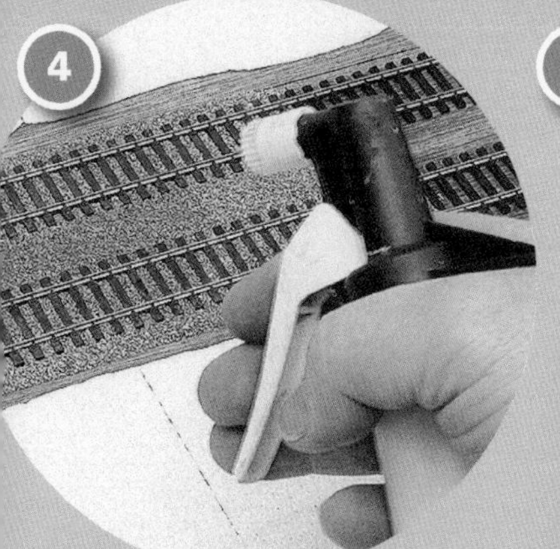

Next 'wet' the ballast by 'misting' it with water from a garden spray, the water should have a few drops of detergent added to minimise the surface tension effect.

5

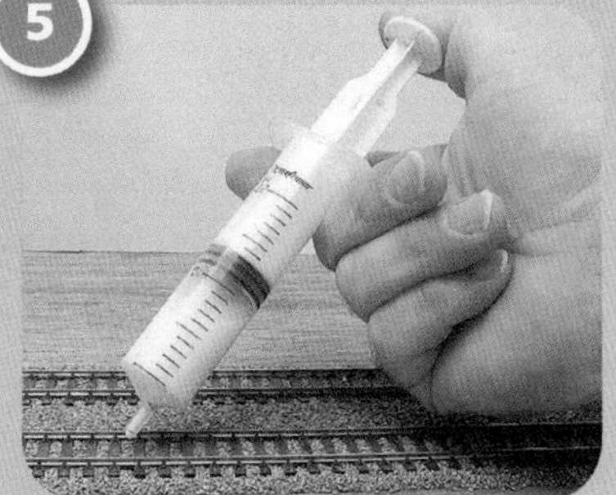

Once wet, a one part waterproof PVA glue/three parts water solution (again with a few drops of detergent) is gently dripped onto the wet ballast using an eye dropper or syringe held about 10mm above the workpiece. It will take a few days for the ballast to dry out thoroughly and some areas may need to be glued a second time.

6

The final step is to paint the ballast and the rail sides, this is optional, but particularly recommended when granite chippings have been used as these often dry to an unrealistic pale green colour once the glue has set. A thin wash of mid brown/grey acrylic colour or thinned enamel paint brushed over the dried ballast and sleeper tops works well. Take great care not to get paint onto electrical contact parts or moving parts of the points.

To operate a point remotely there needs to be an arrangement whereby the tiebar can be moved from one side to the other, thereby moving the blades and changing the route set by the point. This action can be achieved either mechanically using a 'wire in tube' method whereby an operating wire is linked to a switch or knob at the edge of the baseboard (see Fig. 16 on page 66), or electrically using a motor. It is the latter method that we will concentrate on here, specifically the remote operation of points using solenoid type motors.

Power supply for point motors

To install point motors a separate power supply circuit is needed from that for the track. Many 'cased' controllers have an additional auxilliary power output, usually 16V ac, which can be used for this purpose. However, if you are using a controller without an auxilliary output then a separate transformer/power supply needs to be obtained. Gaugemaster is one example of a manufacturer which specialises in electrical components for model railways, offering a large range of cased controllers and transformers (see page 68).

Installing solenoid point motors

The simplest to install in the Peco range of point motors, is the side mounted motor (PL-11) which is designed to be pinned beside Peco Setrack or Streamline OO/HO code 100 points (photo N). There is no need to cut holes in the baseboard because the motor is surface mounted, and it is supplied with colour-coded wires already attached.

N

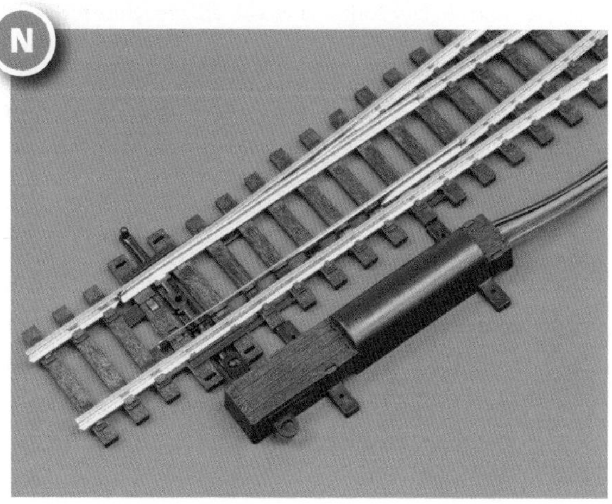

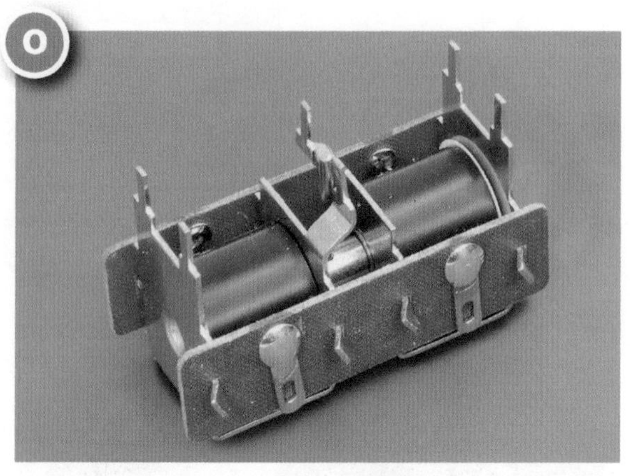

The standard Peco solenoid point motor (PL-10) as shown in photo O, is designed to clip directly to the underside of a Peco point. It requires a 40mm x 24mm aperture to be cut in the baseboard for installation.

A low-amperage version (PL-10W) is available for use with small, low-output transformer controllers.

The standard motor is also available with an extended operating pin (PL-10E) to allow for a smaller sized 9.5mm dia hole in the baseboard. However, a plastic mounting plate (PL-9) is required to install this version (photo P). A low-amperage variant is also available (PL-10WE).

Non-soldered connections

Peco solenoid point motors are supplied with solder tags for connecting the electrical wires, however, there are now products available to aid installation without the need for the modeller to be proficient at soldering. Intended for the PL-10 series motors, the Peco wiring loom (PL-34) comprises spade connectors which are a push-fit onto the point motor terminal tags, with the other ends tinned for connecting to a screw terminal block (PL-39). See pages 68 and 69 for further information on these easy to use solderless connectors.

Operating switches

Even if you intend to use a digital control system to operate your locos, you can still use a traditional analogue point control system for changing points. Indeed many modellers still do, as it eliminates the cost of providing accessory decoders for all the points (see page 68 for further explanation). Consequently it is still quite common to see switches for changing points fitted into a mimic diagram on a centralised layout control panel (photo Q). Peco passing contact switches (PL-26R/Y/B/W) are designed specifically for the purpose of firing the solenoids, in that they provide a short burst of current when the switch is operated (photo R).

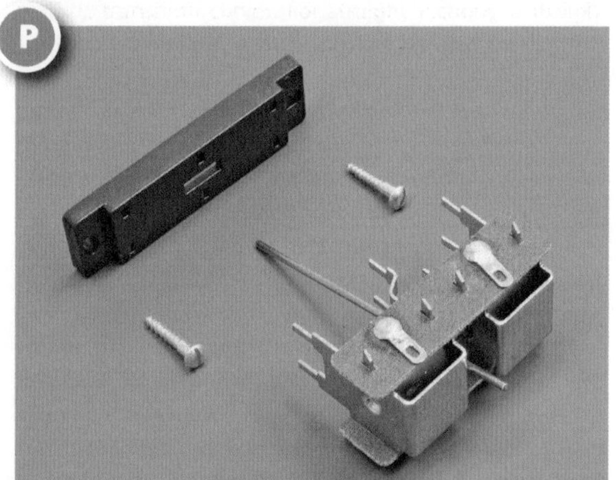

INSTALLING A PECO TWIN SOLENOID POINT MOTOR (PL-10)

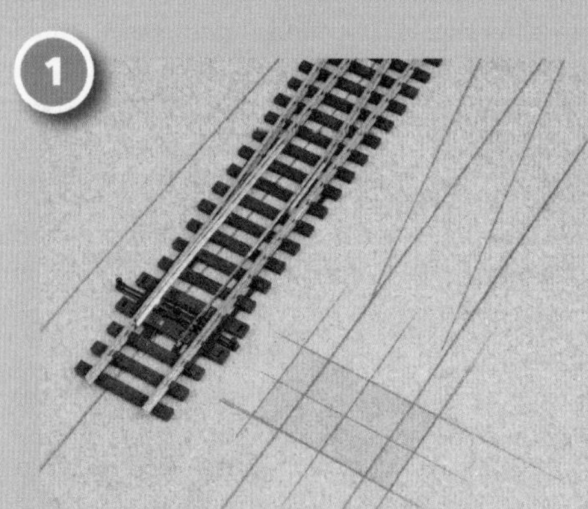

With the outline of the trackwork drawn out on the baseboard, the centre point of the tiebar is marked, around which a 40mm x 24mm box is drawn.

The aperture can be cut out by drilling a series of small holes around the inside edge, and then cutting through with a saw. The edges can then be sanded to a smooth finish, as illustrated.

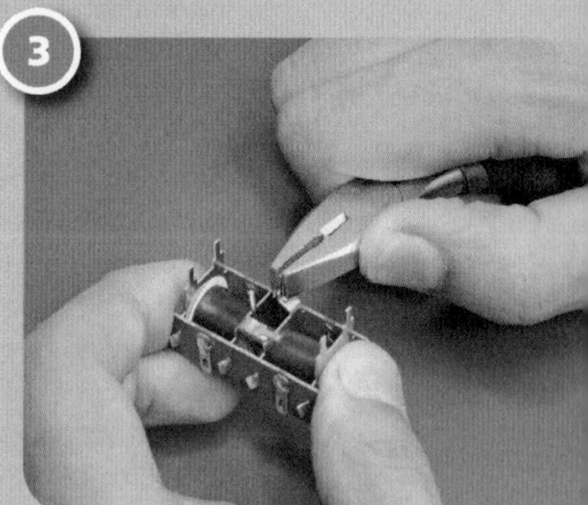

To fit the PL-10 series motors to Peco OO gaug points, the central pair of legs – which are use when the motor is clipped to an N gauge poin need bending over at 90° using a pair of pliers

Right
The Peco passing contact switches (PL-26) are intended for use with the Peco twin solenoid point motors and are available with levers in red, yellow, blue or white. The Peco mounting plate (PL-28) enables these switches to be fixed to a control panel, as illustrated in photo Q.

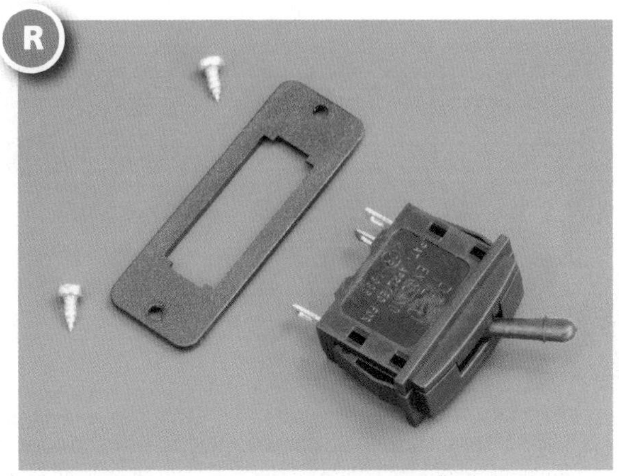

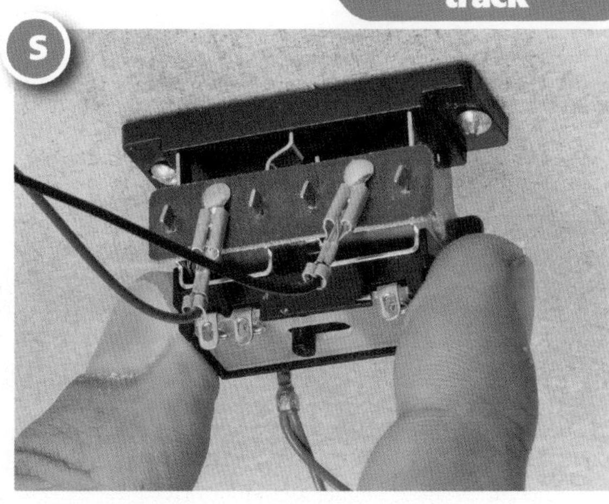

Installing PL-10 twin solenoid point motors

If you choose to use electric point motors instead of hand operation or wire-in-tube methods, the solenoids need to be fitted before the track is finally secured in place with either glue or pins. Below is a short step by step sequence showing how this is done, although remember if you prefer you can use the longer operating pin motors and mounting plates (as opposite; photo P), you can avoid the need to cut such large holes.

Fitting accessory switches to PL-10s

Some of the points, crossings and slips in the Peco track ranges which have live (Electrofrog) frogs must be fitted with an electrical switch to change the electrical polarity of the frog in conjunction with switching the route. There are numerous ways to achieve this, but perhaps the easiest method is to use the Peco accessory switch (PL-13). This is designed to be clipped to the underside of a PL-10 series motor, as illustrated in photo S such that the motor switches both the point blades and the frog polarity simultaneously. Note that wires have yet to be attached to the tags on the switch, whilst wires for the motor are shown fitted in position. Peco push-on terminal connectors (PL-31) can be used to connect up the PL-13 switch with the wire connections on the pointwork item.

Wiring twin solenoid point motors and accessory switches

With all your point motors and accessory switches in position, it is now time to turn to the actual wiring. Although full instructions are supplied with all Peco items, you can find out more about this aspect of layout construction by turning to our section on Controlling Your Railway on page 54. Specifically, for point motor and accessory switch wiring, turn to pages 68-71 which covers basic point motor wiring as well as other important aspects, such as wiring of multiple point motors, operating point motors simultaneously, installing capacitor discharge units (photo T), and also the alternative method of 'probe-and-stud' point motor switching.

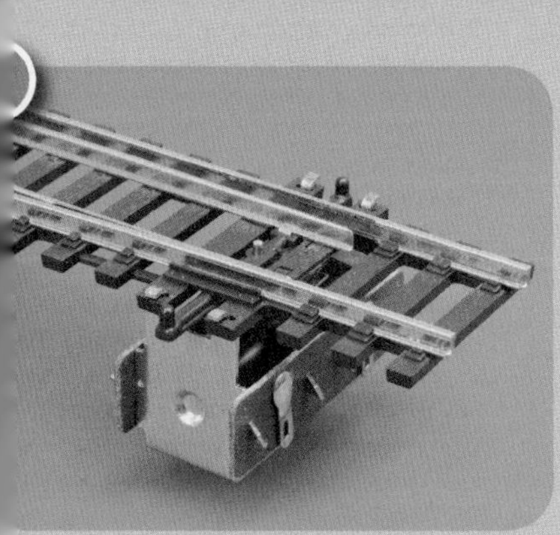

e outside pairs of legs clip through holes in e sleeper base of the point, here a Peco code) large radius one. The legs' tops can then be ded over to retain the motor in position.

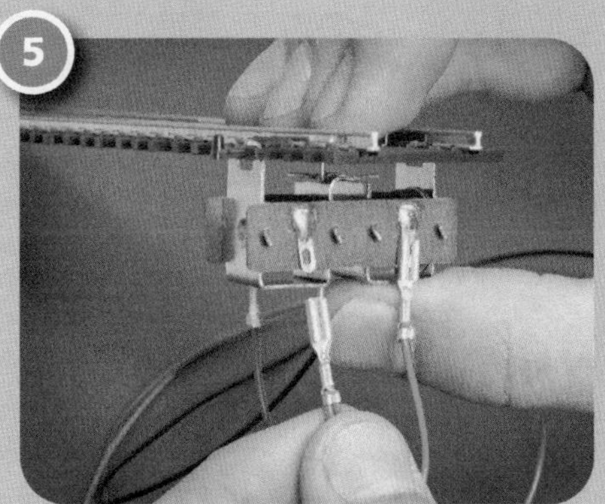

The Peco wiring loom (PL-34) makes for straightforward connecting up of the point motor without the need for soldering. Once the wires have been attached, thread them through the aperture.

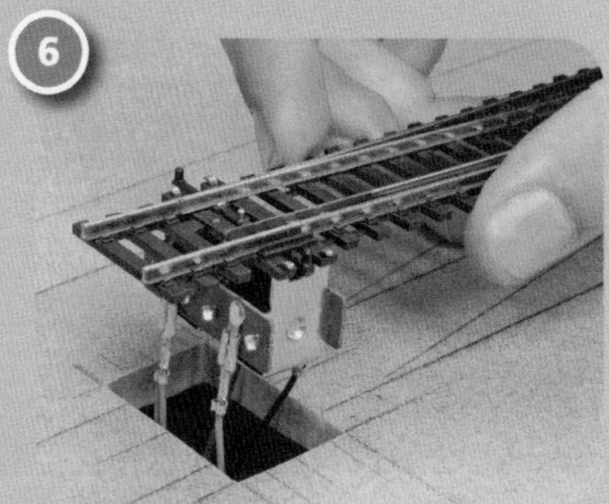

The point can now be fixed in position on the baseboard with track pins. NB this 'working example' excludes the cork or ballast foam underlay which would usually be used between the track and baseboard surface.

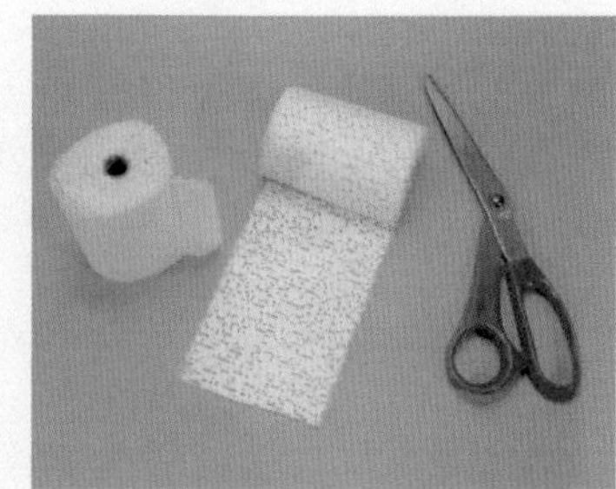

Above
Peco Scene PS-36 Landform plaster bandage is ideal for making the hard shell for the landscape substructure. It is ready to apply straight from the packet.

Modelling the landscape

The term landscape refers to those elements of scenery on a layout which represents the countryside through which the railway runs. It encompasses all the features of rolling hills, embankments, cuttings, bridges and tunnels and is thus distinct from other elements of model railway scenery, such as buildings, stations, townscapes, etc.

In some ways it is perhaps one of the easiest aspects of building a model railway. It is relatively inexpensive to produce, does not demand special skill to execute and most will find that pleasing results can be achieved quite quickly. However, with several established methods used in landscape modelling the greatest difficulty can be deciding which method to adopt.

Methods of the landscape

For construction purposes, model landscape can be divided into three key elements; a sub-structure, a hard shell, and a 'scenic' surface layer. Each of these elements can be built using any of the different techniques shown in the panel on page 37 – opposite.

Fig. 1 shows the sub-structure built up from expanded foam blocks cut from a 25mm thick sheet. Expanded polystyrene is suitable, as is Styrofoam (a more dense insulation foam board), both are available from DIY outlets and builders' merchants. 'Hot wire' cutting devices were once popular, but the quickest way to cut foam sheet is with a sharp kitchen carving knife or bread knife – though do take care and consider wearing safety gloves. The blocks

Right
One way to create the scenic sub-structure is to use garden wire netting. Here it is being covered with Peco Scene Landform plaster bandage.

are cut and shaped to the desired contours and glued in place with white PVA wood glue. Our step-by-step sequence on page 38 shows this method of construction.

Fig. 2 shows a traditional method popular in the past which is far from costly and uses materials readily to hand. Offcuts of insulation board are cut to the profile of the hillside and secured in position about 30cm apart. Crumpled newspaper is then packed into the space between the profiles to give additional support and strips of card are stapled and glued across them to form a light-weight mesh.

The use of chicken wire to form the sub-structure (Fig 3) also dates back many years. This is particularly suitable for large expanses of landscape, or when an open top type baseboard is being used.

The second key element is the hard shell. This can also be made using different techniques; plaster impregnated bandage, plaster based filler, or the patch system.

Plaster-impregnated bandage (above right) is available from model shops, such as Peco Scene Landform, and is used to produce a thin, resilient shell. It is cut into strips, dunked in water and then laid criss-cross over the sub-structure, finally being smoothed by hand before it dries. Two or three layers applied this way are generally required and the method works best with a firm sub-structure, such as with polystyrene blocks or chicken wire.

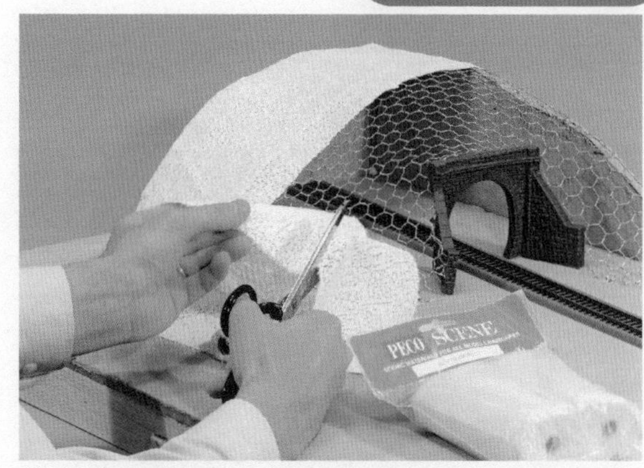

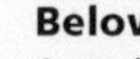

Below
A section of the landscape on Bob Petch's OO gauge layout *Shillinghurst.*

METHODS OF FORMING THE LANDSCAPE

Fig. 1 Expanded polystyrene sub-structure

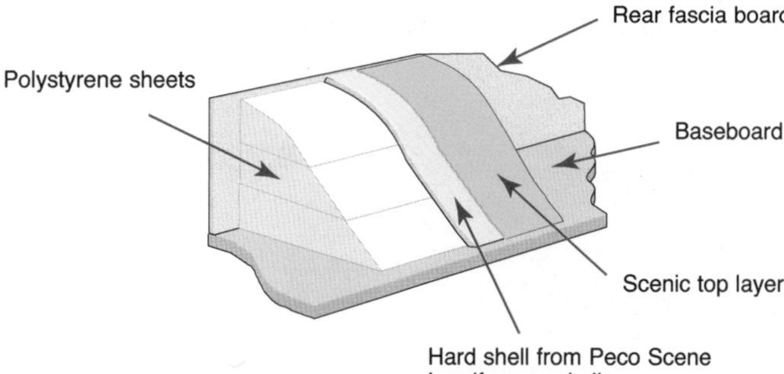

Fig. 2 Card and paper sub-structure

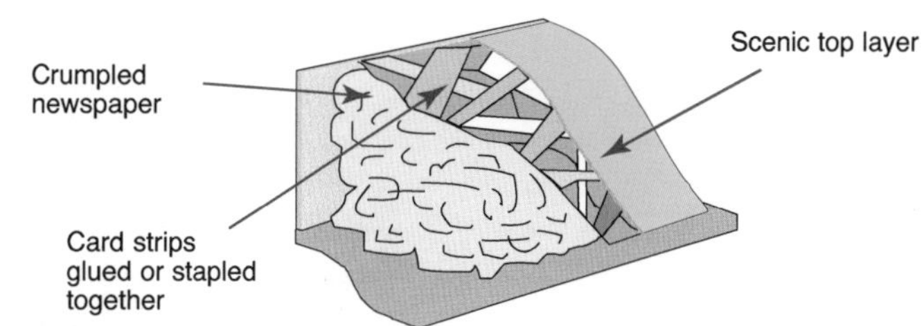

Fig. 3 Wire netting sub-structure

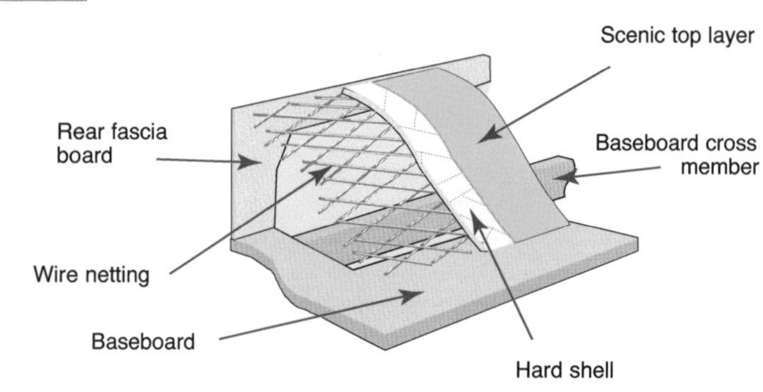

CREATING THE LANDSCAPE STEP-BY-STEP USING EXPANDED POLYSTYRENE FOR THE SUB-STRUCTURE

Whichever method you use to build the sub-structure, the first stage is to fit the edge profile boards. These are cut to shape from thin ply or hardboard with a fretsaw or electric jig saw and glued and pinned into position with softwood offcuts. DIY joining blocks add extra strength.

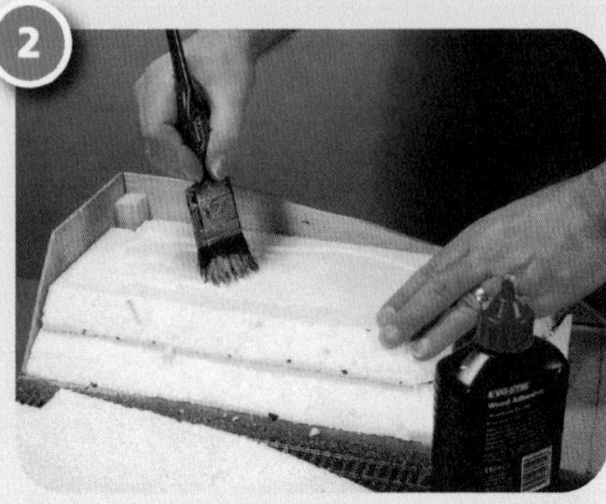

For this sequence, 25mm expanded polystyrene sheet is being used for the sub-structure. It is marked up, cut to the desired shape and fixed in place with PVA wood glue which is applied thickly with a large brush. The sheets need weighting down for 24hrs until the glue sets.

The sub-structure is finished off with a hard outer shell, in this case DIY plaster-based filler is mixed and applied with a palette knife. Alternatively, plaster impregnated bandage (such as Peco Scene Landform) or the patch *papier-mâché* method, can be used to create the shell.

With scatter materials for ground cover, first apply a coat of earth coloured paint. Leave to dry, then, working on small areas at a time, brush on a 50-50 mix of glue/water and cover it generously with a coat of fine scatter. When dry, you may need to do this again to achieve good coverage.

Next, protect other areas of the layout with some old newspaper and spray the working area lightly with diluted glue (about 75-25 water/glue). Don't spray the glue too heavily as it will run or form puddles, or worse, wash away the previously applied layer of fine scatter.

Sprinkle some coarse scatter onto the sprayed area to represent tufts of grass and weeds, this time covering only selected patches of the base layer. To finish, add a little fine pale yellow or pale brown scatter on top to represent highlight areas and leave to dry for about 48hrs.

An alternative way to make the hard shell is to use DIY plaster-based filler, such as Polyfilla. This is mixed up according to the instructions and spread on with a palette knife or putty knife, finally being smoothed off to the desired contours with a palette knife and a dampened decorating brush.

The plaster-based filler method is illustrated in our step-by-step sequence and can be used successfully only with a solid sub-structure such as polystyrene. Other sub-structures will require a fine scrim, such as hessian or Peco Scene Landform, before the top plaster layer can be applied with confidence.

The patch system uses rough squares of newspaper pasted in position to form the hard shell. Known as the *papier mâché* method, it is light and inexpensive, though it does take some time to complete, as three or four separate layers are usually required. It can however be used on most sub-structures and is especially suited to the card strip system.

The final element of the landscape is the top scenic layer and again there are various ways to represent this, such as using a fine scatter material as shown above. More methods of applying the top scenic coat are described on pages 39-41 but first we need to consider the installation of any civil engineering structures – bridges, tunnels, retaining walls, viaducts, etc – which are best fitted during the construction of the sub-structure.

Bridges and tunnels

Bridges, tunnels, retaining walls and the like, are essential features of the railway landscape. They keep gradients to a minimum and allow the railway to cross over roads, rivers and valleys or pass under hills and mountains. Even on a flat landscape overbridges for roads, lanes and farm tracks are quite common.

Bridges of course come in all varieties, sizes and designs and unless you are modelling a specific prototype, there are many kits available to assist the modeller.

Opposite right
Bridges are usually built up as separate items, as are tunnel entrances, and fitted into the baseboard at the desired location. The scenic sub-structure is then built around the unit as shown, using your preferred method.

Fig. 4 – creating a drop-section

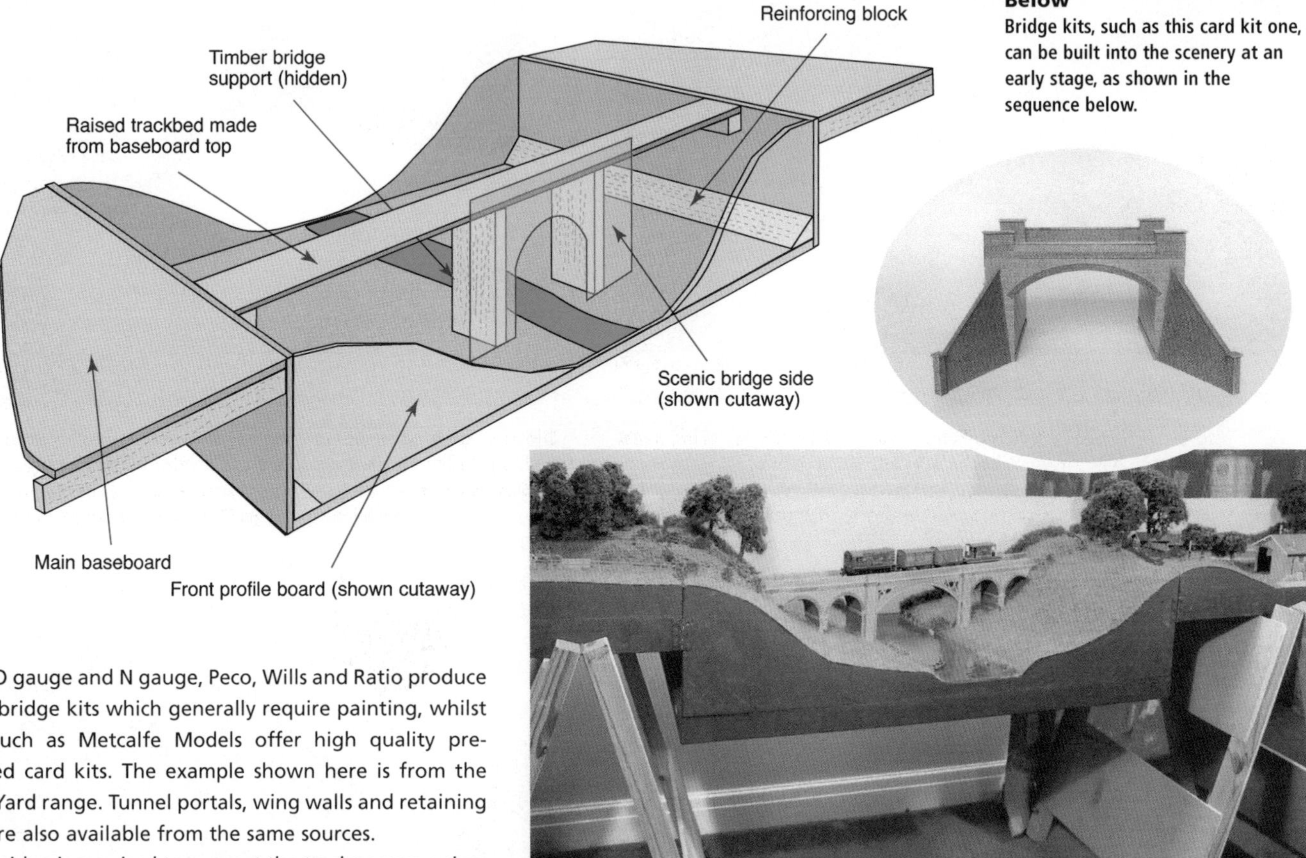

Below
Bridge kits, such as this card kit one, can be built into the scenery at an early stage, as shown in the sequence below.

In OO gauge and N gauge, Peco, Wills and Ratio produce plastic bridge kits which generally require painting, whilst firms such as Metcalfe Models offer high quality pre-coloured card kits. The example shown here is from the ModelYard range. Tunnel portals, wing walls and retaining walls are also available from the same sources.

If a bridge is required to support the tracks across a river or valley, then the trackbed will require adequate hidden timber supports, as shown opposite.The bridge walls and arch are purely cosmetic. Overbridges that carry no load other than the scenic finish can be constructed without extra support, the kits themselves being strong enough.

To incorporate a bridge into the landscape, firstly put the kit together following the manufacturer's instructions. Next, before any of the surrounding landscape sub-structure is built, secure the completed unit in its location on the layout, as shown here. The earthworks are then built up around the bridge using your preferred sub-structure construction method.

As a general rule, the slope of embankments and cuttings should be constructed at an angle of about 45°. There are exceptions however, and rock-faced cuttings and retaining walls can be almost vertical in alignment. In our example below, the sub-structure is again being created from expanded polystyrene. A thin plaster shell will be applied and carefully blended close up to the bridge to seal any gaps prior to finishing with the scenic top layer.

With tunnel construction, the tracks are hidden entirely beneath the sub-structure. Dummy tunnel walls and roof are built up around the tracks out of thin ply sheet. The portal and wing walls are from the Peco range and are simply glued in position as shown below. Edge profile boards are fitted and the rest of the landscape is then built up around the tunnel using your chosen method.

Adding the scenic top layer

The third element of landscape construction is the scenic top layer; this is the visible layer representing grass and undergrowth, or just plain earth.

Above
Here's a drop section made as per the diagram in Fig 4. It formed a scenic extension to an early OO gauge layout called *Etton* built by Peter Goss, who later went on to build the award winning *Rowland's Castle* and *Worlds End* scenic masterpieces.

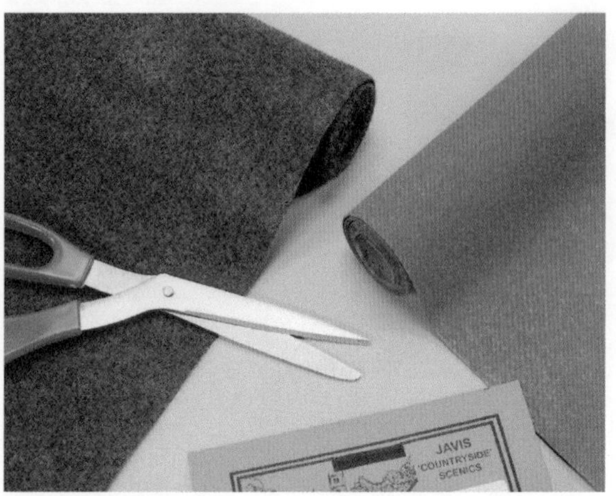

Left
Fibre mats come in a variety of sizes and colours and can be trimmed to shape with scissors. The lengths of fibres differ greatly, from fine weave to represent a trimmed lawn to more loose and 'hairy' types for replicating long grass.

These days, there are several ways that modellers use to create the scenic top layer. Essentially though, these fall into just two basic methods; the 'mat' method and the 'scatter' method.

With the mat method, the grass or earth, is created using a fibrous mat of flexible material that is glued tightly over the hard shell of the landscape. Proprietary mats are available from firms such as Hornby, Javis, Heki, Busch, etc, and are pre-coloured and available in various 'textures'. These simply need cutting to the required shape and fixing down with PVA glue. Further layers of undergrowth and detailing can be attached to the surface at a later stage.

Numerous other common household materials are used by modellers as scenic mats. These include soft toy fur fabric, medical lint, fibrous carpet underlay and even insulation matting from old cars! These materials mostly require colouring to represent grass etc. Whole mats can be coloured prior to laying by dyeing with commercial fabric dyes, such as the Colron range. Once in position, additional shades can be blended in with powder, acrylic or poster paints.

Alternatively, colouring can be undertaken after the plain matting has been laid in place. Use powder or poster colours and add a little PVA glue and a drop of detergent to the solution to help the paint to flow through the fibres and remain fast when dry.

The alternative 'scatter' method probably dates back to the days when dyed sawdust was used by modellers to represent grass and turf. Materials have improved somewhat since then, especially those available commercially, though the method of application is still the same in principle, in that the scatter fibres are sprinkled onto a pre-glued surface and left to dry, as shown in the step-by-step sequence shown on page 38.

Commercial scatter materials are now much more sophisticated and colourfast than they used to be, and include; natural wood-fibre based flock powders; granular particles made from ground-up foam rubber and cork; and fine synthetic fibres which can be made to 'stand upright' like blades of grass by using a 'static' applicator.

There are now lots of manufacturers offering scenic scatters of all types including; Hornby, Peco, K&M, World War Scenics, Woodland Scenics and many more of continental origin. There is now a huge variety of colours and different textures, and all are widely available from model shops.

Left
Grass mats allow an area of scenery to be covered quickly and easily. Simply cut to shape and fix to the hard shell with glue. Where folds occur, slivers can be cut out, or the material simply overlapped. Further colouring or detailing can be added afterwards.

Right
Scatters from fibrous flock or finely ground foam rubber and cork have been around in the hobby for decades and are still very popular despite the recent rise in the use of 'static' grass. However, modellers have plenty of choice, and can find a method which suits them best.

Non-static applications rely on the particles being sprinkled onto a layer of PVA glue solution painted on to the hard shell which has been pre-painted with an earth colour mix. Work on small areas at a time and sprinkle a few different shades, adding coarser textures afterwards to represent thicker growth and long grass. A good idea is to mix a few shades together before use; about 80% of the mix is made up of the main colour, with two or three lighter/darker shades making up the other 20%.

For static applications, which use pre-coloured synthetic fibres, you need a special device called a 'static applicator' There are several types on the market from which to choose. Some resemble a tea strainer, whilst others look more like a tea caddy! However they all perform the same job, which is to apply a static electrical charge to the fibres as they are sprinkled onto the glue. This makes them stand upright until the glue dries to create a very realistic grass-like appearance. The basic method is shown in the sequence below, and as with powders, the fibres can be premixed to vary the final shade.

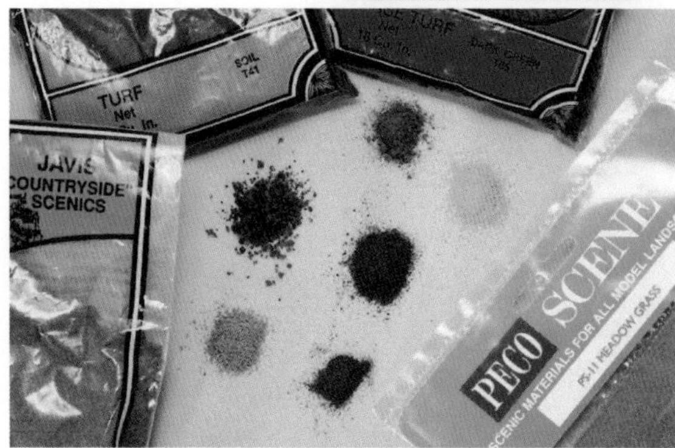

Both mat and scatter methods have advantages and disadvantages and often modellers make use of them side by side to create the desired effect. As with all aspects of modelling, practice and experience make all the difference, however, creating grassland is not an exacting task and any mistakes can easily be re-done until satisfactory results are achieved.

CREATING A SCENIC TOP LAYER USING THE STATIC GRASS METHOD

1

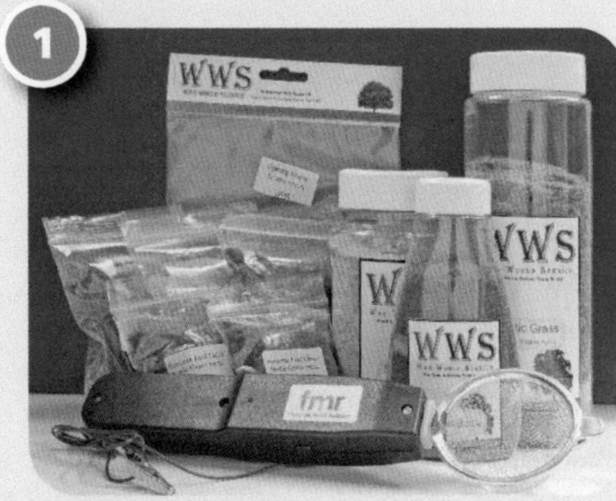

The main difference from conventional flock or ground foam scatter is that the fibres are synthetic and are given a static charge just before they are sprinkled over the glue. The applicator can be of the metal strainer type (as shown above) or wire colander, both of which are battery powered and safe to use.

2

The surface to be covered in grass is first painted an earth colour to hide the white plaster. When dry, and with the fibres ready mixed as desired, apply a coat of PVA adhesive over the entire area. This should be fast tack, but slow drying, to allow the grass fibres to penetrate once thay have been scattered.

3

An important aspect of static grass application is the 'earth' connection. A nail is driven into the layout to which the applicator's loose wire is attached via the crocodile clip supplied. This is to maintain the static charge (between the metal strainer and the layout) along which the charged fibres will align and thus stand up.

4

With all the area covered by the sprinkling, and before the glue dries, the applicator is waved gently over, but not in contact with, the fibres whilst it is still switched on. This further encourages the fibres to stand upright, as the effect of the charge is greater, the closer the applicator is to the fibres themselves.

5

Disconnect the applicator and the 'earth' terminal and leave the glue to dry thoroughly. Once this has occurred, the fibres will be safe to handle without them being loosened. The effect can be built up with successive applications of charged fibres, but the glue should be sprayed on, as brushing it on could flatten the previously applied layer.

6

When finished the overall effect is of a grassy bank. The fibres come in various lengths so short, neatly trimmed lawns, or rough areas of longer grass can be created. Here we have a neatly kept embankment for the steam age railway. Further tufts, weeds and small shrubs can be added with a dab of glue to represent rough areas and uncultivated land.

A4 No.2512 *Silver Fox* heads a northbound 'Silver Jubilee' service past Gas Works Signal cabin on Cliff Parsons' *Gresley Beat* layout. This section of his railway depicts an urban landscape scene in North London and is detailed with allotments, industrial buildings and some splendid Victorian terraces built by Geoff Taylor.

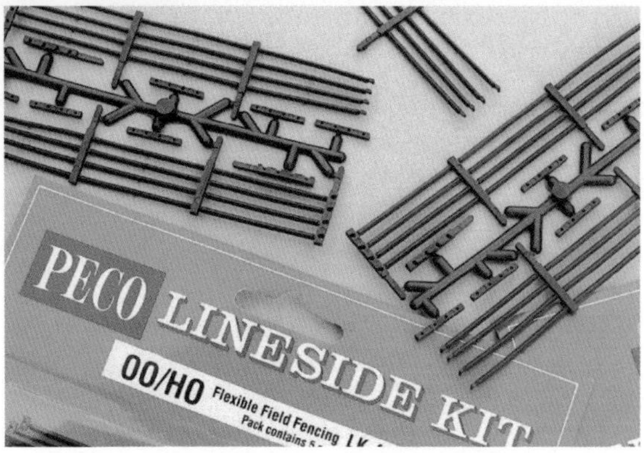

Above
Ian Graham's scenic layout *Mereton Junction and Allchurch* which includes examples of many of the scenic elements described in this section.

DETAILING THE LANDSCAPE

With the basic shape and colouring of the landscape completed, we now turn our attention to developing realistic scenery by adding all the details which transform the bare hillsides into woodland, farmers' fields, townscapes and urban sprawl – whichever takes our fancy.

Countryside scenery will include farmland, woodland, hedging and fencing. There may be a stream, river or pond, and perhaps rock faces to railway cuttings and embankments. In urban areas detail will include retaining walls, arches, boundary walls and all sorts of buildings, from simple huts to huge mills and factories (see page 46 onwards). Whilst basic landscape has to be built up from scratch using raw materials, a lot of detail can be added using commercially available accessories.

Lineside fencing

Fencing is a characteristic lineside feature of the British railway scene and in the popular gauges is well provided for by the trade. Most commercial fencing comes in plastic moulded strips about 200mm (8") long, though some types are made from etched brass.

Moulded fencing strips tend to be rigid and can only be fitted easily onto a level landscape. Where fencing is required to run across the undulating contours of an embankment or cutting, the post and rail style Peco Flexible Field Fencing kit (right) is the ideal solution. This product can be fitted in a few minutes and is designed to be bent around the contours of the scenic base whilst keeping the posts upright. It is available for N, OO and O Gauges and comes ready coloured in brown plastic. The individual strips just need clipping together with the aid of a small metal blade until the required length is achieved (as shown below).

The whole length is then transferred to the layout where holes corresponding to the fence post pegs are made with a bradawl in the hard shell of the landscape as shown in the top picture. The fencing is then pushed into the holes for a tight fit – lower picture. Alternatively each post can be secured with a blob of clear adhesive (such as Bostik or similar) to provide added strength.

Already, this simple and easily fitted addition begins the transformation of basic bare landscape into realistic scenery. Additional colouring and weathering can be applied using a dry brushing technique if desired.

Alternative fencing styles are available from Ratio for OO gauge (with a steadily expanding range for N and O gauges). This includes; wire and post, 'Midland' style (with sloping palings), 'GWR' wooden paling and spear point railings, 'Southern' style concrete sectional fencing and a modern wood planking type. Commercial fencing kits are ideal for speed and ease of fixing, especially where long lengths have to be fitted quickly. For those who prefer, fencing can be constructed from scratch using fine obechi strip wood. This method replicates the construction of the real thing, where posts and palings are cut individually and glued in place. It results in very realistic fence work but is time consuming.

Hedges and bushes

Hedges are to be seen all over the countryside, especially acting as boundaries around fields. There are dozens of ways of representing them on the layout from the use of naturally occurring plant materials to man-made fibrous substances.

Ready to use commercial products include dyed lichen and different types of strips supplied with or without foliage. Brands such as Peco Scene offer packs of dyed lichen bushes in various colours. These simply need pulling gently to shape and gluing in place on the landscape base. K&M makes flexible hedgerow strips for OO and N gauges

which come complete with green scatter foliage already applied (above). These items can be gently shaped to fit over undulations and only require glue to fix in place.

For extra realism, you can make your own bushes and hedges. Materials like horsehair, lichen or 'sea foam' can be pulled into clumps, sprayed with adhesive and covered with scatter material to represent the foliage. Some household materials can be pressed into use such as nylon scouring pads, bottle brushes and even stuffing from old cushions and car seats has been used. Also of interest is an ultra-fine fibre material called Postiche; this is perhaps better known as theatrical hair. To use, a wad of fibres are teased away from the hank and fluffed up into a bush-sized ball. This is then sprayed with adhesive and sprinkled with coarse flock, as below (note that hair lacquer can also be used as a cheaper alternative to spray adhesive).

It is also ideal for creating patches of undergrowth. The fibres are teased out into a thin fluffy blanket and glued to the scenic base. The area around the patch is then masked off with old newspaper, as shown in Fig. 5, given a coat of spray mount adhesive and gently covered in scatter

Fig. 5 – masking off the layout when using spray adhesives

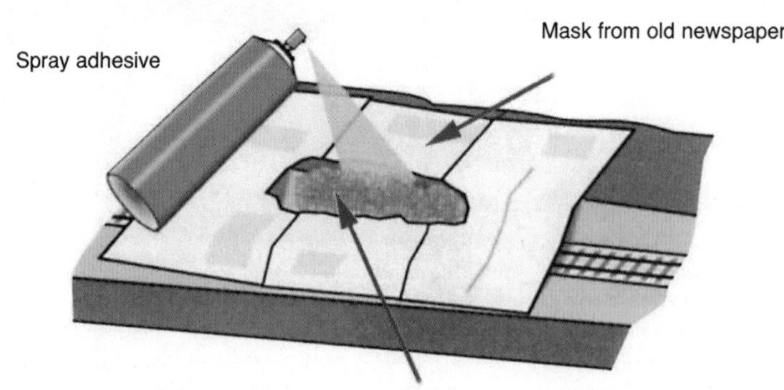

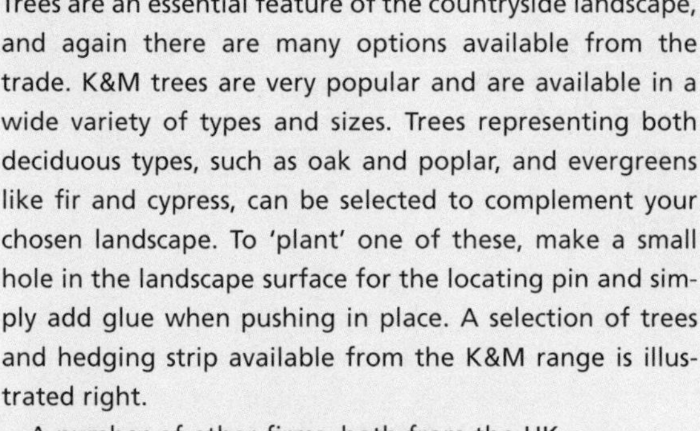

materials. All fibrous materials can also be used in this way to create undergrowth and shrubbery of different densities and textures, such as lichen as above.

Trees

Trees are an essential feature of the countryside landscape, and again there are many options available from the trade. K&M trees are very popular and are available in a wide variety of types and sizes. Trees representing both deciduous types, such as oak and poplar, and evergreens like fir and cypress, can be selected to complement your chosen landscape. To 'plant' one of these, make a small hole in the landscape surface for the locating pin and simply add glue when pushing in place. A selection of trees and hedging strip available from the K&M range is illustrated right.

A number of other firms, both from the UK and abroad, offer all types of trees in ready-to-use form, so even the most inexperienced of modellers can easily achieve realistic results.

When arranging trees on the layout, place them so as to look natural. Small groups should have the tallest trees in the centre with shorter ones around the outside. Individual trees often look best placed within hedgerows, at corners of fields or around gated entrances. Clumps of trees are useful to help disguise scenic breaks around bridges and tunnels, for example.

Main picture
Another scene on Ian Graham's magnificent layout showing fields, rough pasture and outcrops of trees.

For those who wish to make their own trees there are numerous methods from which to choose. Tree making can be split into two distinct stages of construction; the fabrication of the trunk and the application of foliage. Trunks can be made from carefully selected 'cuttings' of naturally occurring woody plants such as privet or moorland heather. More complex tree 'skeletons' can be made from twisted wire. Florists' wire and various gauges of copper electrical wire have all been used to good effect, though the process can be time-consuming. Bundles of wire are twisted together to firstly form the main trunk, then the branches and finally the twigs. The whole structure can then be soldered or glued together for added strength and finished off with a bark layer made from plaster filler. There are also pliable trunk kits available from the trade in plastic and whitemetal.

Unless you are modelling an autumn or winter scene, all these trunk varieties require foliage. The first choice for representing leaves is probably commercial foliage matting, which is cut into irregular shapes, teased out and glued onto the branches with general purpose adhesive. Horsehair, polyfibre, postiche or teased out scouring pads can be used to bulk out the tree before coarse scatter material is added.

Finally, if speed is the priority, try using 'sea foam' trees. This type of tree is a delicate plant material treated with preservative which just requires foliage. To do this, take one piece and spray it evenly with some suitable adhesive such as 3M Spray Mount or dip it into well diluted PVA adhesive. Next place the tree into a container filled with a coarse grade scatter. Rotate the tree in the scatter (left) and sprinkle on some extra bits by hand until all the surface is covered. Tap the tree gently to remove any loose scatter and then plant it into the landscape shell in the usual manner, though do take care as the trunks are very delicate and can easily snap off. Sea foam is available from several scenic firms.

Rock faces

When railway cuttings are made through solid rock, retaining walls are often unnecessary, the rock itself being the supporting structure. A traditional method of representing rock faces is to use cork bark (below), a lightweight, rock coloured material available ready to use from model shops. Again, some planning is required at the landscape building stage and often it is easier to build in the cork bark as you go along. In the UK, sheer rock cuttings are rare and more often rock faces appear as outcrops within embankments. When in place add plenty of scatter material on the top surfaces and amidst the cracks and crevices to represent vegetation.

Another method is to use offcuts of polystyrene tiles or fibre board glued vertically together so as to represent rock strata. The visible face is given a thin coat of plaster to hide the fibres or granules and when hardened, coloured with water-based paint.

Finally, rock faces can be made by hand using crumpled cooking foil and plaster casting techniques. A number of firms make rubber 'rock moulds' which allow individual outcrops to be cast in either plaster or resin.

Retaining walls

Retaining walls and arches are a common feature of the trackside in both urban and rural areas. Again, some advance planning to accommodate these items is required when building the scenic base. Often, such walls may be an integral part of the baseboard structure and the visible part is merely the cosmetic facing (see Fig. 6).

Prototype retaining walls can be constructed from brick, stone or concrete depending on location and period modelled. For the modeller there is a choice of materials to use as wall facings depending on your preferences. Building papers, such as those from Superquick, are ready coloured and just need cutting to shape and pasting onto a suitable card support. Moulded plastic builder sheets in brick or stone, includ-

Below
Ron Curling's Scotrail layout *Sharraine* featured rock faces made from cork bark. Plaster castings, small rocks and even painted coal fragments have been used for this scenic feature, but cork bark is light in weight and easily worked.

Right
Retaining walls on the Pecorama 'loft' layout *Peckwick Rye* were made from Wills brick arch walls.

Fig. 6 – elements of a retaining wall

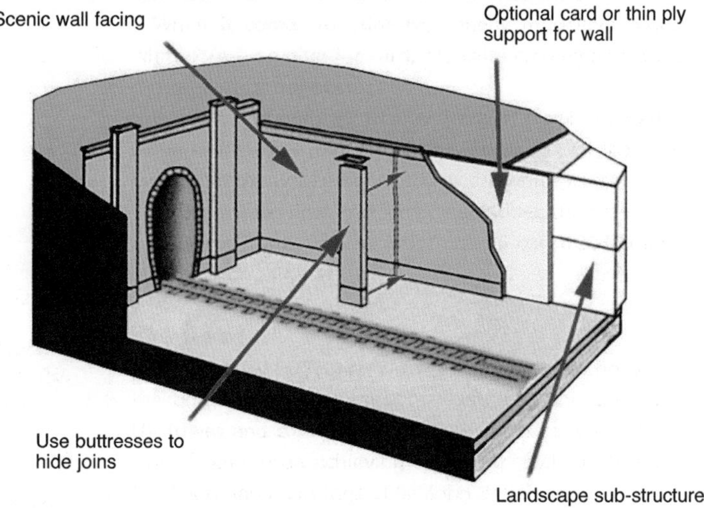

Fig. 7 – creating a small pond

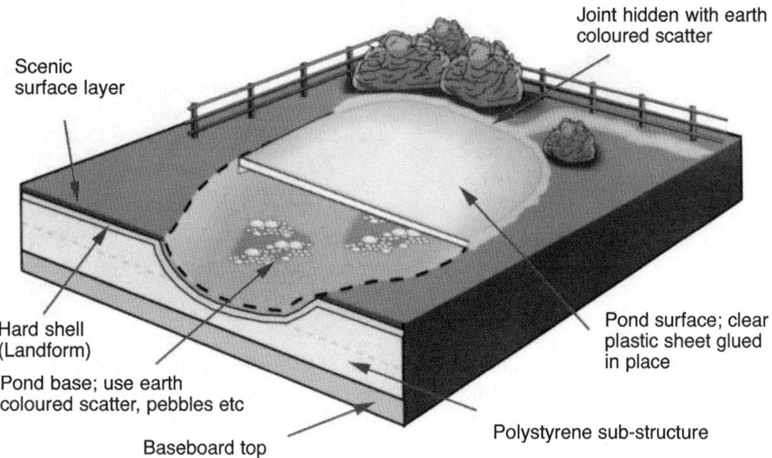

ing arch structures such as those made by Wills, provide some texture and relief and can be installed without extra support. Further variety, in plaster or resin cast sections, can also be obtained.

Simple water features

Small water features are an attractive addition to any layout and here we look at creating a simple pond or stream as in the scene below, made by Len Weal.

Bear in mind that some advance planning for such a feature is necessary when modelling the basic landscape. Typically, you will need to create a hollow or trough to represent the bed of the pond or stream. This should not be very deep, about 5mm will be adequate for still water as the impression of depth is created by the colour and texture of the bottom.

For shallow water, use fine sand or scatter for the banks and the base of the pond or stream, gluing it with PVA adhesive in the usual manner. The water surface is a piece of transparent plastic sheet cut so as to match the shape of the hollow. Fix in place with some clear glue and add some more fine sand or scatter to hide the edge of the sheet (see Fig. 7). To represent deeper water, simply paint the base a dark grey/green before adding the plastic 'surface' sheet.

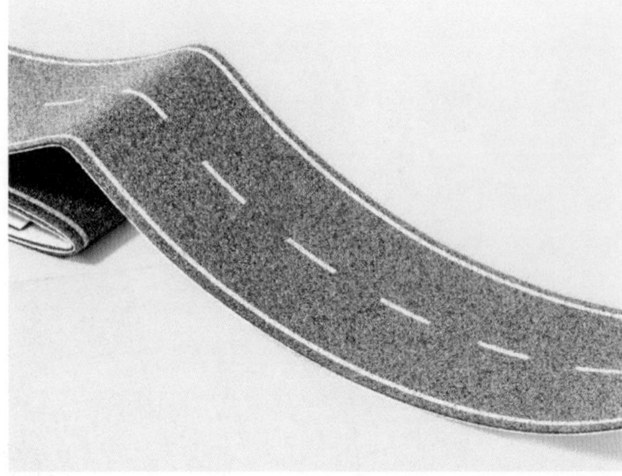

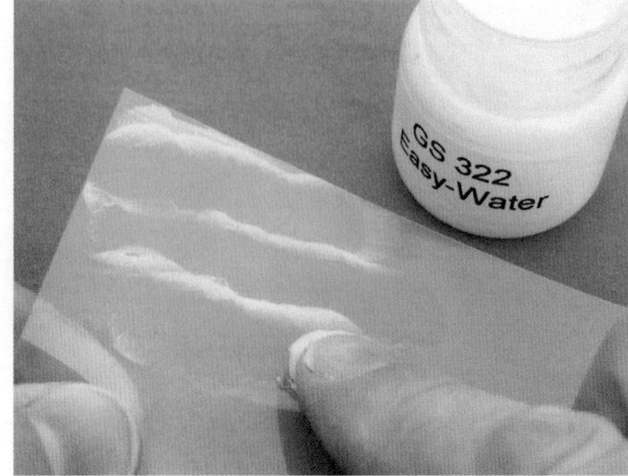

Ripples can be added on top of the plastic sheet using a special white acrylic gel which dries transparent. The gel is supplied by Green Scene under the brand name of Easy Water. Smear a thin layer on the surface of the plastic and with the forefinger, gently press and push the gel into little ripples before it dries (above).

There are numerous other ways of replicating water surfaces. One very popular method is to paint the river or seabed on the baseboard surface, and cover with several coats of gloss varnish. This eliminates the need to create a hollow in the baseboard itself, and is the method used to create the sea on *Morwenstow Riverside* (right), the OO layout by the Redruth Model Railway Society.

Roads, tracks and paths

Commercial roadway systems are available from various firms, such as Gaugemaster which offers a self adhesive roadway system made by Noch (top left). The European firm Faller, manufacture and market a complete working roadway system which uses battery-powered vehicles that follow wires buried beneath the surface.

Making your own roads is simple and inexpensive, though again you will need to plan where you intend to have them and create level foundations at the landscape construction stage. Road surfaces can be made from various materials depending on what finish is required. Cobblestones or granite setts can be represented with embossed plastic sheet, such as that in the Wills range, cut to the required shape and glued down (as illustrated on Tony Bucknall's *Lydgate*, above left).

For tarmac surfaces thin card, treated with paint and talcum powder gives pleasing results. Cut and glue the card in place, then, working on short stretches at a time, paint the top surface with a mid-grey paint and sprinkle it liberally with talcum powder before it dries. Press the powder gently into the paint and leave for an hour or so. When dry, vacuum and dust off the excess powder to leave a realistic pale grey patchy road surface. Rough tracks and paths are best made from earth coloured scatter materials sprinkled on glue. Finally finish off your roads and tracks with fencing or hedging down each side.

Cameo scenes

Small details are the finishing touches which bring a layout to life and allow you to give the model your own personal touch, setting it apart from the rest.

Right
The background on Mike Thomas's *Whitley South Dock* in OO, is an example of one method of depicting distant scenery – in this case layered building 'flats' (see overleaf).

There are hundreds of scenic accessory items available in all the popular gauges, some ready to use and others which require painting or assembly.

To get the best effect, create small individual cameo scenes to form focal points for the viewer rather than try to fill every square inch of landscape (such as illustrated bottom left on *Market Lindum*, a OO layout built by members of Hull Miniature Railway Society). Include figures in suitable poses and groups, talking or working together, rather than in random and isolated positions.

ADDING THE BACKGROUND

It is a widely held belief that superb model railway layouts need lots of space, and those who live in average-sized homes don't have sufficient room for such grand schemes. Up to a point, this is perhaps true, but as a consequence, modellers have derived all sorts of ingenious solutions to overcome the problem. Modelling a branch line, a cameo shunting scene or a locomotive depot are alternative ways of squeezing layouts into small areas, but other methods which involve foreshortening background scenery have also been used for many years. Such techniques mean that the non-railway landscape occupies less of the available space, allowing more of the baseboard area to be filled with track.

Below
There's plenty of scenic depth on *Morwenstow Riverside* from the Redruth MRS.

This final section examines some of the different methods used to model the background, and in particular describes how to create an illusion of distance in the narrow strips that lie between the tracks and the rear edge of the baseboard.

Simple backgrounds

Even the simplest of backgrounds can be sufficient to provide a frame or border to the railway; without one the layout will merely look like a test track.

At its most basic, a lineside fence and a strip of grass is a start, but a small embankment, perhaps featuring a stone wall, and some bushes and shrubs from lichen will add depth and create a pleasing boundary (above). This can all be squeezed into a strip as little as 1" (25mm) wide if need be and is an ideal solution for the really space-starved modellers amongst us.

Layered backgrounds

If a little more depth is available, the simple background can be developed further by adding two-dimensional scenic layers or cut-out building façades. The photo below shows a layered background built this way. It consists of a low embankment and concrete fence which has been enlarged by the addition of a single sheet façade representing the gable ends of a factory unit. A thin strip of shrubbery has been added between the factory layer and the fence to increase further the illusion of depth. The final component is another single sheet layer which represents the roof of the factory. Because the layered background is only a two-dimensional scene, the roof angle has to be chosen very carefully so that the perspective appears reasonably correct from most viewing positions. A low angle, as shown here, usually works well for most viewpoints. Note also that the end of the factory has been disguised by the addition of a 'thin' tree.

Low relief backgrounds

When a bit more space is available we can make use of buildings modelled in low relief.

The term 'low relief' refers to structures where only the front (or back) façade is modelled to scale. The other elevations of the building are considerably foreshortened and the whole structure is built up as a thin element, but not totally flat (as in the previous example).

The foreshortening is achieved by making roof pitches steeper and by making items such as gable ends and bay windows shallower, as shown in Fig. 8 (below). Generally, 'low relief' embraces structures that vary in depth from just a few millimetres up to about 50mm.

A variation on this approach is half (or even two-thirds) width buildings which can be constructed for similarly confined sites. These are sometimes called 'half relief' structures and do not include foreshortened elements; rather, all elevations are built to the same scale and same degree of detail.

In principle, all these variations are used for the same purpose; to create an illusion of depth by careful positioning towards the rear of the layout. As a rule of thumb, the thinner the low relief element is, the further towards the back of the layout it should be placed. However, in cases where available space is such that only a very narrow baseboard can be accommodated, then there will be no alternative but to place very thin low relief structures close to the trackside.

Another aspect to consider when using low relief structures is the viewing angle. This is quite critical since foreshortened buildings look rather peculiar when viewed from the side. Consequently place them so that viewing is generally restricted to the front elevation and note that a

Fig. 8 – elements of low relief structures

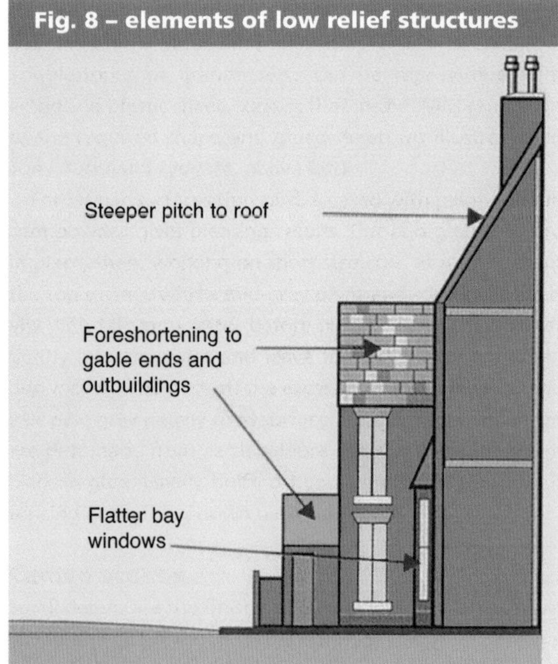

Fig. 9 – tips for using low relief structures in the background

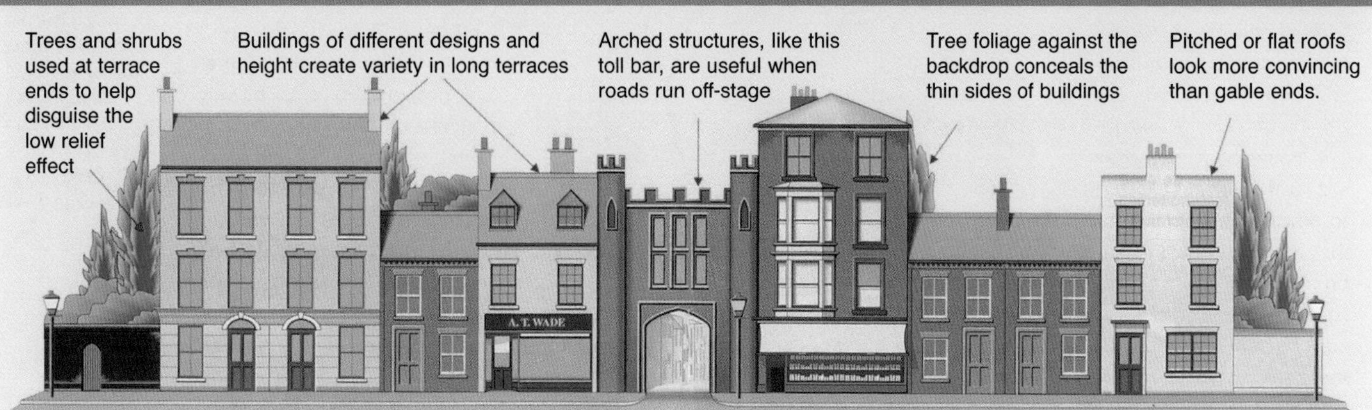
Trees and shrubs used at terrace ends to help disguise the low relief effect
Buildings of different designs and height create variety in long terraces
Arched structures, like this toll bar, are useful when roads run off-stage
Tree foliage against the backdrop conceals the thin sides of buildings
Pitched or flat roofs look more convincing than gable ends.
A. T. WADE

row containing several buildings of different styles and heights usually works better than just one or two large buildings. Indeed, raising one's eyes above normal shop-front level on a stroll down the high street of any British town, you could be surprised to see how varied the architectural styles can be.

Position all the buildings tight up to each other in a terrace, rather than with gaps between them. The ends of the terraces (where the low relief effect is most obvious) can be hidden behind carefully positioned trees, shrubs or billboards. Another trick for disguising a row end is to have a gatehouse or 'toll bar' in the line-up, since such items are thin prototypes to begin with (see Fig. 9).

Woodland or forest can also be represented on the background with just one or two strips of 'flat' trees arranged in low relief. Choose dense foliage types and include shrubbery and undergrowth around the base of the trunks. Alternatively, use a high boundary wall, such as those which surround large country estates, and simply model the tree tops growing over the wall.

Building kits

Low relief building kits in card (such as the low relief Metcalfe Models terrace housing, right) are suitable for creating city, town and village backgrounds. Firms such as Metcalfe Models offer a wide variety of these designs, which are pre-coloured and, being very easy to construct, are suitable for beginners.

The full-depth building kits from these firms are suitable for conversion into low relief models by splicing them lengthways to provide two 'half' relief buildings.

The construction of both card and plastic building kits (and scratchbuilding your own buildings) is described in detail in our Skills Workshop sections (pages 78, 82 and 86).

Roads and rivers

Not all background scenes include buildings; you may want roads, rivers or other landscape features in the background area of the layout.

With roads and rivers which run lengthways to the layout, they can simply be modelled as half or one-third width. This works well as long as viewing angles are restricted to the front, but difficulties can arise when such features run across the layout from front to back.

As a road, track or river regresses into the distance, it

Right
Making rivers disappear off scene can be done easily by using a bridge as a scenic break, as illustrated here on Willie Smith's *North Tyne Light Railway.*

Fig. 10 – simple forced perspective

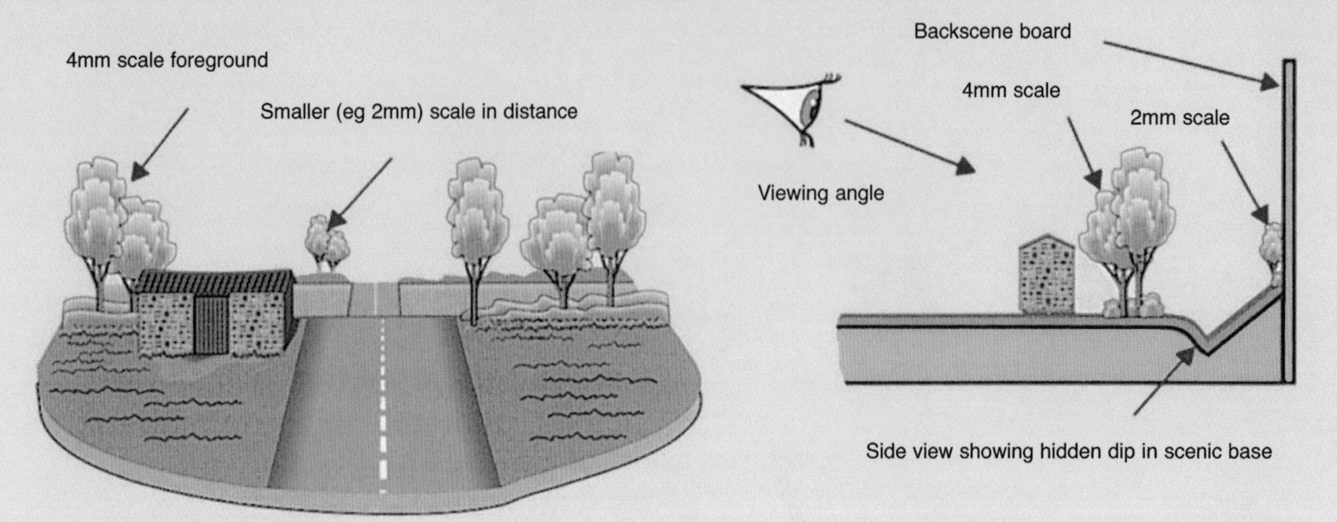

progressively becomes smaller and narrower as a result of the laws of perspective. Modelling this effectively can be difficult but a few tricks from the modeller's toolbox can be applied as follows.

A river which runs off the back of the layout can be made to appear as if it continues somewhere by running it under a bridge. The bridge is positioned on the back edge of the baseboard (as shown on the previous page on Willie Smith's *North Tyne Light Railway*) where it acts as a scenic break, hiding the fact that the river ends abruptly at the baseboard edge.

The illusion that the river continues beyond the bridge can be enhanced by the addition of a small mirror positioned behind the bridge arch.

With minor roads or tracks, a simple five bar gate can be located at the edge of the board to act as the scenic break. Whilst for larger roads, to help disguise any rapid foreshortening, a useful trick is to take them over a hump or brow in the scenery and model the distant part of the road in a reduced scale (see Fig. 10). This is a simple form of 'forced perspective' and works well provided it is not viewed from an acute angle at the front. The technique is also useful when a roadway has to be blended into a backscene.

Forced perspective

Low relief modelling is a way of forcing the perspective on a layout by squeezing up the space between the middle ground and the background. True forced perspective modelling actually uses models of differing scale in the scene as well as foreshortening techniques. The idea has been around for many years and probably has its origins in the film industry, where the technique was used extensively before the advent of computer-generated imagery. Today, more and more modellers are experimenting with the methods and creating truly stunning effects. Although the principles are easy to grasp, they require care in their execution, and viewing angles have to be restricted selectively to ensure optimum results.

In its simplest form, on a layout we may use 4mm scale OO gauge equipment and track, but incorporate 2mm scale/N gauge buildings and accessories into the background (below). The critical factor is the placing of the various objects in relation to each other. This is best done by eye on a trial and error basis; in fact it is worth mocking-up the distant buildings in card to see how they fit into the scene before committing yourself to buying kits or building models. Buildings that are intended to be even more distant can be reproduced at still smaller scales, perhaps

being nothing more than simple hand-drawn cut-outs, or photographs cut from magazines.

At its most complex, forced perspective involves constructing buildings in their true perspective image. This means that building lines converge as they move away from the viewer such that the back of the building has to be modelled to a smaller scale than the front of the building. The modelling is thus quite demanding, as elements that are normally square or rectangular such as doors and windows, have to be reproduced in trapezoid shapes in order to retain their perspective.

Using mirrors

We mentioned above that a small mirror may be used under a bridge to create the illusion that a river flows on into the distance. The same principle can be applied to streets and roads and even stations and sidings.

The trick is to position the mirror perpendicular to the scenery and such that from normal viewing positions the image cast does not immediately look like a reflection of the adjacent layout. Experienced modellers have been known to use large mirrors instead of backscenes at the ends of layouts to recreate large swathes of countryside, as indeed, illustrated below on Ian Allcroft and Dave Oliver's 7mm scale *Bridge Norton* layout. However small, strategically placed mirrors can be equally effective. To work properly, the sides of the mirror must be concealed behind the walls of adjacent buildings with the top edge hidden by an overbridge, covered gantry or walkway. In the example shown above, on Richard Peake's *Castle Wharf Yard,* the mirror edges have been concealed by the corrugated iron building which creates an archway. The effect is that the wharfside and siding appear to continue through the arch.

The particular advantage of a mirror is that it reflects all the ambient light and colour of the modelled area towards the viewer at the same brightness and contrast level. In the model above, a painted scene (instead of the mirror) would be shaded by the building's shadow, and a modelled scene, even in forced perspective, would require its own lighting.

The final element of layout construction is the two dimensional backscene fitted at the rear and ends of the modelled scene. Further details on the creation of these can be found in the Practical Guidance section on page 72.

Above
Look carefully through the archway on the corrugated iron building to spot the mirror.

Below
Two mirrors located at opposite ends of *Bridge Norton* created this scene – can you see the joins?

Controlling your railway

Of all the aspects related to building a layout, the one which causes most concern to new starters, and indeed experienced modellers, is that of installing the track wiring and linking up a train controller. With a basic train set, this is fairly straight forward: you plug the controller wires into the track clip and away you go, the difficulty comes when you install points and want to run more than one engine on the layout. Moreover, the arrival of Digital Command Control as an alternative to traditional 12V dc control for model railways has further complicated understanding (see comparison notes on pages 12 and 13).

However, whilst many of the practical 'wiring' issues on a layout are relevant to both DCC and 12V dc systems, some are appropriate to either one system, or the other. Accordingly, we have highlighted some of the section descriptions with a coloured tab to indicate to which control system the advice is compatible. This could be either, or both, systems depending on the topic.

12V dc operation is still widely used but DCC is steadily gaining popularity. Should you wish to know more about Digital Command Control, we would direct you to our 'Shows You How' booklet No.17 which provides a good overview of the system and its capabilities.

Below
Digital command control offers the ability to operate an extensive layout without many switches. Alan Munday uses Lenz equipment to control his OO layout *Stevenstown* (RM April 2012).

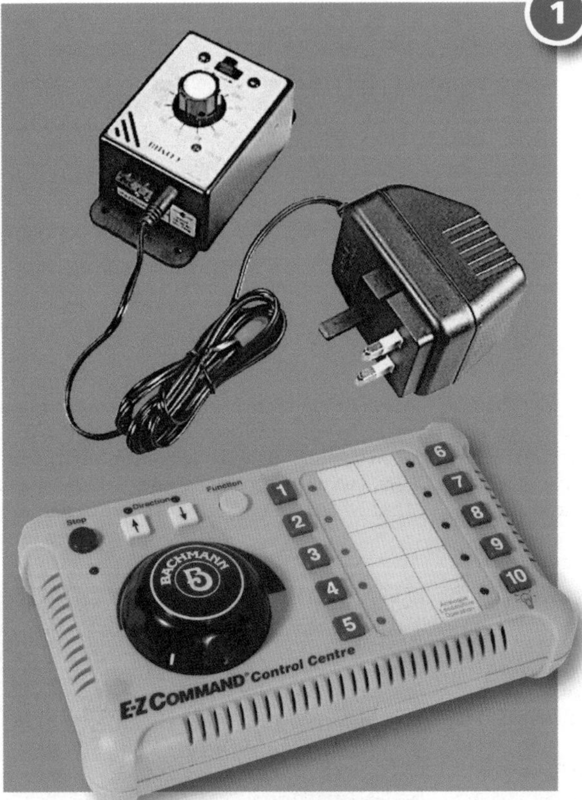

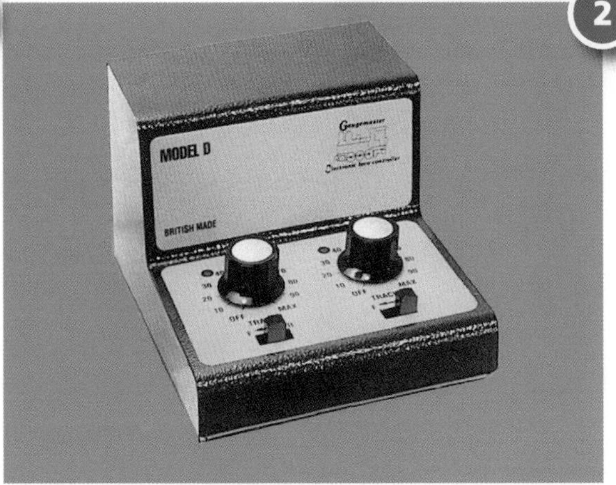

Basic layout controllers

DCC & 12 Volt

Firstly, let us consider the minimum equipment you will need to operate a locomotive on a layout. This will be a 'mains transformer' and a 'speed controller' (also referred to as a 'track' controller by some manufacturers). Numerous designs and combinations of these items are available from model shops and both analogue and digital versions are available.

For those on a limited budget, economy units such as the Bachmann E-Z Command console (for DCC) or the Gaugemaster 'Combi' (for 12V dc) are ideal for smaller layouts (photo 1); both are supplied with separate transformers.

Some analogue 12V dc controllers are available as integral 'Cased Controllers', which have the mains transformer, speed controller and necessary circuitry all in one box. Cased controllers such as these are available with up to four integral speed controllers, thus allowing control of up to four trains simultaneously, but, either a single or twin speed control version (photo 2) is usually enough to begin with. Most also include an 'auxiliary output' to allow you to provide power to other electrical accessories (such as point motors) or to add on another speed controller later.

Several DCC systems are available as a single cased 'console' unit; such as the Hornby Select, Digitrax DCS 50 or the ZTC 611, but all require to be connected to an external transformer.

Hand-held controllers

DCC & 12 Volt

Hand-held speed controllers (often called 'walk-about' controllers) require to be powered by a separate transformer, or from the auxiliary output of a cased controller, and do not have an auxiliary output themselves (photo 3). They are fitted with a long cable and are particularly useful if you have to move up and down the layout to uncouple trains at different locations. Since a separate transformer is necessary, the wiring is a little more involved than with an integral cased controller, but still well within the capabilities of the beginner. Many DCC systems use predominantly hand-held units, such as the Gaugemaster Prodigy Advance illustrated (with external transfomers), and today even mobile phones and tablet PCs can be turned into a controller.

Feedback and inertia controllers

12 Volt ONLY

These are slightly more complex versions of standard 12V dc controllers. Feedback controllers include special 'feedback' circuitry to maintain a constant train speed. They are useful on layouts with gradients, and improve slow speed performance, but are unsuitable for decoder-fitted locos on 12V dc only layouts.

Inertia controllers also include extra circuitry, switches and control knobs to allow you to set up a predetermined simulation of the acceleration and braking of your locomotives, thus adding an extra dimension to the operating. Both Feedback and Inertia controllers are more expensive than standard ones, and with the advent of DCC have

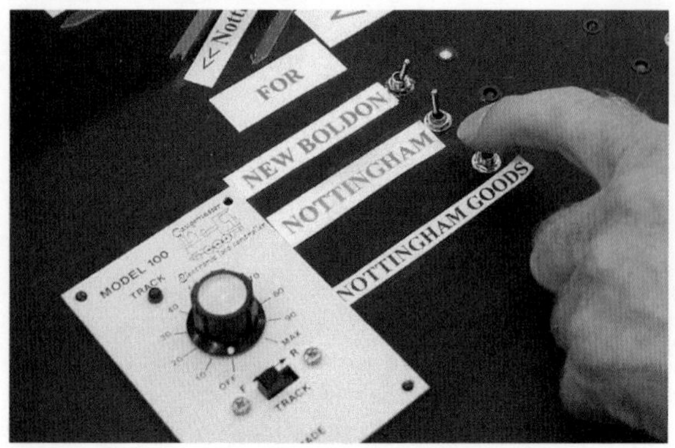

Fig. 1 – track feeds from a controller

Controller

+ve (feed wire)

-ve (return wire)

Far left
A panel-mounted Gaugemaster unit fitted into the Soar Valley MRC's extensive layout *Dorehill St Stevens* (RM September and October 2009).

fallen out of favour, particularly as all the features they provide are to be found in many DCC systems anyway.

Panel mounted controllers

12 Volt ONLY

Also less popular with the advent of DCC. Panel mounted versions of some manufacturers' speed controllers are still available. These are of 'open frame' design with all the components mounted onto the underside of the front indicator panel. They are for fixing within a separate control console, or for mounting into the rear fascia board of the layout. For more details on their application see page 65.

Two-rail wiring principles

DCC & 12 Volt

Whether you have chosen a DCC or 12V dc control system, powering up the layout to get the trains running is identical in each case. At its very simplest, the output wires of the controller are connected to the track, one to each rail, at a position known as the track feed. With a simple layout, such as an oval of track, only one track feed needs to be installed. As layouts become more complex it becomes necessary to install more than one track feed as we shall see later.

By established convention in two-rail wiring, one rail of the track is said to be powered positive (+ve), whilst the other rail is said to be powered negative (-ve). Wires to the +ve rails are often referred to as 'feed' wires, whilst those to the -ve rails are referred to as the 'return' wires. Thus each track feed has a 'feed wire' (+ve) and a 'return wire' (-ve). In this section we shall colour code these as red for the feed (+ve) and blue for the return (-ve) – see Fig. 1 (above right). Also, as we shall see later, sections of rail can become isolated from the controller (via the changing of a point for instance) and thus be at neither polarity. Such sections, when isolated, are unpowered and consequently shown colour coded as black.

When planning your wiring, you can use this colour convention to help you to avoid mistakes. Using coloured pens, draw one side of the track as the red rail and the other side as the blue rail. If your track design is such that at some position a red rail meets a blue rail, then a short circuit will occur. To overcome this problem an insulated rail joiner needs to be inserted in the rail at the point where the two rails meet. You will find this basic rule especially useful if you plan to use points and crossings with Electrofrogs (live frogs) – see under 'Adding Points'.

Layout wire

DCC & 12 Volt

For most low voltage layout wiring applications using either DCC or 12V dc, 0.2mm dia. multi-strand 'equipment' wire is most suitable and can be soldered with ease. There are numerous varieties available and reels can be obtained from selected model shops, specialist dealers (such as those who attend model railway exhibitions or advertise in Railway Modeller), some DIY outlets, motorists' shops and high street electronic retailers. DCC users planning to run lots of trains and powered accessories should use heavier gauge wire for the DCC 'power bus'. Do not use old mains flex or cable, as this is far too heavy, and also could be confused with mains wiring with possible serious health and safety consequences.

Track connections

DCC & 12 Volt

Even with just one track feed there has to be an actual physical connection between the wire and the rail itself. This can be achieved with either a proprietary 'power connecting clip', such as the Peco ST-273 (photo 4) or a soldered joint to the base or side of the rail (photo 5). Soldering requires a little more skill (see pages 103-105) but provides a permanent and more discreet connection to the track. You can now use the new power feed rail join-

Connecting wires to rails

4

Proprietary power connecting clips (left) do not require any soldering, and are easy to use. Simply bare about 20mm of wire and twist it back on itself a couple of times. Then, using a fine screwdriver, push the bare end firmly into each clip. A soldered joint (right) will form a permanent connection to the rails, and looks more discreet. Feed wires are generally run under the baseboard and brought up through small holes as shown. For soldered joints you will need a fine-tipped iron (max 25W output should suffice), electrical solder with rosin cored flux, and a means of cleaning the rail such as a fibreglass brush. For full details on soldering see page 105.

5

ers from Peco (see page 30) which avoid the need to solder, and thus the possibility of accidental damage to the plastic sleepers which can occur during the soldering process. For further information on this important topic, see under the tracklaying section, beginning on page 26.

Adding points

DCC & 12 Volt

Very few layouts consist solely of an oval of track as shown in Fig. 1; most modellers add points, crossings and sidings to make the layout realistic and more interesting to operate. However, when points are introduced into the formation they affect the electrical status of the track. This is because they also act like electrical switches when the route is changed over. Exactly how points affect the electrical status is dependent on the electrical properties of the points being used. Fortunately there are only two types of point to contend with: those with so-called 'dead frogs' and those with so called 'live frogs' ('frog' is a colloquial term for the crossing V part of a point). In the Peco Streamline ranges of track, points with 'dead frogs' are called Insulfrog and those with 'live frogs' are called Electrofrog.

At the outset, you need to be aware of the electrical properties of the points you are using as this will affect the way you wire the layout up, as explained later. Peco Setrack points in OO gauge and N gauge are all Insulfrog, but the Peco Streamline range includes both Insulfrog and Electrofrog types in some, but not all, of the various gauges of track available. Consult the Peco catalogue for more information on the availability of the two types. Both types are equally suitable for DCC or DC control.

Insulfrog or Electrofrog?

DCC & 12 Volt

Insulfrog points, as the name suggests, have an insulated tip to the frog (crossing nose) about 8mm long.

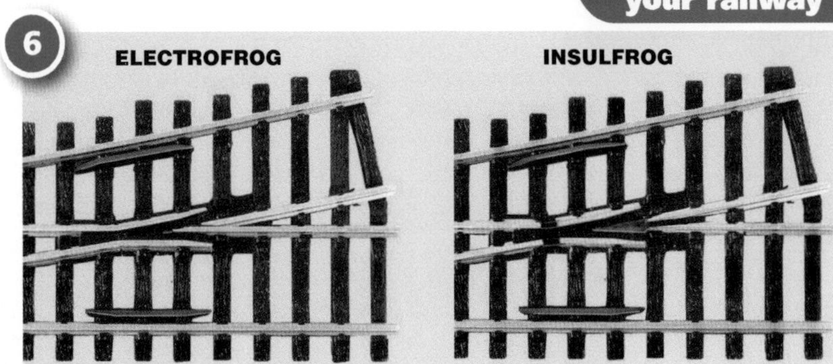

From a running point of view, this short unpowered gap at the frog tip means that current pickup by the locomotive is interrupted as the wheel passes over it. Normally, this should not be a problem, as other wheels on the locomotive will collect current from elsewhere on the track; however, if for some reason there is not another wheel collecting current (as may be the case with a short wheelbase loco, or possibly the other wheels need cleaning) then the loco stalls abruptly.

Electrofrog points have a full metal frog nose and automatically switch the frog to either the +ve side or the -ve side as required by the route set. The benefit is that there is no unpowered gap at the frog tip, thus minimising the chances of the loco stalling as it passes slowly over the frog. Compare the differences between the two types of point in photo 6.

Ostensibly then, Electrofrog points offer better running reliability, particularly at slow speeds, but because the frog is always powered (see Fig. 2b), either positive or negative depending on the route set, then insulated rail joiners have to be used at certain positions in order to eliminate any chance of rails at opposite polarities connecting together and creating a short circuit. Insulfrog points, when set to one route, automatically isolate the blade and

Fig. 2 – Insulfrog and Electrofrog points

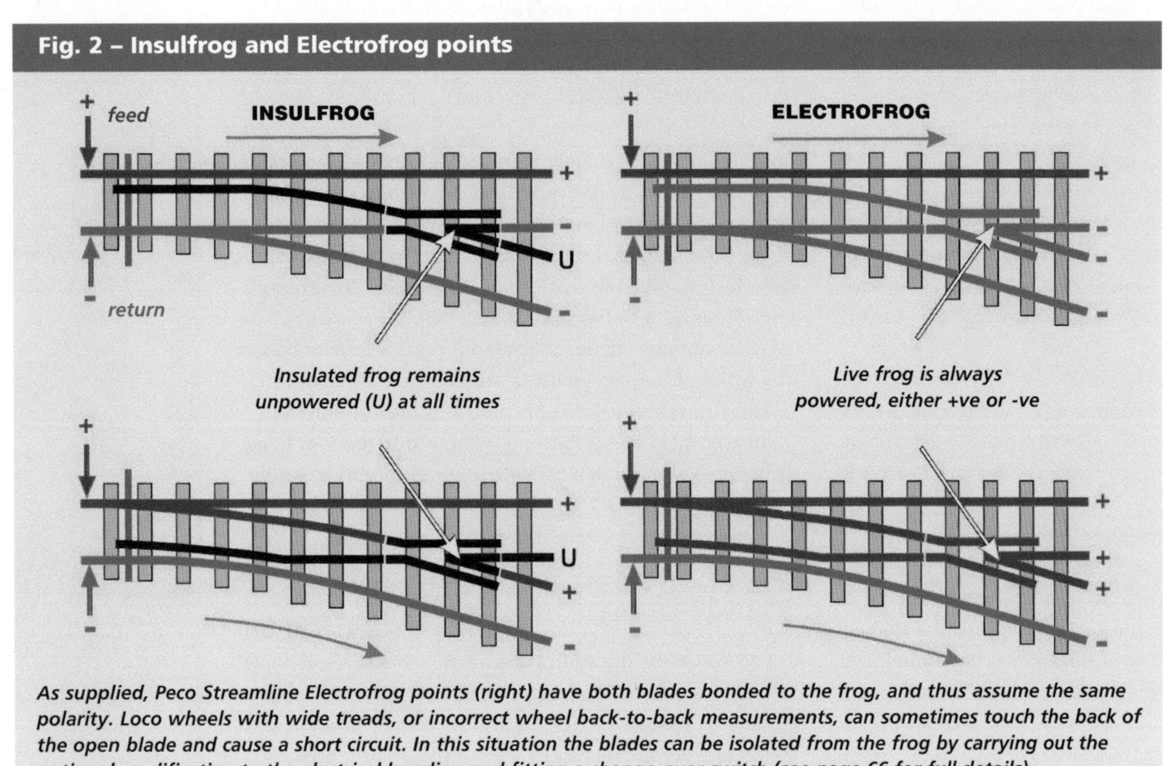

As supplied, Peco Streamline Electrofrog points (right) have both blades bonded to the frog, and thus assume the same polarity. Loco wheels with wide treads, or incorrect wheel back-to-back measurements, can sometimes touch the back of the open blade and cause a short circuit. In this situation the blades can be isolated from the frog by carrying out the optional modification to the electrical bonding and fitting a change-over switch (see page 66 for full details).

frog rail to the other route, i.e. the one not in use (see Fig. 2a), and thus, in most situations, insulated rail joiners do not need fitting. Note however, if you plan to use two analogue controllers on a double track oval layout, you will need to fit insulated joiners to isolate the track sections powered by the different controllers; this applies to both Insulfrog and Electrofrog points.

To explain this in more detail, look at Fig. 3 and compare the effects the different types of point (Insulfrog or Electrofrog) have on a simple oval layout, then follow the various steps as the layout is expanded in Fig. 4.

Note that the last two diagrams in Fig. 4 are for 12V dc only, but by way of a comparison, Fig. 5 on page 60 shows the same twin track formation wired for DCC only. Although the wire runs are less complicated, the middle siding still requires a pair of feed and return wires in order to ensure the two kick-back sidings can be powered.

Positioning track feeds and rail breaks

DCC & 12 Volt

As can be seen from the preceding series of diagrams the positioning of track feeds is actually quite straightforward; place track feeds at the leading end (toe) of a point to ensure that all sidings accessed via the point can be powered. This generally applies to both Insulfrog and Electrofrog points in most instances. The major difference is that where there is a possibility of a live frog being back-fed from either of the trailing ends of the point, then a rail break and an insulated joiner must be inserted. This situation will usually occur on any oval, passing loop or headshunt feeding kick-back sidings. (This requirement to fit rail breaks at frogs is also necessary when using a DCC system with Electrofrog points.)

DCC and self-isolating points

DCC ONLY

The self-isolating facility of Peco points can sometimes be a drawback with DCC as it is often desirable to have all the tracks on a layout powered-up, or 'live', even when the points are set against them.

This would be particularly important if your locomotives are fitted with DCC lighting and sound: for instance, you may want a stationary diesel locomotive to stand in a loop or dead-end siding with its lights on and its engine sound 'ticking over'. If the siding point is set against it, then normally it will be electrically isolated and the DCC auxiliaries

Fig. 3 – using Insulfrog (left) and Electrofrog (right) points in an oval DCC & 12 Volt

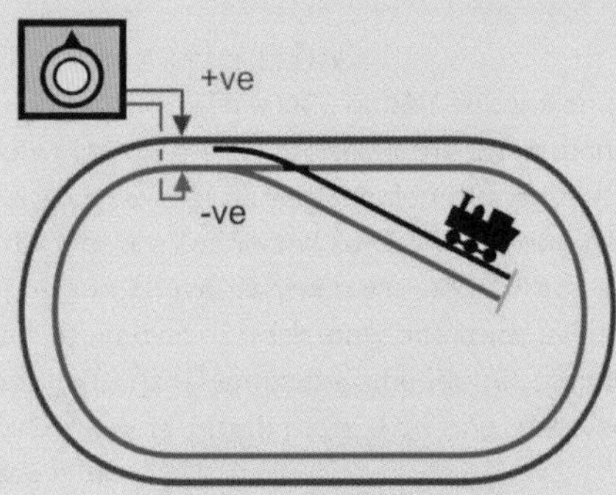

The basic oval with a siding, with one feed and the point set for the main line. One rail of the siding (black line) is isolated by the point and thus unpowered. The loco on the siding cannot therefore be powered and will remain stationary.

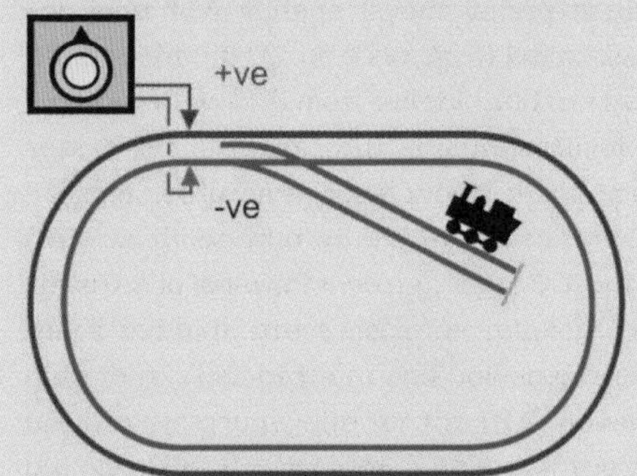

Here, with the all-live frog, there is no problem with the point set for the main line. The siding has both rails -ve, but as they are of the same polarity, the loco in the siding cannot be powered and will again remain stationary.

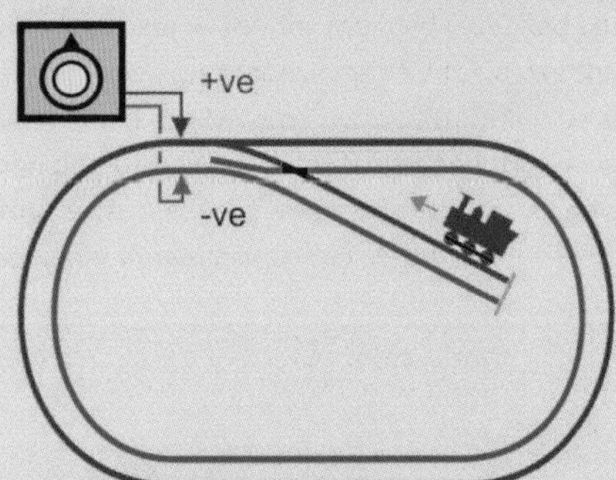

The same diagram as above but with the point set to the siding. The electrical status of the oval remains the same, but both rails to the siding are now powered +ve and -ve, allowing the loco to be powered and move off in the direction set by the controller. This also applies to DCC control systems – but see also the section on DCC and self-isolating points.

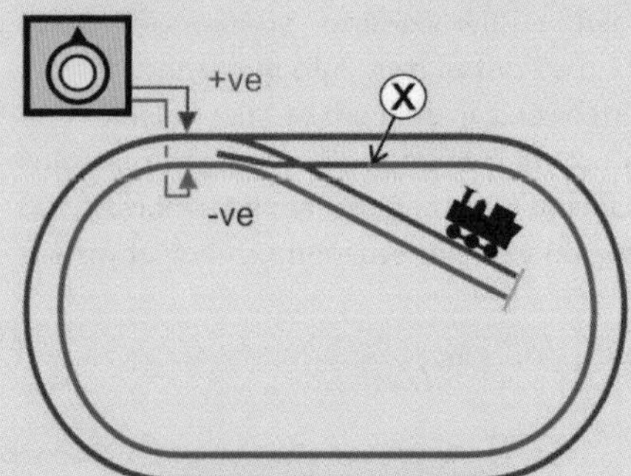

Change the point and the frog becomes +ve; the rails to the siding are now +ve and -ve and in theory the loco should move, but trace the -ve rail right around the loop and at position X it meets up directly with the +ve rail. This will create an instant short circuit. To prevent this situation, an insulated rail joiner has to be installed in the rail at X.

Fig. 4 – Insulfrog (left) and Electrofrog (right) points in more complex situations

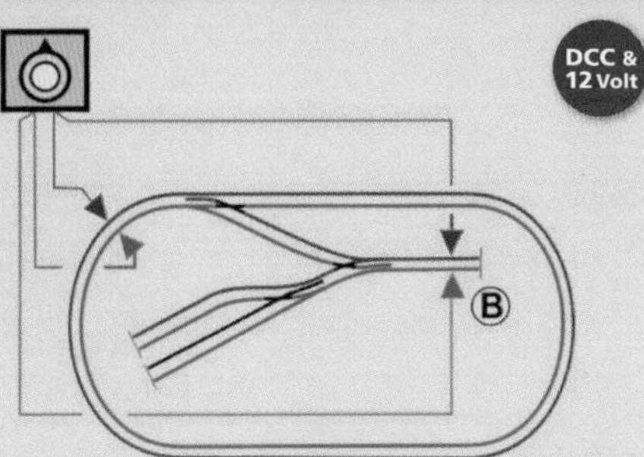

The basic oval in Fig. 3 has been expanded to include two kick-back sidings. An extra track feed and return is now required at B, otherwise a loco in the kick-back sidings cannot be powered, even with the points set correctly. This applies to DCC users as well – but see the section on DCC and self-isolating points, page 58.

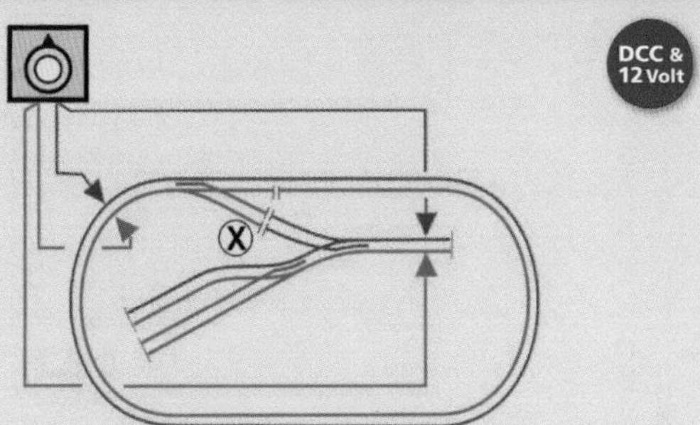

As with the Insulfrog points set-up, an extra track feed has to be installed in the headshunt. However, this time a double rail break at X has to be installed to isolate the two Electrofrogs from each other. This again applies to DCC – but see also the section on DCC and self-isolating points, page 58.

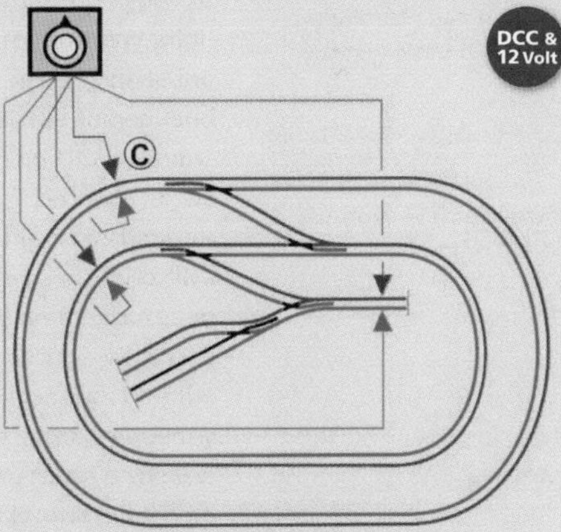

Another oval has now been added on the outside to make the layout double track. An extra feed and return is needed at C in order to allow trains to run around the new circuit. Providing that we are still using the same 12V controller or a DCC controller, no extra rail breaks or insulated joiners are needed.

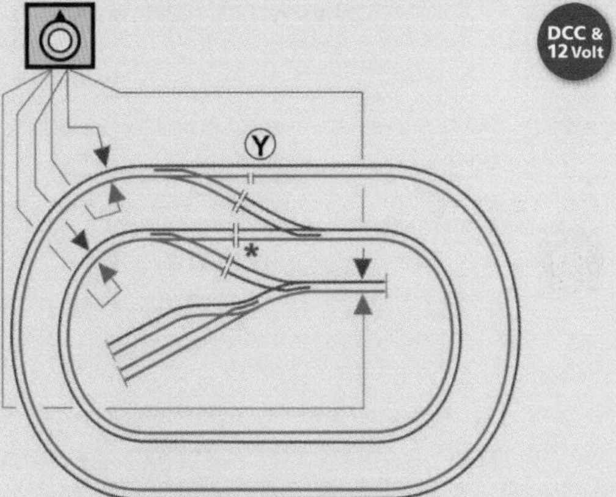

*Adding the outer oval and new crossover requires the original single rail break (at *) replacing with a double rail break and a new double rail break between the Electrofrogs of the new crossover. Don't forget to install a rail break on the inner rail of the outer circuit as shown at Y.*

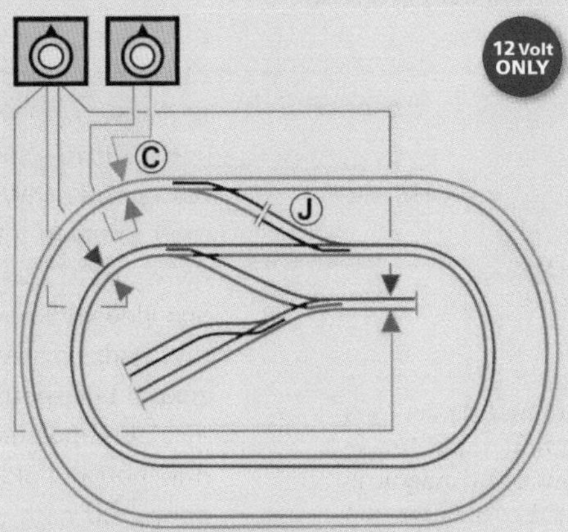

To run two trains independently on the two circuits with 12V control, a second 12V controller is fitted at C (coloured orange for the +ve and green for the -ve). To eliminate crossfeeding of power from the outer circuit to the inner circuit and vice versa, two insulated joiners have to be installed at J. To run a train from the inner circuit to the outer circuit, set the points correctly and simply set the two speed controllers to the same speed and direction.

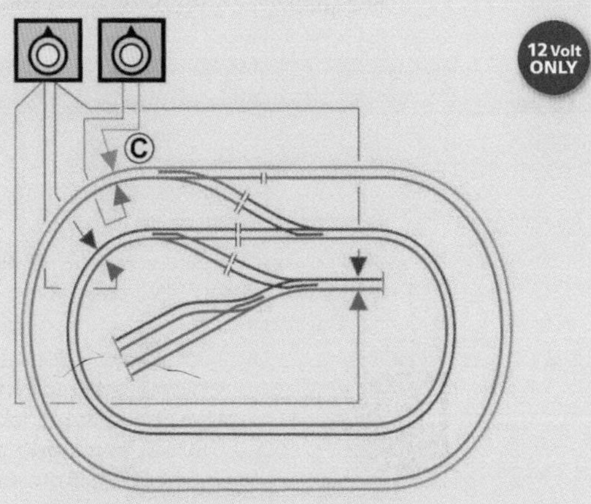

Switching the outer oval to a second controller requires no further alterations to the track, as the existing double rail break will suffice. Again, to run a train from the inner circuit to the outer circuit, set the points correctly and simply set the two speed controllers to the same speed and direction.

Fig. 5 – Insulfrog (left) and Electrofrog (right) points in a DCC powered twin track oval

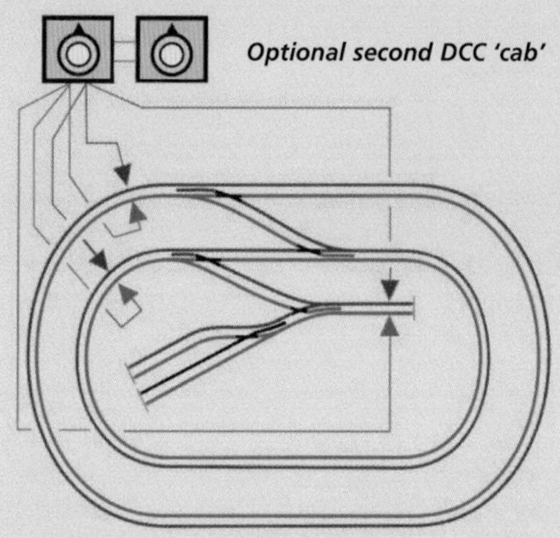

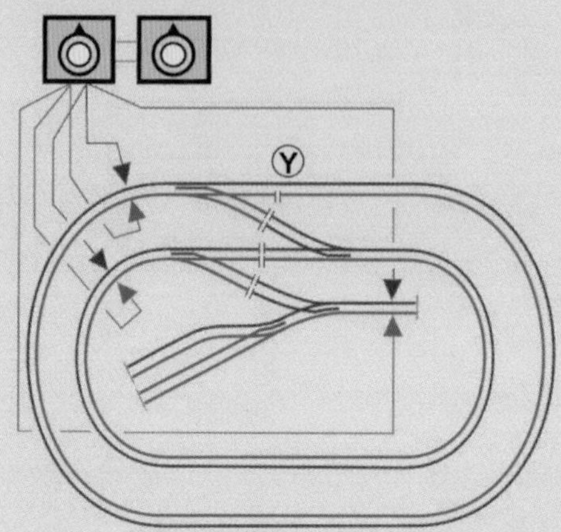

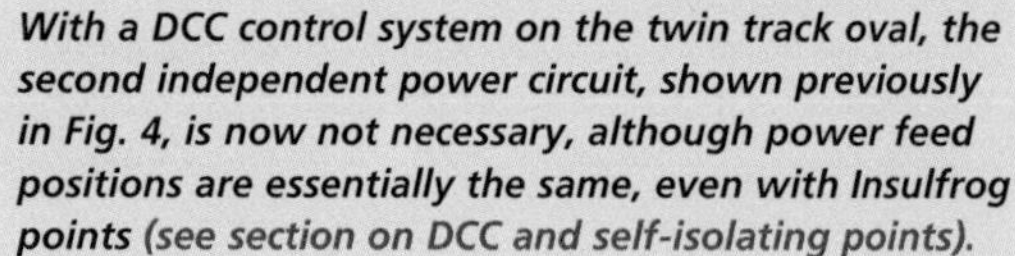

With a DCC control system on the twin track oval, the second independent power circuit, shown previously in Fig. 4, is now not necessary, although power feed positions are essentially the same, even with Insulfrog points (see section on DCC and self-isolating points).

Likewise, with Electrofrog points, the power feed positions have to be retained and insulated rail joiners still installed when the live frogs are laid back-to-back: and also at position Y on the outer oval.

will not function. You therefore need to over-ride the self-isolating feature of the sidings' points, and this is easily accomplished by the addition of link or jump wires installed between the main running rails (or DCC power bus if fitted) and the isolated siding rails as shown below; Fig. 6a for Insulfrog points and Fig. 6b for Electrofrog.

If the sidings are not dead end (ie they are loops) the link wires will still be required with Insulfrog points. With Electrofrog points, depending on your track configuration and positions of feeds and insulated rail joiners, some link wires may still be needed.

Track control sections

12 Volt ONLY

As layouts expand and experience develops, many modellers split the trackwork into separately switched electrical control sections. This enables one loco to operate on part of the layout whilst two or more are held stationary on different parts which are isolated from the power. Taking our double track oval in Fig. 4 (using one controller only) we can install on-off switches (also known as SPST – single pole, single throw) in the +ve feed wires from the controller. Fig. 7 shows the new configuration, each of the three sections can now be switched on independently, so switching (1) and (2) on, allows one loco to be operated on the inner and onto the outer oval, whilst a stationary loco can be held in the sidings. You will see also that we have joined the -ve powered return wires together rather than run each one back to the controller. This saves wire and a little bit of time and is a simple version of what is known as 'Common Return'.

Fig. 6 – link wiring for DCC control systems

For over-riding the self-isolating features of points.

a) Insulfrog points

Link wires

b) Electrofrog points

Insulated rail joiners

As can be seen, the installation of link wires to overcome the self-isolating feature of the points is the same for both types. The only difference is that insulated rail joiners must be used with Electrofrog points, as indeed they must also be with 12V dc, although see the Special Note in the adjacent panel.

DCC & INSULFROG POINTS – SPECIAL NOTE

Insulfrog code 100 points and code 75 slips and crossings can be used with DCC control systems without modification and without the use of insulated rail joiners between pairs of points laid back-to-back. However when a track feed is connected after (ie downstream of) the frog, the two frog rails will be at opposite polarity. The metal ends of these rails are embedded very closely together in the plastic crossing vee, a design feature to keep the length of the dead section to an absolute minimum. Depending on how the point is laid relative to adjacent track, some older loco wheel treads have been found to bridge the tiny gap (see illustration) as they pass over and create a momentary short circuit. With 12V control, this momentary short circuit is overcome by the momentum of the locomotive, and at worse a little spark is generated, but the loco continues on its way. With DCC however, the smallest hint of a short circuit and the system cuts out. If this problem occurs with your models, the way to overcome this is to fit insulated joiners to those frog rails where a potential backfeed might occur (as you would for an Electrofrog point). Ordinarily, you do not need to fit insulated rail joiners with Insulfrog points, but it is often worthwhile doing so if you plan to use DCC, as it offers a virtual guarantee for a trouble-free future.

Fig. 7 – adding track sections to a 12V dc controlled twin track oval layout

12 Volt ONLY

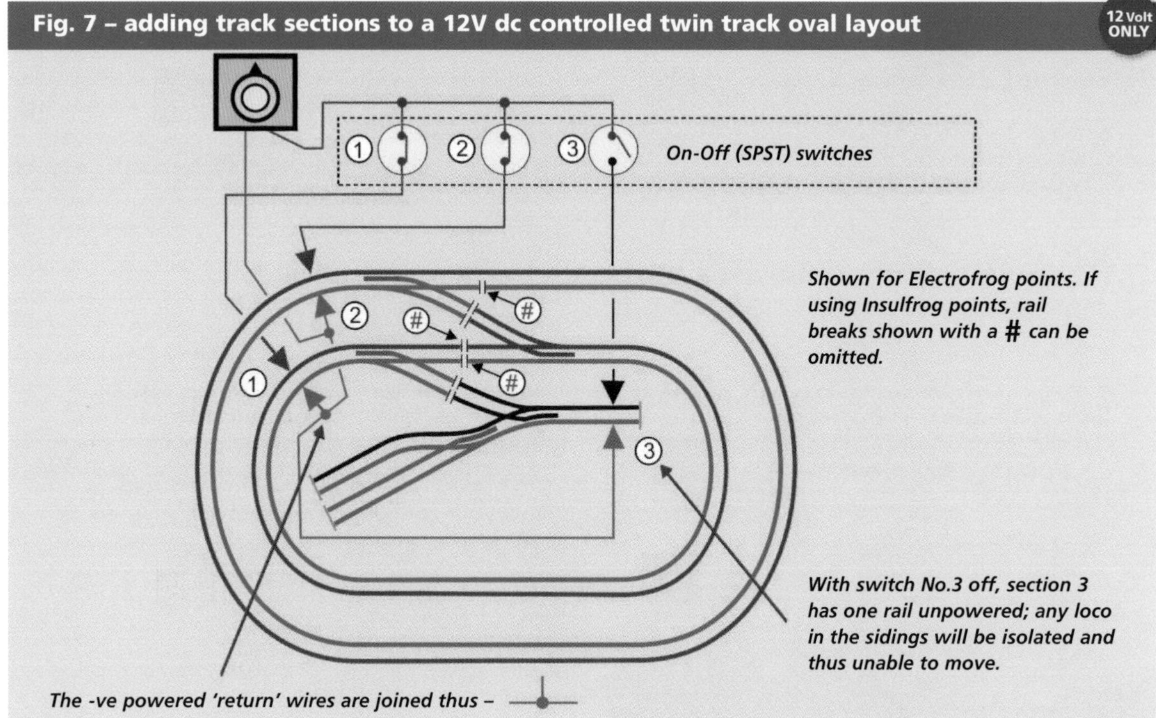

On-Off (SPST) switches
Shown for Electrofrog points. If using Insulfrog points, rail breaks shown with a # can be omitted.
With switch No.3 off, section 3 has one rail unpowered; any loco in the sidings will be isolated and thus unable to move.
The -ve powered 'return' wires are joined thus –

When sectioning your layout, it is always good practice to fit double rail breaks between the sections, even when using Insulfrog points as this ensures that sections you want isolated do not get powered when the points are changed over.

Isolating sections

12 Volt ONLY

Track sectioning is often extended to layout features such as locomotive sheds where several separate sections may be fitted along each shed road to allow the storage of many locos. These are called isolating sections (also referred to as 'dead sections') and are used on dead end tracks, such as loco shed roads as previously mentioned and those found at a terminus station where a train loco has to be halted at the buffers whilst another loco couples onto the rear of the train and draws the rolling stock away.

Isolating sections can be wired up as independent sections connected back to the speed controller in the manner as shown in Fig. 5, but a simpler way is to make a break in one rail with a fine-tooth saw and wire an on-off switch across it as in Fig. 8. Considerable runs of wire will be saved if the switch is located adjacent to the rail break at the baseboard edge, but, if the wires are to be run back to a central control position, the best option is really to wire it as an additional track control section.

A simple isolating section can be made using the Peco PL-20 switch. This just clips into the track across the rail break and although not very realistic on the visible scenic parts of the layout, they are ideal for creating isolating sections in fiddle yards (see glossary page 122).

Both track control sections and isolating sections are rarely required with DCC layouts as locomotive power is switched on and off by the system handset.

Reversing loops

DCC & 12 Volt

A reversing loop is a track formation used to enable a whole train to be turned around and sent back along the same route. They are most often to be found on 'Out-and-Back' and 'Dumb-bell' layout configurations, either as a single track reverse loop or as multiple storage loops in the fiddle yard section. Because each rail returns back onto itself, the problem of opposing polarities occurs, this time affecting both rails. Firstly the loop has to be isolated fully from the rest of the layout using twin rail breaks at each end. If you are using DCC, then you need to connect to the loop rails a special item known as a 'reversing module' which works automatically.

Fig. 8 – simple isolating section

12 Volt ONLY

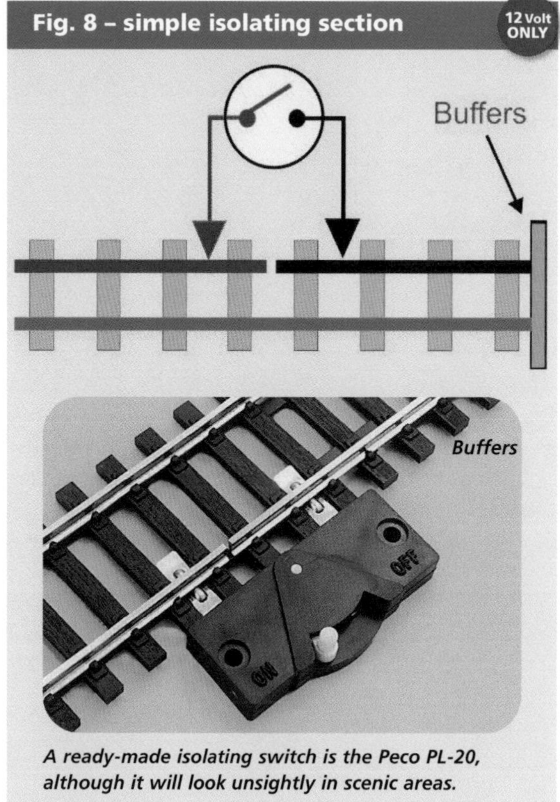

A ready-made isolating switch is the Peco PL-20, although it will look unsightly in scenic areas.

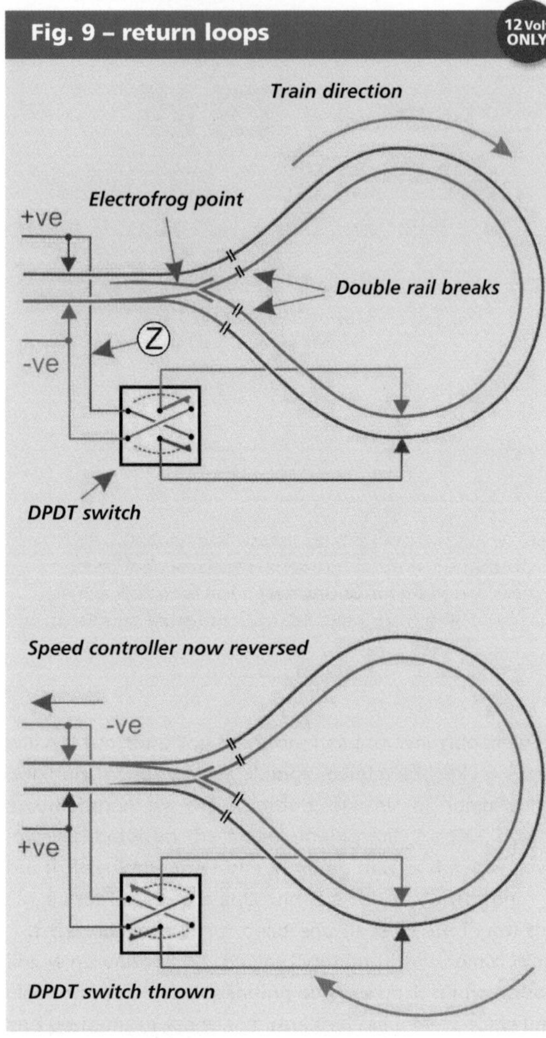

With analogue control, the issue is more complicated. Power is fed to both rails via a double pole changeover switch (known as a 'DPDT' switch – double pole, double throw). The switch is wired as shown and, as long as the left-hand track feed remains powered, it will always provide power to the loop at one polarity or the other. (In other words, the DPDT switch does not allow the loop to be switched off. To switch the loop off completely, fit a separate on-off switch in the feed wire at Z, or use a centre-off DPDT switch instead).

To run a train onto the loop, the point is set and the DPDT switch thrown as shown in Fig. 9. The electrical status of the loop will allow a train to be brought in from the left. When the whole train is inside the loop, it must be brought to a halt. After the point and the DPDT switch are both changed, the train can then be brought forward out of the loop by turning the speed controller up, but in the reverse direction. Because the polarity has to be changed over mid-way in the manoeuvre, it is the reason why the loco must always be brought to a halt with two-rail conventional DC wiring.

Installing section switches

12 Volt ONLY

Once we begin to include separate electrical sections on our analogue controlled layout, the question of where to put the switches themselves arises. It is perfectly possible to fit the switches alongside the relevant track feed on the layout, or along the baseboard edge opposite the track feed position (see Fig. 10). Such a system would require less wire to install, and is fine for small cameo-sized layouts, but on larger layouts, and in particular ovals or continuous runs, it would be cumbersome and potentially confusing to operate. There would also be a lot of walking up and down the layout to flick the switches on and off. So, most modellers choose to put the section switches in a central location on the layout next to the speed controller, creating what is traditionally known as the 'control panel'.

In its simplest form this need only be a row of numbered or colour-coded switches, and an easy way to build one is to use the Peco switch mounting console (PL-27) with Peco lever type switches (PL-22, PL-23, etc) as in photo 7. The switches simply clip into the console which in turn is screwed to the baseboard. A terminal block strip is fitted on the underside of the baseboard beneath the console so that the wires to and from the switches can be threaded through (photo 8) and later connected to the speed controller and to the corresponding track sections. Fig. 11 shows how the switches and terminal blocks are all linked up. Note that the feed from the controller is simply looped from one switch to the next within the console. As the lay-

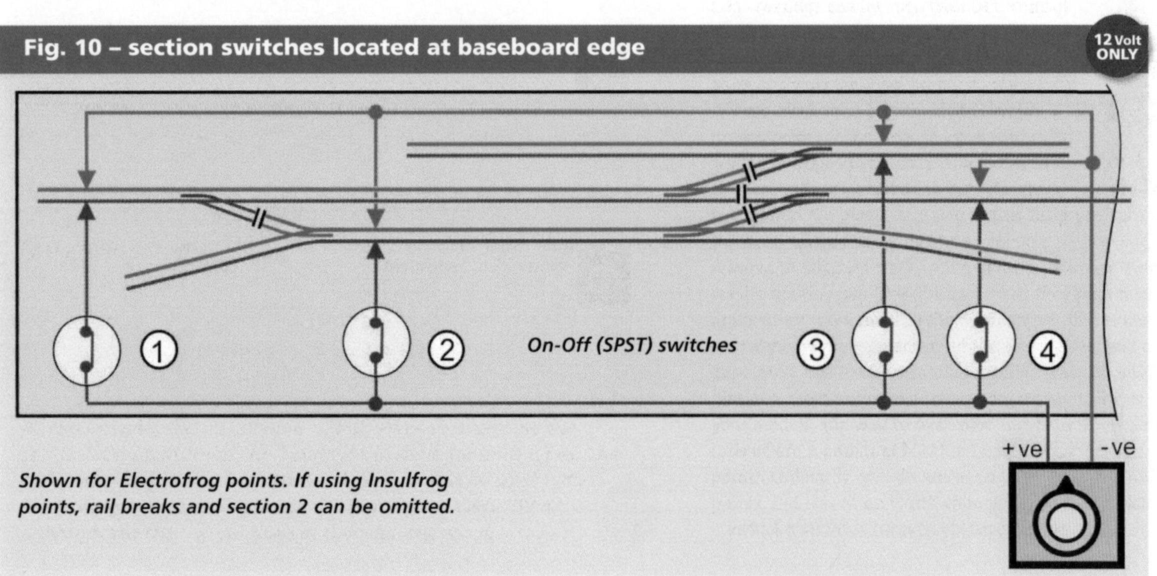

Shown for Electrofrog points. If using Insulfrog points, rail breaks and section 2 can be omitted.

Fig. 11 – console wiring

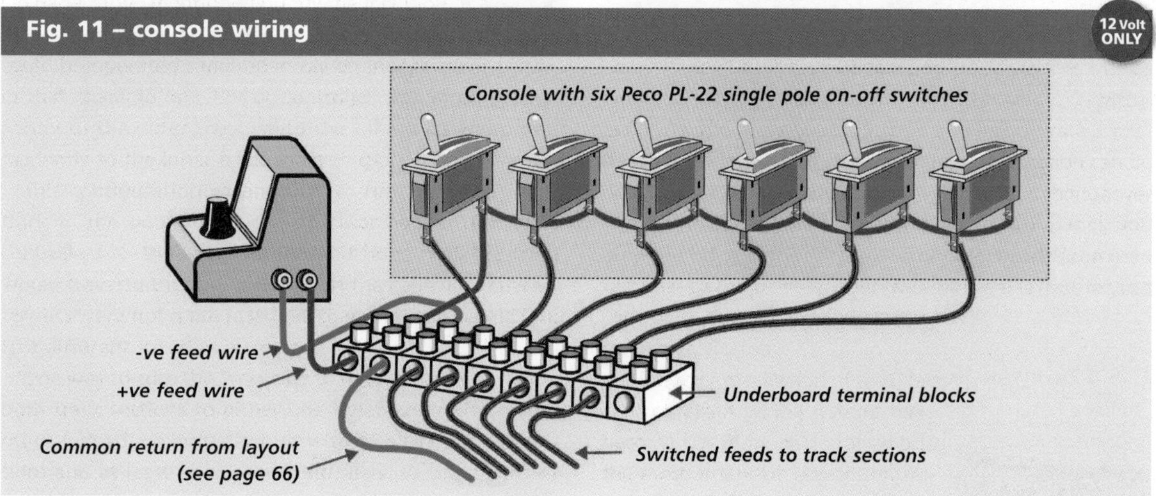

out expands additional consoles can be added as required, although the photo shows the wires soldered to the switch terminals.

On more complex layouts, or when the track plan is finalised before construction begins, switches can be mounted on a flat panel and arranged either in rows or within a mimic track diagram with each switch placed at the corresponding section position. Fig. 12 illustrates how such a mimic panel might look for our twin track oval layout described in Fig. 7.

The speed controller can also be built into the panel, if using a flush mounting 'open frame' one as per the example on page 56, or sited to one side if using a 'cased controller' version, or attached via a cable, plug and socket if using a 'hand-held' version. Materials which can be used for making the panel include plywood, MDF sheet, plastic/acrylic sheet and aluminium sheet. As holes need to be cut to accommodate the switches, etc, choose whichever material you find easiest to work with. If you are using the Peco lever switches and flush mounting plates (PL-28), then

Fig. 12 – a simple panel with flush-mounting controller and mimic diagram

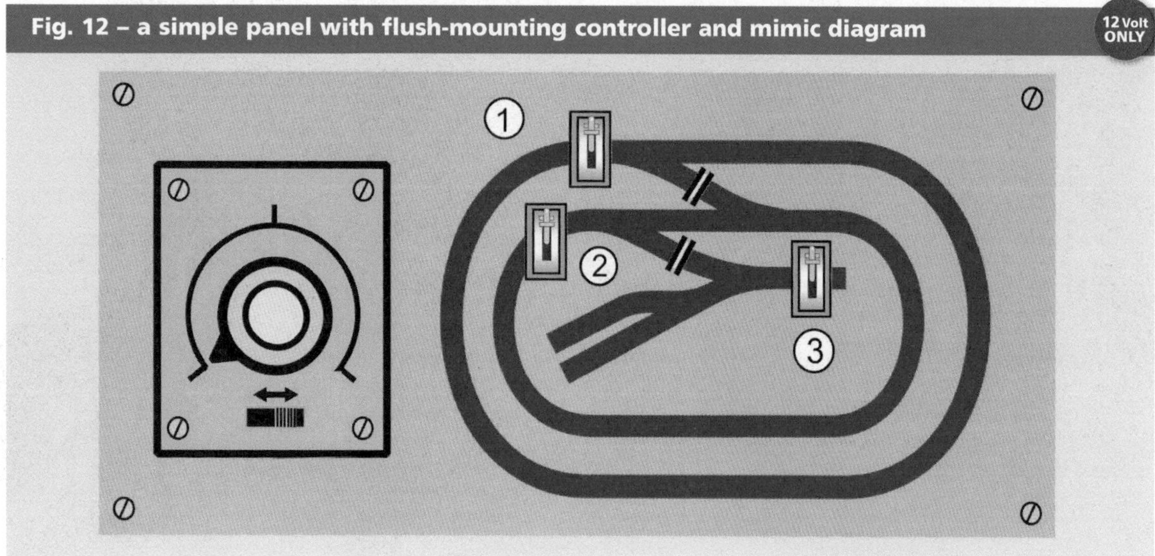

Fig. 13 – the common return principle

12 Volt ONLY

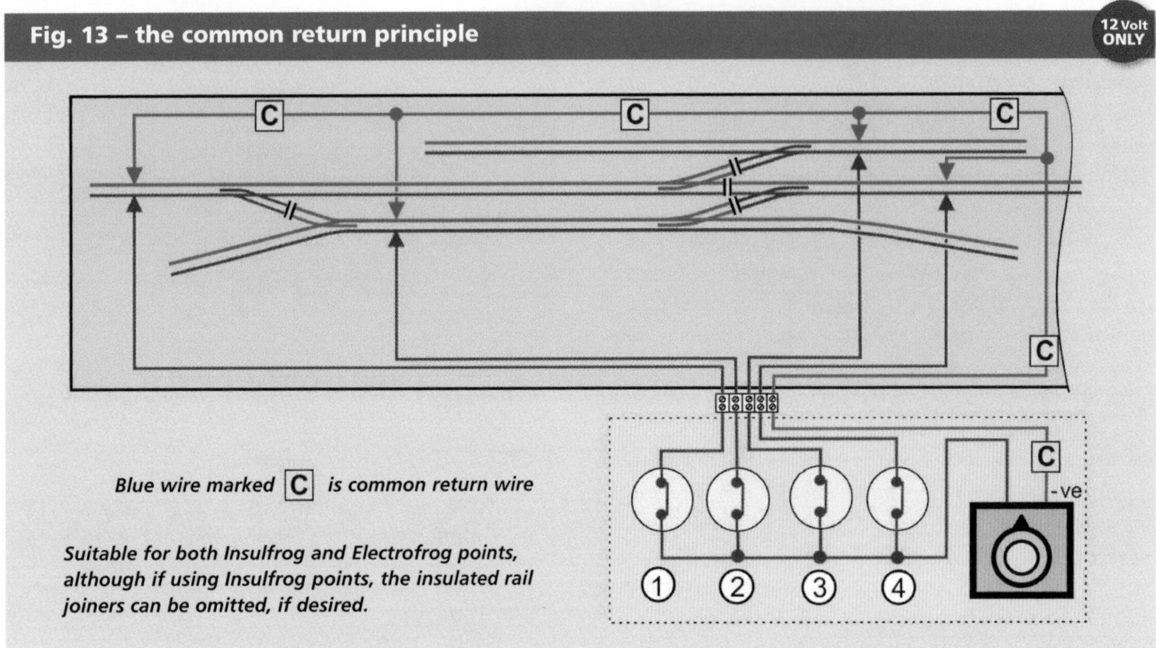

Suitable for both Insulfrog and Electrofrog points, although if using Insulfrog points, the insulated rail joiners can be omitted, if desired.

oblong holes need to be cut out. Note also that an external mains transformer is recommended and should be connected to the panel only by the 12V feed and return wires for maximum safety.

The 'Common Return' principle

12 Volt ONLY

Common Return is the name given to the wiring configuration in which all the -ve return wires from the track sections on an analogue-controlled layout are linked up to one wire which loops around the layout and runs back to be connected to the speed controller's -ve terminal. In Fig. 13, we have redrawn the wiring diagram featured in Fig. 10 to show how it would appear if the section switches were contained within a console frame. However, the blue return wires are not affected and still connect to a single common wire which is routed back to the speed controller's -ve terminal. This is the basis of a common return wiring system and the main benefits are that it saves on wire and minimises the number of connections to the panel/controller and at board joints on portable layouts.

When setting out to install common return wiring for the track sections, it is important to assign which rails on the layout will be the 'common' rails and to use the designation throughout. This is not difficult; on an end-to-end layout choose either the nearest or furthest rail, on a continuous run circuit, select either the inner or the outer rail. Don't forget however that special rules apply where reversing loops and triangular junctions occur.

Track section circuits and auxiliary control circuits for point motors, colour light signals, etc (see page 70), should all be wired up using an individual common return for each circuit The rule then: *always use a separate common return for the track circuits and separate ones for each of the auxiliary control circuits.*

As an aside at this stage, for a direct comparison, it may be helpful to observe how the layout shown in Fig. 13 may

Fig 14 – DCC version of the layout shown in Figs. 10 and 13

DCC ONLY

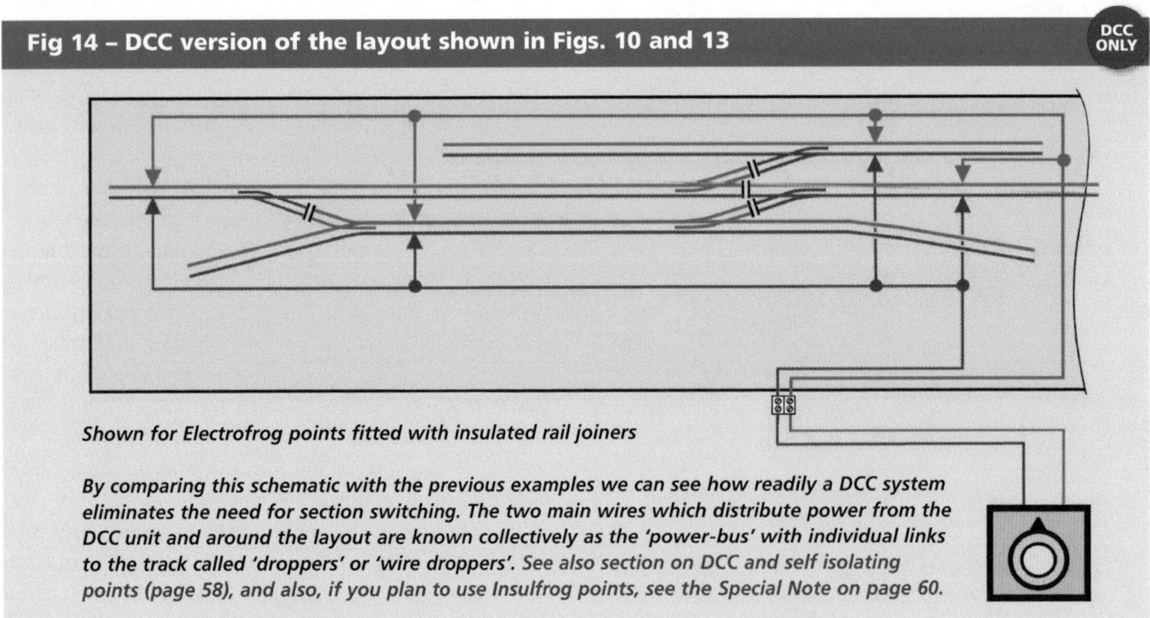

Shown for Electrofrog points fitted with insulated rail joiners

***By comparing this schematic with the previous examples we can see how readily a DCC system eliminates the need for section switching. The two main wires which distribute power from the DCC unit and around the layout are known collectively as the 'power-bus' with individual links to the track called 'droppers' or 'wire droppers'.** See also section on DCC and self isolating points (page 58), and also, if you plan to use Insulfrog points, see the Special Note on page 60.*

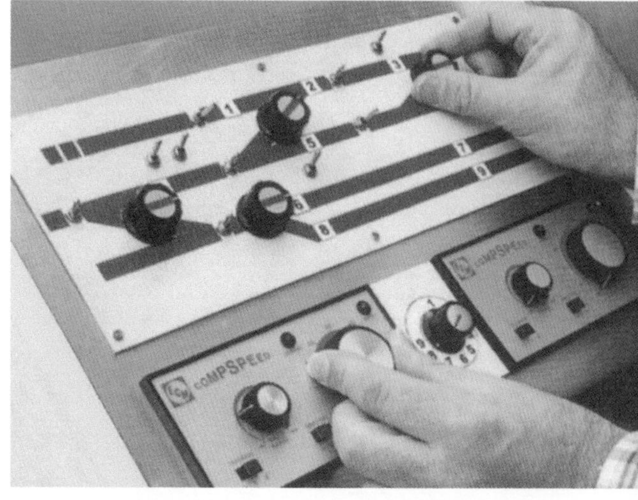

Right
With cab control, the speed controllers (at the bottom of the panel) can be assigned to different parts of the layout via two-way toggle switches. The rotary switches operate points and the numbers on the panel refer to positions of uncoupling magnets.

be wired for use with DCC, as indeed seen in Fig. 14. The +ve feed wires are now all linked together in a formation we could call 'common feed' as it mirrors the circuit as drawn for the common return. In DCC, however, these two 'common' feed and return circuits are usually referred to as the 'power bus' which distributes power around the whole layout.

Fig. 14 is shown for Electrofrog points. If using Insulfrog points, the number of feed and return connections could be reduced, but don't forget if you want to have all the track and sidings permanently live when using DCC, you will have to add more feeds and links, as explained under the section DCC and self isolating points on page 58.

Cab Control

12 Volt ONLY

On page 61 we mentioned briefly the inclusion of a second controller on analogue layouts so that two trains could be operated simultaneously on independent tracks. In that example one 12V dc controller was wired permanently to the outer track whilst the other was wired permanently to the inner track and sidings.

This configuration meant that to run from the inner track to the outer track, the operator had to turn both controllers to the same setting and hope that the train would traverse the join smoothly. If the controller characteristics were not quite matched, then the train would jerk to a different speed as it crossed.

One way to cure this would be to have a means to switch both track sections to either one speed controller or the other. Indeed, on larger layouts with many more track sections and at least two speed controllers, such a means of switching some, or all, of the sections between one controller or the other was always very desirable to increase operating flexibility, ie either of the controllers can be used to run a train anywhere on the layout.

This system is known as 'Cab Control', where the speed controllers are designated 'Cab 1' and 'Cab 2' respectively and track sections can be switched between 'cabs' via two-way (changeover) switches (SPDT). The changeover switches also incorporate a 'centre off' position so that the respective track section can be switched off completely. Providing that the changeover switches are installed in a centralised control panel, you only need to run one feed wire from the switch's common terminal to the track section; thus wiring a layout for cab control is not really all that much more complicated.

With the introduction of DCC, cab control layout wiring systems have become less fashionable for all but the most ardent of 12V dc control devotees. Accordingly we will not deal with it in depth in this book, but those wanting to find out much more are referred to the Peco Shows You How booklet No.5, *Wiring the layout – part 2 for the more advanced.*

Below
With sophisticated wiring, even a large 12V dc layout is perfectly capable of being operated single-handed, as demonstrated by David Dobbs and his *Allerton Gardens* layout (RM February 2013).

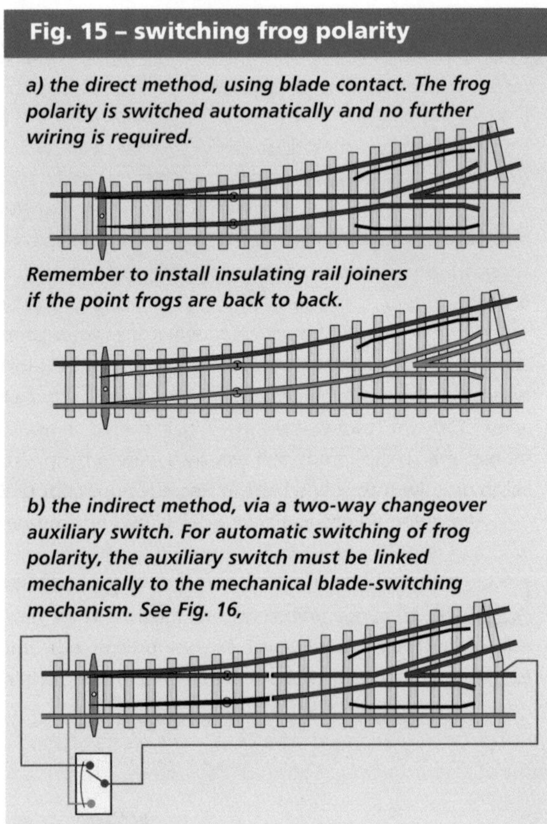

Fig. 15 – switching frog polarity

a) the direct method, using blade contact. The frog polarity is switched automatically and no further wiring is required.

Remember to install insulating rail joiners if the point frogs are back to back.

b) the indirect method, via a two-way changeover auxiliary switch. For automatic switching of frog polarity, the auxiliary switch must be linked mechanically to the mechanical blade-switching mechanism. See Fig. 16,

Peco Streamline points and crossings

DCC & 12 Volt

Because of their ingenious design, all points and crossings in the Peco Streamline Insulfrog ranges (including all the Setrack systems) and most in the Electrofrog ranges, are ready-to-use out of the box

Insulfrog points should be considered when you want to keep the layout wiring as simple as possible. Because they have a fully insulated frog, they do not require any modifications or additional switching or wiring. With Electrofrog points, however, the polarity of the live frog has to change over when the blade direction of the point is changed. This is why layout wiring with Electrofrog points can be slightly more involved: they must have power fed only from the leading end (toe) of the point, and rail breaks and insulated rail joiners must always be installed between two point frogs when they occur back-to-back, as with a crossover or loop, or when laid in a continuous oval (see section 'Insulfrog or Electrofrog?' on page 57 for a full explanation of this).

The switching of frog polarity is self-activated by blade contact with many Electrofrog items, however some points – for example (in OO) the asymmetric three-way point and the single and double slips – because of their complexity, require this to be done indirectly through a separate switch and extra wiring.

OO code 75 left-hand, right-hand and Y points normally self-activate, but they also have the option to have the frogs wired up via a separate switch. This has the advantage that older-type model locos and stock can be used with these points as the separate switching option eliminates the possibility of short circuits occurring between the open point blades and the backs of wide loco wheel flanges and treads; a factor equally important when using DCC control (How to set up the separate switching option is described on the instruction leaflet).

Fig. 15 shows schematic diagrams of the two alternative methods of changing frog polarity on a standard OO code 75 point. Fig. 15a shows the self-activated switching method through blade contact alone, whilst Fig. 15b shows the indirect method via a separate two-way changeover switch (SPDT), as would be the case with the separate switched option. The switch has to be mechanically linked in some way to the point tiebar, such that when point direction is changed, the switch is activated and the frog polarity changes simultaneously. If you plan to operate your points electrically, using Peco PL-10 series point motors, the frog switching can be done easily by clipping on a Peco PL-13 Accessory Switch and wiring it up accordingly. The 3D illustration Fig. 16a shows how this is achieved on a three-way point which needs two point motors of course, though the principle for ordinary two-way points is identical.

If you don't want to use electric point motors, it is possible to operate points manually using the 'wire-in-tube' method. The operating wire is linked through a hole drilled in the knob of a slide switch, fitted at the edge of the baseboard. Fig. 16b shows how this is achieved.

Crossings and double junctions

DCC & 12 Volt

Crossings are often called 'diamond crossings' because of their obvious diamond-like shape. They occur in double track junctions and scissors crossovers, or where

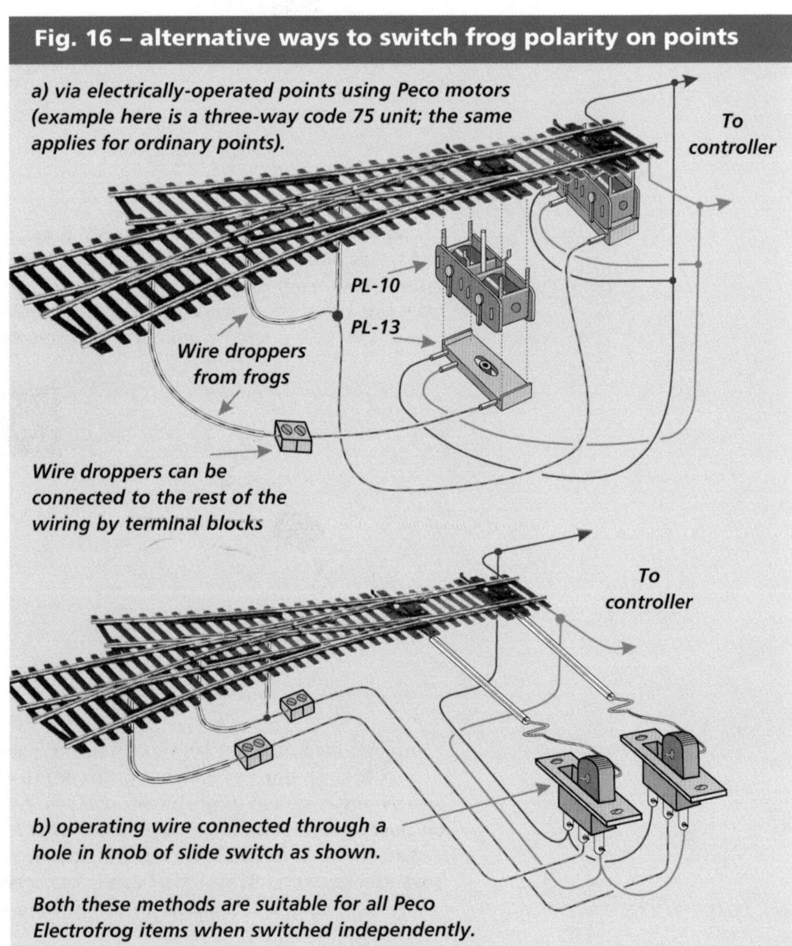

Fig. 16 – alternative ways to switch frog polarity on points

a) via electrically-operated points using Peco motors (example here is a three-way code 75 unit; the same applies for ordinary points).

Wire droppers can be connected to the rest of the wiring by terminal blocks

b) operating wire connected through a hole in knob of slide switch as shown.

Both these methods are suitable for all Peco Electrofrog items when switched independently.

Fig. 17 – diamond crossings

one route crosses several parallel routes diagonally. They can also be found in freight yards, harbours and industrial sites where sidings might be required to criss-cross each other at random.

In the Peco OO code 100 Universal and Setrack ranges, all crossings are available only as the Insulfrog type. As such, they are ready-to-lay and do not require any additional wiring or switching: they simply need connecting into the rest of the trackwork via metal rail joiners and work equally well on 12V dc (analogue) and DCC systems.

Electrofrog crossings in all Peco ranges do need to be laid in conjunction with separate switching mechanisms for the frog polarity. In each crossing there are two 'live frogs' which must be switched depending on the route set. As there are only two routes through a crossing – which we can refer to as 'normal' and 'transverse' (see Fig. 17 – the normal route can be thought of as the most frequently used or 'main' route, whilst the transverse route is the less frequently used route). In this case, only one switching action is needed via a DPDT (double-pole double-throw) switch. At its very simplest, a manually-operated DPDT toggle switch would suffice, as shown in Fig. 18, but the operator would have to remember to switch it over each time the transverse route was selected, otherwise a short circuit would occur when the loco attempted to move over the crossing.

Usually, to run a train over the transverse route of a crossing, an adjacent point leading into that route has to be changed. So by mechanically linking the DPDT switch to the point actuating mechanism, the polarity of the crossing frogs can be switched automatically. When using Peco point motors, then you need to install a PL-10 with a Peco PL-15 Twin Microswitch assembly, wired as a DPDT switch as shown in Fig. 19. If your layout is powered by only one 12V dc speed controller, or a DCC system, then this arrangement can be used at double junctions and scissors crossovers. (Note that if two, or more, analogue dc controllers are being used, such as at a double junction with up and down lines controlled separately, then the wiring can be a little more involved and is described in more detail in our Shows You How booklet No.21 *Wiring the layout – part 3 points and crossings.*)

At these junctions only one point has to be fitted with the switch mechanism for the crossing frogs. In the case of a double junction, this must be the point which directs trains across the transverse route of the crossing.

For more details on double junctions and scissors junctions see our Shows You How booklet *Wiring the layout – part 3* as above.

Fig. 18 – manual frog switching for an Electrofrog crossing

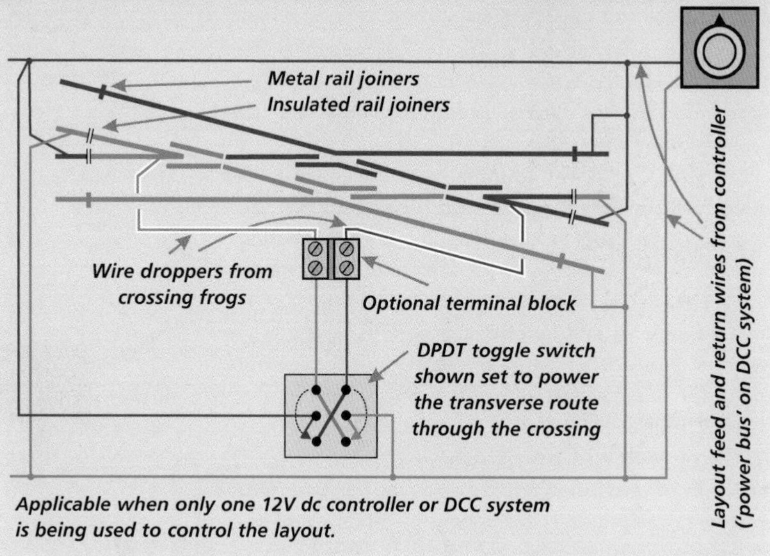

Applicable when only one 12V dc controller or DCC system is being used to control the layout.

Fig. 19 – automatic frog switching for an Electrofrog crossing

For double track layouts when only one 12V dc controller or DCC system is in use. For wire-in-tube operated points.

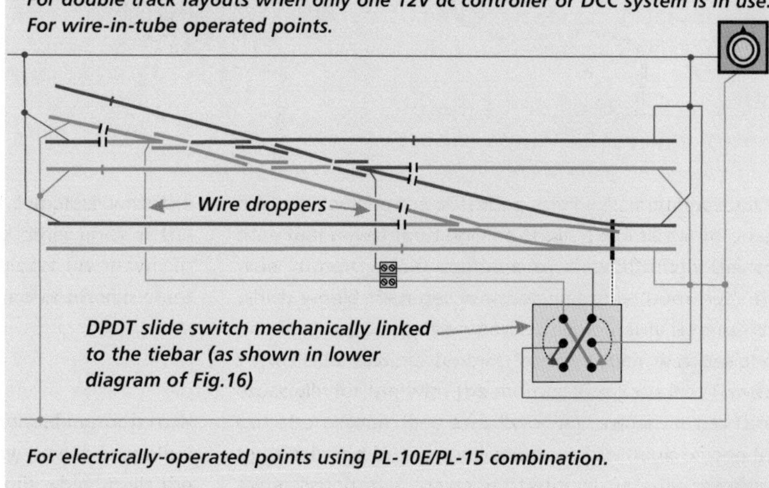

For electrically-operated points using PL-10E/PL-15 combination.

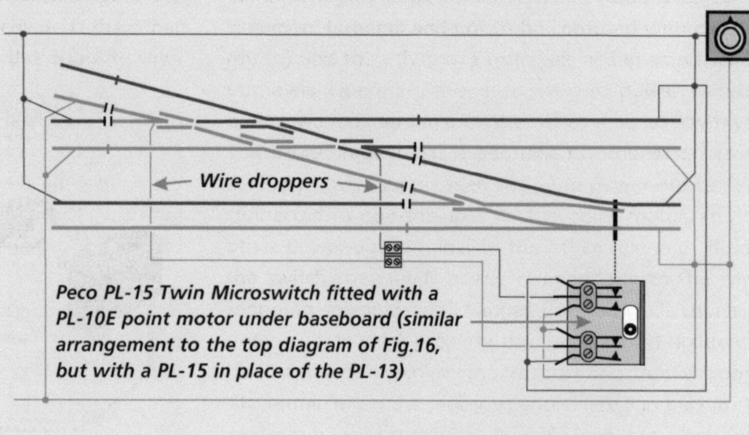

Single and double slips

DCC & 12 Volt

Slips are similar to crossings but have a tiebar and sets of blades at each end to change the route setting. This means that just as with points, frog polarity switching (when required) can be achieved via changeover switches mechanically linked to the blade operating mechanisms.

Insulfrog slips are ready-to-lay and do not require additional wiring or switches providing you are using only one analogue controller, or a DCC system, on the layout. It only becomes complex if you are using two analogue controllers (as with up line and down line) and again extra information can be gleaned from our Shows You How booklet *Wiring the layout – part 3*.

When wiring Electrofrog slips they must be treated as independent electrical sections with their own feed and return, but must again have frog polarity changed indirectly by switches linked to the blade operating mechanisms; either slide switches for manual operation, or PL-10/PL-13 combinations for electric operation. Note that the switches change the polarity of the frogs at the opposite end of the slip as shown in Fig. 20.

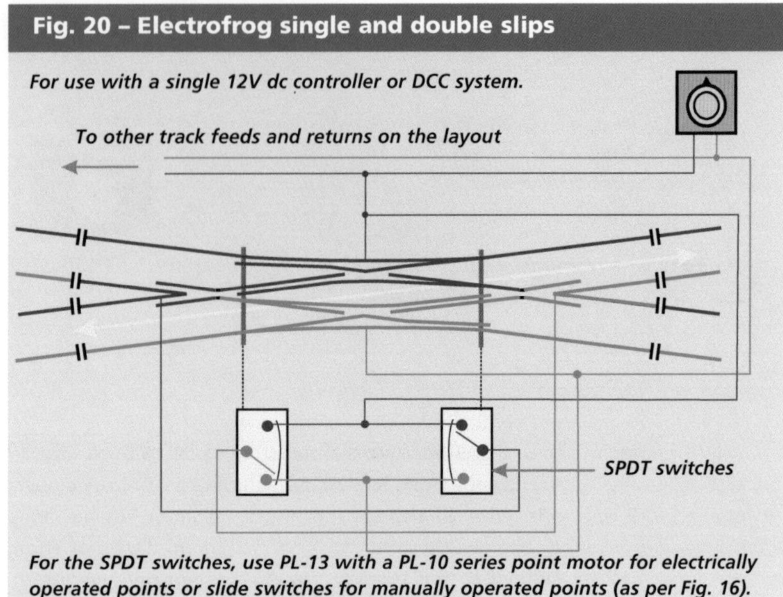

Fig. 20 – Electrofrog single and double slips

For the SPDT switches, use PL-13 with a PL-10 series point motor for electrically operated points or slide switches for manually operated points (as per Fig. 16).

Wiring electrical point motors

DCC & 12 Volt

Although all Peco points and crossings can be operated by hand straight from the box, the remote operation of them is often desirable and, as we have seen above, sometimes necessary if we are to have automatic switching of the live frogs.

Accordingly, the electrically operated point motor is most often the first accessory layout builders install after the track wiring is accomplished.

DCC or traditional point motor control systems – which is best?

Point motors, including solenoid types, can be operated via a DCC system providing you install accessory decoders for them. You will have to do this If you want to fire the point motors via the keys on your DCC system handset or console, or even operate them on a computer screen, via a click of the mouse, or touch-screen facility.

However, the traditional method of operating point motors from an auxiliary 16V power supply is likely to be the cheaper option, and may be easier to install.

Indeed, many DCC devotees continue to operate their trains digitally, but choose to use a traditional system for their point operations. (Installing accessory decoders for points is covered in our Shows You How booklet No.17 *Introducing DCC*.)

So if you settle for the traditional method you will need to install a separate circuit for the point motors. For those controlling the trains with 12V dc, many cased analogue controllers have an additional 'auxiliary' power output (usually 16V ac) which can be used for this purpose (photo 9). If you do not have an auxiliary output on your controller or use a DCC system, you will need to obtain a separate transformer/power supply such as a Gaugemaster M1 cased unit for the point motor circuitry.

Types of point motor

There are several designs of point motor to choose from; the twin solenoid type, such as the Peco PL-10 and the PL-11 side mounting ones; the slow action motor, of which the Peco SmartSwitch or Circuitron Tortoise motors are examples; and the servo motor type, which is gradually being made available commercially. The solenoid type works on an instantaneous supply of power, whilst others work on a constant supply in conjunction with either integral switching, or external circuitry (photo 10).

Peco PL-10 solenoid motor

The Peco types can now be installed without having to resort to the soldering of wires. For the PL-10, the Peco PL-34 Wiring Loom can be used: the spade connectors simply push onto the terminals on the motor casing as shown (photos 11 and 12). The other ends of the loom are connected to the rest of the wiring using standard plastic

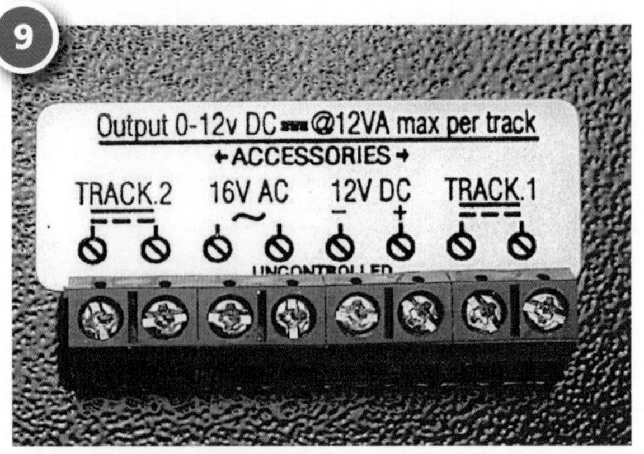

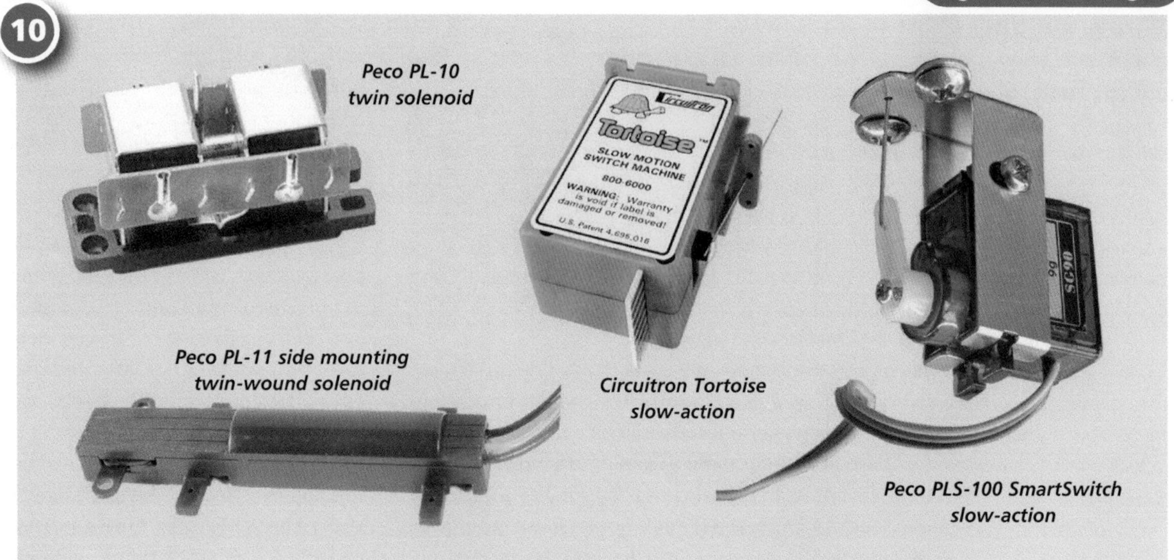

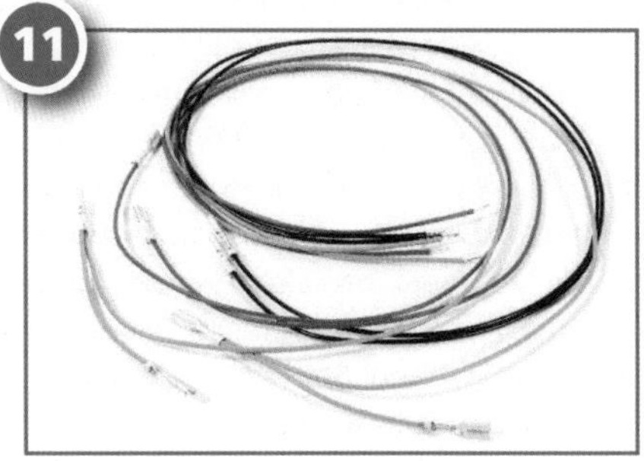

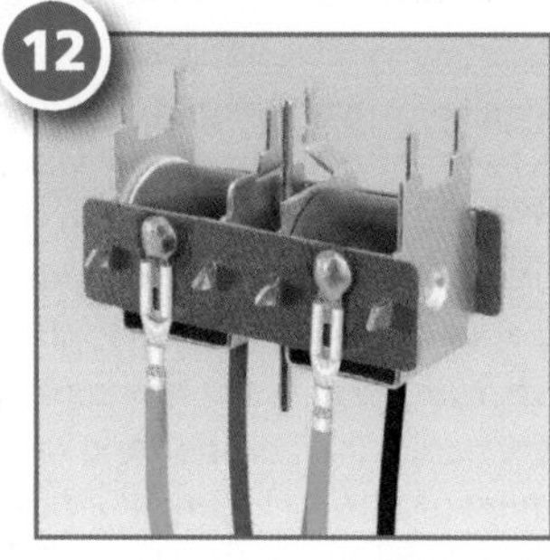

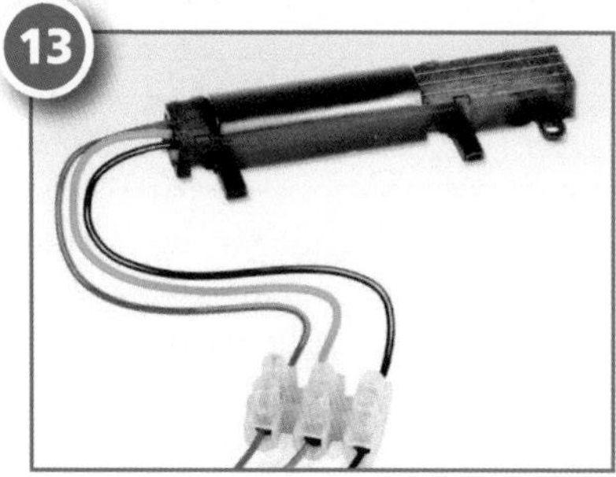

terminal blocks. The PL-11 is supplied complete with the wiring pre-fitted, it too just needs the other ends of the wires connecting up using terminal blocks (as shown in photo 13). Many other makes of point motor often require connections to be soldered.

Basic point motor wiring

The principle of operation of a twin solenoid motor is really quite simple. To activate it one way, power is applied momentarily to one of the solenoid coils which pulls the operating arm across to that side. To activate it the other way, power is applied momentarily to the opposite solenoid coil, pulling the operating arm back. It is important to note that power must only be applied momentarily, otherwise current would continue to flow through the coil which would then get very hot and may 'burn out'. The simplest way of applying power momentarily is to use the Peco PL-26 Passing Contact Switch which was designed especially for use with the motors. The Peco PL-26 switch can also be described as a 'two-way' switch. It has three terminals and in this application we can think of one terminal acting as a 'power-in' terminal (usually called the 'common' terminal and not to be confused with common return) and the other two terminals acting as power-out terminals. Operating the lever switches power to either one power-out terminal or the other – hence 'two-way'. The power-in terminal is permanently connected to the auxiliary power supply feed with one power-out terminal connected to one solenoid on the point motor, and the other power-out terminal to the other solenoid. Flicking the switch over feeds power momentarily to the corresponding solenoid and changes the point. Of course, in order for it to work properly, the full electrical circuit must be completed. To achieve this, return wires from the opposite terminals on the motor solenoids are run back to the auxiliary power supply. Fig. 21 explains this in more detail showing how both PL-10 and PL-11 point motors are wired. At all times the point motor wiring (from the 16V ac auxiliary supply) and the track wiring (from the controlled 12V dc supply) must be completely isolated from each other.

(A two-way switch is generally known as an SPDT switch – single pole, double throw. The PL-26 passing contact switch is a unique design of SPDT switch for this purpose.)

Fig. 21 – wiring Peco solenoid point motors

Peco PL-10 point motor
Peco PL-26 passing contact switch
Peco PL-11 point motor
Momentary pulse
Rear terminals of PL-10 linked together
Terminal blocks
Feed wire
Return wire

Wiring multiple point motors

It is possible to power many point motors on a layout from just one auxiliary power supply and, since only one point is usually switched at a time, there is no theoretical limit to the number of motors which can be connected up. Only if you wish to operate several point motors simultaneously might the power supply (rated in amps) need upgrading, although the installation of a capacitor discharge unit will help in these situations.

For many layout applications, however, we only need to wire up all our point motors and their respective switches to operate one at a time. To do this the switches are wired into a 'parallel' circuit with all power-in terminals on each PL-26 switch linked together, and the power-out terminals of each switch wired to the relevant solenoid terminals of the corresponding point motor

On occasions, you might wish to change two points together, such as with a crossover or run-round loop. To do this you simply wire the pair of point motors so they can be operated by the same switch. Though bear in mind, as mentioned above, in so doing you are taking twice the power from the auxiliary supply at one go.

Capacitor Discharge Units (CDUs)

This is a piece of circuitry used with twin solenoid point motors only. It boosts the power output at the moment of switching and helps to overcome any excess friction in the sliding part of the motor as well as ensure a more positive throw of the point. The extra power boost is also useful when firing more than one motor simultaneously as described above, and more powerful 'heavy duty' versions are available for use when many motors are required to be operated in rapid succession when setting up routes.

An example of a CDU unit is available as Peco-Lectrics item PL-35. They are simply wired into the auxiliary power supply feed and return wires as shown in Fig. 22.

Fig. 22 – adding a Capacitor Discharge Unit

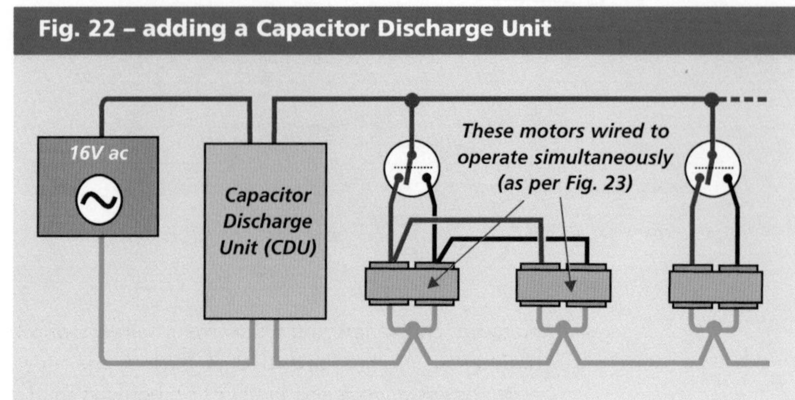

Probe and stud point motor switching

If you are using a mimic diagram style of panel you can cut down on the number of switches needed by using the probe and studs method.

Basically, two metal studs are screwed into the panel instead of a two-way passing contact switch. The studs effectively replace the two 'power out' terminals of the switch, and 'power in' is provided by a metal probe on a flexible lead which is touched momentarily onto the stud corresponding to the solenoid of the point you wish to change (photo 14). Fig. 23 shows this in a schematic form.

The component parts for this method are available in the Peco range; probe (PL-17) and studs (PL-18). An additional benefit of this system is that you can set up a route swiftly by touching all the relevant studs in quick succession. The method is only suitable for use with solenoid type point motors, and use in conjunction with a Capacitor Discharge Unit is recommended.

A possible drawback with this system is that you cannot tell instantly to which route the point is set. However there are methods by which route indicator lamps could be fitted into the panel such that when the points are switched

Fig. 23 – probe and stud wiring schematic

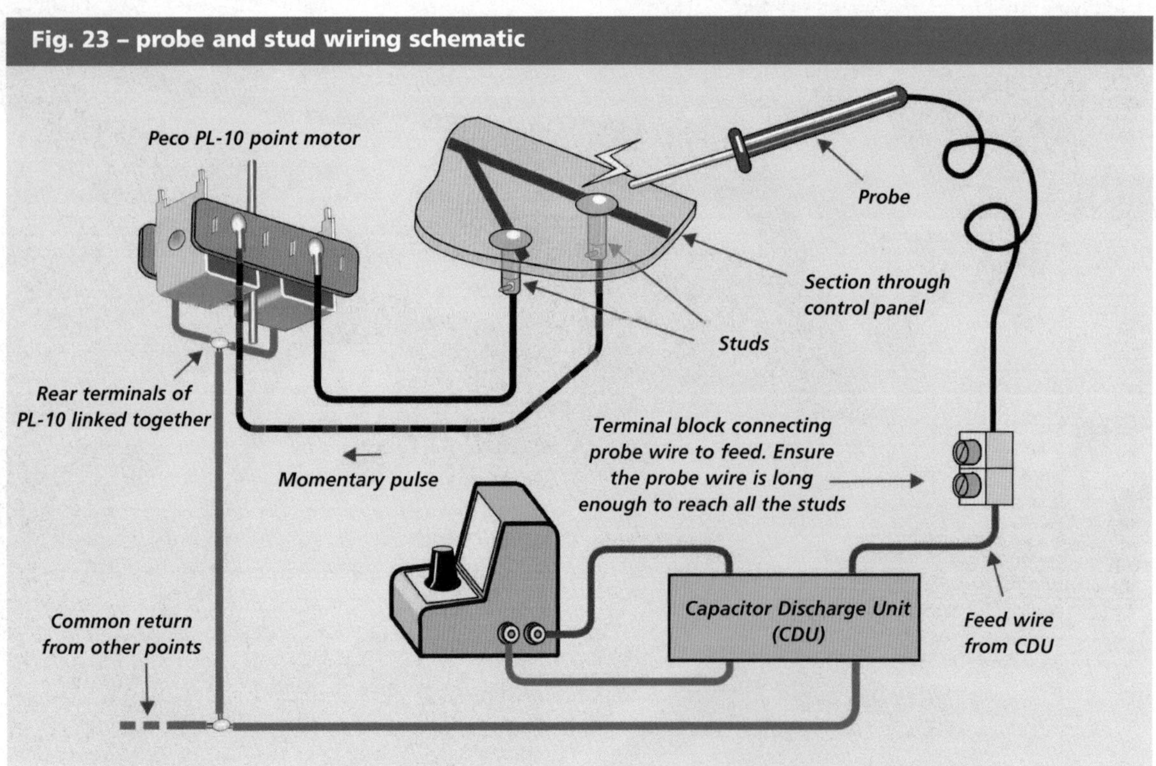

the relevant lamp lights up. One method is to use the Peco PL-13 accessory switch on the underside of the point motor and run wires back to the panel to energise the relevant bulb (or LED). Although the switching circuits for the lamps are elementary in themselves, the wiring can become quite involved if a lot of points are used and, further, a separate power supply for the lighting circuits is required.

So opting for the DCC point control option as described above, could well be a viable alternative, but as with many aspects in the hobby, there are always pros and cons with each option.

Servo-operated point control

The new Peco SmartSwitch is a versatile way of operating points, signals and other accessories; see Fig. 24.

Fig. 24 – The Peco SmartSwitch

The SmartSwitch servo control system is a recent addition to the Peco range of electronic products, providing an alternative means of automated operation for points and semaphore signals. Servos are miniature dc electric motors which are coupled to a gearbox and an integral electronic circuit, to provide very low gearing and up to 180° of very precise and powerful movement.

simply a matter of plugging the control board, servos and remote servo programming boards together with the leads supplied. The only external wiring required (to be fitted by the user) is that to the toggle switches, and to connect a separate auxilliary 12V dc power feed to the input connections on the SmartSwitch control board; on DCC installations the power feed can, if desired, be taken from the track.

The SmartSwitch kit offers enough components to get started, and indeed may be sufficient for smaller layouts with limited pointwork and signalling. However, because most installations will require additional servos, these can be obtained individually, and 1000mm extension cables cater for occasions where there are longer distances between a servo and the control board. Additional control boards are also available for situations where there is in excess of four servos used.

Also available separately is a SmartFrog optional circuit board that can be used in combination with a servo to change to polarity of the frog. It needs wiring to the control board, the track power and the frog itself (it also needs its own auxilliary 12V dc supply). Regardless of the amount of servos used on an installation, only one programming board is required.

DCC operation

Digital control of the SmartSwitch servos is possible by connecting a Peco SmartSwitch stationary decoder (ref.PLS–135) to the control board. Each servo can be assigned its own unique address number, so that they can be individually controlled via a DCC controller. This also enables the servos to be operated without the toggle switches, if desired.

More details can be found online at www.peco-uk.com, where there is also a link to a video which introduces and demonstrates the system.

Advantages of SmartSwitch

The Peco system is designed as essentially a 'plug and play' installation with comprehensive, illustrated instructions to make its use as straightforward as possible.

The main advantages of using a servo to operate a point or semaphore signal are that it allows precise control over the pitch of the throw, is less noisy (than the 'zap' of a solenoid) and the speed of the throwing action can be adjusted to suit. The physical size of a servo assembly is also a lot smaller than other types of slow-action point motor, making it much more versatile and suitable for confined spaces.

Servos can also be used to operate crossing gates and other moving features on layouts, and are powerful enough for use with all scales and gauges up to G. There is also the advantage that SmartSwitch servos are powerful enough to throw a Peco point without the need for modification, or removal of the over-centre spring.

SmartSwitch – what you get in the box

Peco offers SmartSwitch as a complete starter kit in a box (ref.PLS–100) with sufficient servos and components to operate four turnouts. The electrical circuitry is very easy to connect up as it is

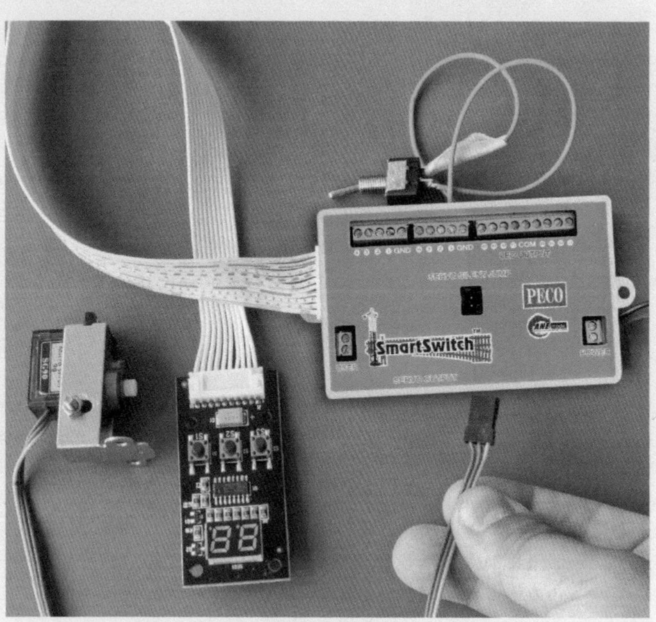

Adding a backscene

Above
Pre-printed backscenes, such as these perennial favourites from the Peco range, finish off the scenery very well.

Perhaps the final phase of constructing a layout is to add a backscene. This helps to frame the modelled area and provide a means of concentrating the eye on the scene, rather than allowing it to drift off and focus on what lies beyond the layout, which might be a plain wall, or the rest of the room.

Commercially printed backscenes

The quickest way to provide a backscene is to make use of one of the many pre-printed types which can be obtained from the local model show. These include those by Peco, which has a large range of different scenes, all of which are very popular (above) and inexpensive. There are also photo-realistic types of backscene available through firms such as Gaugemaster. Essentially these items are not dissimilar to a roll of wallpaper, and indeed can be pasted onto a suitable backscene board in much the same way, although it is important not to let the prints get too wet during the application process.

Hardboard, or thin MDF sheet, is probably the most suitable material for the backboard and needs only to be screwed to the rear of the layout baseboard, once the sheet has been attached and left to dry.

Creating your own backscene

If you want to have a unique and individual backdrop, one solution is to select colour photos from magazines and calendars, cut out the building elements and arrange them in a montage on your own backboard. When you are happy with the arrangement the pictures can be glued in place.

Above
A photo-realistic backscene in place on *Alloa East* by Gareth Rowlands. This N gauge layout was in the April 2010 RM.

Right
A selection of artists' materials which can be used to paint your own backscene. Tester pots from DIY stores are a good choice when only a small amount of paint is required.

Left
The backscene on Richard Lane's *Oakbourne* layout (see RM November 2007 and July 2009) was created using photographs and painted areas, built up collage-style.

Richard Lane used this technique many times as illustrated on his *Oakbourne* layout.

Hand-painting a backscene

For those modellers who want to have a go at hand-painting their own backscene, we have included the methods used and described by Andy Peters. A modicum of artistic talent is required but the methods Andy uses are not difficult to get to grips with. His normal backscene material is white-faced hardboard which he gets from his local timber merchant who cuts it to size for him. The material is easy to paint and work with, and can even be bent relatively easily to make a curved backscene.

Paint

The materials Andy uses are very basic and inexpensive. To block in the sky he uses a tester pot of Dulux First Dawn matt emulsion. He works with acrylic colours for the painting in the main scenes, using brands such as Reeves or Winsor & Newton, and purchased from the likes of Hobbycraft, The Range, or any good art shop.

Start with the sky

If your backscene is removable then all the better, as doing this on a flat surface is easier than working in the vertical and possibly 2' away from you.

Andy always starts with the sky, having first decided what the background subject matter will be. You will have to choose yours to suit your layout. Using the tester pot and the integral pot-lid brush, he starts at the top of the board: with this combination of paint and board you don't get a solid blue sky effect, it is more broken and natural, which stops it looking top-heavy. Paint should be applied one third down the board and be faded out a bit towards the bottom to leave a white-ish sky at the horizon (see photo 1). Have a look on a bright day, as that is how it most often is: but it is important not to be too fussy and over-work the sky. At this stage you can add clouds if you want to or you can wait for the paint to dry completely; either way, just get a bit of damp tissue and dab it around in a fluffy cloud shape (see photo 2).

Reference pictures

If you can find reference pictures of the area you wish to replicate, all the better; if not look in a few books for pictures of trees, hills, mountains etc.

Next, Andy sketches some idea of where the landform elements will go and checks it against the modelled scenery; a wonderfully-painted valley or mountain peak should not be obscured by a building on the layout.

Likewise, note where the bottom of the scene will be in relationship to the layout scenery, as there is, again, no point in painting detail elements too low or too high. Sunlight direction is another crucial factor; decide from which side the sun shines for painting shadows etc.

In the step-by-step sequence Andy has included a mountain just to show how easy they are to paint. He starts with a mix of white, the smallest amount of blue – as any blue is a very powerful colour – and has a tiny bit of crimson ready to use. He first picks out the overall shape and then adds a touch of light grey to add depth to the shaded side, then with a wet brush, adds a touch of the crimson and blends it in (see photo 3).

For rolling hills, start with the horizon: remember, if you are in a valley your horizon will be well up the back board, and if you are on high ground there will be a low horizon.

Using a similar colour mix to the mountains pick out some distant hills; the further away they are the flatter they will be. Again, as with the mountain, you can add some grey to show contours and shade (see photo 4). As you work towards yourself the colours will become greener and stronger.

For the distant treelines and hedgerows across fields, Andy just tones the colour down a bit; don't be worried about shape or form at this distance, just remember to keep the bottom of the hedgerow smooth and the top undulating to represent trees, shrubs and hedges etc (see photo 5). Once you have all your fields in place you can use a clean wet brush and take paint off the 'sunny' side of the fields, which again will add form, shape and highlights the hills (see photo 6).

1 Apply the blue down to one third of the board.

2 Dab on fluffy cloud shapes using damp tissues.

3 Mountains are easy to paint – don't overwork.

4 Distant hills are flatter; add grey for contours.

5 Working 'nearer' the colours are greener.

6 Add form, shape and highlights to the hills.

7 Tree trunks are green/grey to white in colour.

8 Mix yellow ochre and green for foliage.

9 Hedgerows give the rest of the scene distance.

Right
The finished result. If you can make your backscene removable, rest it as here on an easel as it's easier to paint it in the flat rather than reaching over a baseboard that may be 2' or so wide.

Trees

Tree trunks are rarely brown; they vary from a greenish grey to almost white when viewed at a distance on a nice day, and will invariably look lighter then the land around them.

Andy has used a mix of grey and a little green for the main tree, and again he has taken paint off the sunny side of the trunk. He only creates a basic shape, as most will be covered in foliage (see photo 7).

For the foliage you need light and dark shades to represent the leaves. Andy uses a mix of yellow ochre and green and, using a stiff brush, just stipples the tree shape in very lightly, adding a darker mix of green and a very small amount of blue (see photo 8). He doesn't mix the colours on the palette but dabs the brush from one colour to the other alternately.

The bases of trees are always left hidden behind the scenery – either painted or the 3D landscape – as they are very difficult to paint convincingly.

Foreground

For the foreground Andy prefers to use a hedgerow, as this will throw the rest of the scenery into the distance. He does this with almost no water and use the paint fresh from the tubes. He makes up three or four piles of paint, usually a dark green, light green, yellow and brown, and with a stiff brush forces it upwards to give a rough top edge and then add the lighter colours as he goes, wet into wet, so that different shades react in different ways to each other colour as they meet on the board (see photo 9).

The result...

Photo 10 shows the finished backscene fitted behind Andy's O gauge *Trebudoc* layout. Woodscrews are the simplest way to affix the boards to the baseboard frames, although there are doubtless other ways and fittings that can be used to make the backscenes removable if installed on an exhibition layout.

10

Above
A representation of the Cornish countryside on the author's O gauge layout *Trebudoc*.

Right
The backscene conveys a sense of location when trains, such as this china clay working, are absent.

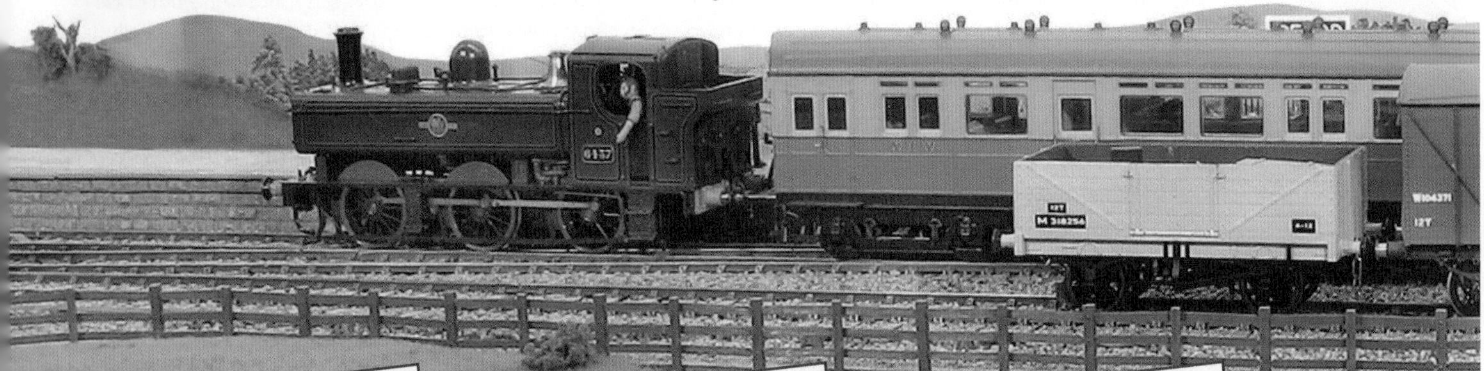

GAZINE PRESENTS THE ...

ITAL ARCHIVE*

- ◀ Special subscriber only covers!
- More than 800 searchable issues
- Invaluable modelling resource
- Easy on-screen navigation
- Regular subscriber offers

DELLER AVAILABLE AT YOUR FINGERTIPS

gital Edition available for your PC, Mac, tablet or mobile device. ‡Overseas? Please visit our website for details.

CALL 01297 626203 OR VISIT www.pecopublications.co.uk

Building cardboard kits

Above
The completed model. The kit is also available in N, ref.PN166; sufficient parts are provided to build two pairs of houses and garages.

Card kits are usually printed in colour on material varying from thin card, paper almost, to quite thick board. Those in the extensive Metcalfe range are in the latter category and recent ones have the parts pre-cut which is a real boon for the inexperienced modeller. The parts are released simply by cutting with the scalpel a short way along a scoreline, which is marked with a blue arrow, and gently pressing the part which 'plops' out of the sheet, perfectly cut out. This fascinating procedure is a large part of the enjoyment of building the kit and is perhaps of most value when it comes to windows, resulting in perfectly rectangular apertures of constant size.

The scorelines mentioned above are lines that are cut only about three quarters of the way through the card. These hold the parts in place on the main sheet until cut through as described in the step by step sequence.

The instruction sheets in a Metcalfe kit are quite clearly written and the constructional illustrations are sequential and very good. Good advice would be to follow the instructions to the letter, although Nick Metcalfe's almost evangelistic plea to 'roll your own' chimney pots from printed paper supplied, rather than use purchased whitemetal or plastic ones, usually falls on deaf ears in the

1 Start by cutting out the card parts from the sheet. Metcalfe makes this very easy as the cutting lines are both pre-scored and clearly indicated with a blue arrow. Use a steel rule to guide the blade safely.

2 The front windows have fine card frames, to which the glazing, including curtains, is fixed. We used Evo-Stik, and Deluxe Roket card adhesive, to construct the kit, although many types of suitable glues are available.

3 One of the completed window frames, showing how a very effective impression of depth is created by the layers of card and clear plastic. Metcalfe kits have good part identification, ensuring all fits where it should.

4 The side and rear elevations of the kit are seen here 'in the flat'. Note the two inner sections of the front elevation, at top left and lower right, which allow the half-timbered front section to stand proud of the rest of the building.

5 The front doors are available in a choice of green or blue, and are neatly printed to represent panelling. Once installed, the doors and windows can be personalised, in much the same way as happens with the real things.

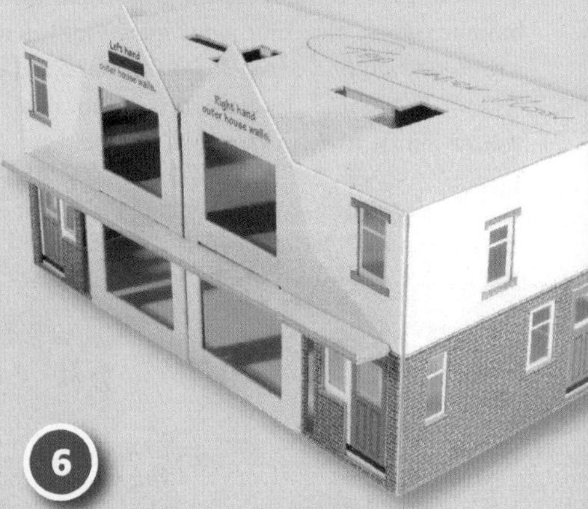

6 The pair of semis is now starting to take shape. The card strengthener at upper storey level can be seen; it also carries a pencilled note ('top inner floor'), as an easy way to identify it from similar-coloured parts in the kit.

Now the roles played by the plain frontage and card strengthener can be understood; here the half-timbered front section is about to be mated to the rest of the building. By this method the porches can be modelled effectively too.

The roof is made from grey card for strength, to which an overlay printed with tiles is fixed. Note the v-shaped notches in the latter, which will allow the large gabled frontage to be represented; the rear is plain roofing.

The chimney stack represents one topping a central flue and back-to-back fireplaces in the real houses. It is made up into a solid block out of card laminations which becomes a close fitting item that is glued in place as shown.

RM Office. Likewise the writer ignores the recommendation to remove all the components from the sheet, placing them face up in neat piles, preferring to keep them in the sheets for as long as possible, until needed.

The card parts themselves are well printed in full colour, giving a realistic effect which would be difficult to achieve for the average mortal with paints and brushes. The kits also include plain grey card, still with pre-cut parts, which form the unseen internal strengtheners and formers which contribute to the strength of the finished models.

When it comes to adhesives, many modellers prefer white PVA-type glue for card, Metcalfe recommends UHU or Bostik Clear adhesives.

It is often suggested that white card visible at folded corners and other joins should be disguised with paint or pencil, but the writer would add 'if the white worries you'. The fine white lines can give the model character and enhance its form, like an artist's pencil construction lines on sketch or painting.

The Semi

The model (ref.PO266) represents semi-detached houses of the 'bogus Tudor' type which proliferated in the suburbs of UK towns and cities in the 1920s/30s and have stood the test of time, even achieving some respectability through the 'Metroland' writings of Sir John Betjeman.

The characteristic half-timbered gables of the frontage were removed first from the sheet, and the windows prepared which, on the front elevation only, have very fine frames. Windows elsewhere in the building are plain printed transparent plastic.

The main body of the house is assembled separately, with the gabled frontage slotted in place at a later stage,almost as a 'styling' feature and not too differently, one imagines from the many prototypes. Two inner floors from grey card help to keep the model square and divide the interior space should the builder desire to add lighting.

The roofs, although of complex shapes, fit very well, and here is an example of an inner structure in plain grey card, with the printed tile effect roof glued over it, again resulting in a strong structure (see photo).

The chimney stack is a good example of the lamination technique which Metcalfe sometimes uses, the stack being glued up from no fewer than 12 grey card layers, encased in a cosmetic brick-effect wrapper. The stack fits snugly into the apertures in both inner and outer roofs,and is crowned by the aforementioned chimney pots.

The completed building locates accurately onto a base card which provides a perimeter of paving stones.

The garden walls are double-sided brick, with a 'sandwich filling' of grey card and tiled tops. The arrangement of the walls is naturally left to the modeller, but the property dividing walls, front and back, have a satisfying upsweep where they adjoin the building, see photo.

Detached garages complete the model and real beginners could start construction with one of these, in order to become accustomed to the 'press out' routine and other simple techniques required to continue.

Kits supplied by

Metcalfe Models & Toys Ltd.,
Bell Busk, Skipton,
N Yorks. BD23 4DU.
Tel: 01729 830072.
www.metcalfemodels.com

Metcalfe products are available from all Peco stockists.

The main building is completed with ridge tiles and chimney pots. The surrounding paving is supplied as a base upon which the building sits, and to which the landscaping can be brought alongside to the builder's preference.

Two garages, of different designs, are included; the newcomer to this type of card kit could well make a start with these and thereby learn the ropes. Interior detail could be provided; how about a miniature model railway?

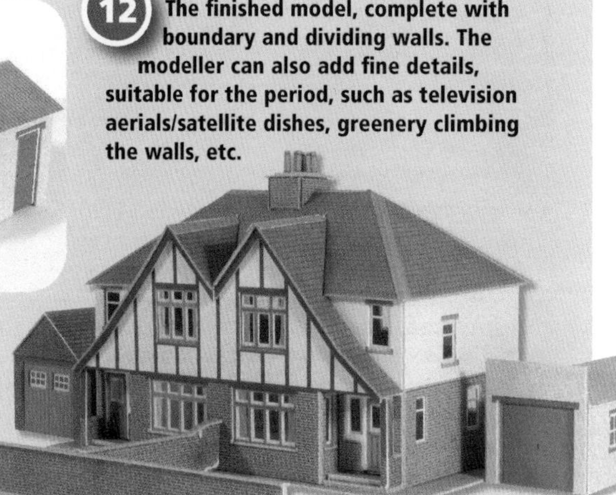

The finished model, complete with boundary and dividing walls. The modeller can also add fine details, suitable for the period, such as television aerials/satellite dishes, greenery climbing the walls, etc.

Modelling with cardboard

Postcard
use for detail work

Cereal packet
laminate and use for structure frames

Mounting board
use for structure frames

Corrugated card
use for scenery formers

Cardboard has been one of the most long-standing construction materials used by railway modellers. Many no doubt will be familiar with its role in scenic structures but its use has seen many different applications over the years. An undated, though quite old, publication, *Cardboard Rolling Stock and How to Build It*, written by E Rankine Gray advocated the use of card along with parts from the then Boscombe-based ERG model railway company. More recent building kits from the likes of Metcalfe and Alphagraphix build on from what had already been achieved by Superquick and Prototype. They in turn probably owe their roots to Hamblings' development of the Merco and Bilteezi sheets of the early 1950s.

The appeal of card kits has survived fads and fashions within the hobby and today there are several manufacturers steadily releasing new kits. Furthermore, you can use card for layout planning mock-ups (eg in conjunction with track templates – see right), support for landscaping, and even for the construction of small baseboards!

Whether you're kitbuilding or using the material for scratchbuilding, there's a whole range of skills, some very basic and others more demanding, that will ensure good results every time.

Summary

Cardboard is undoubtedly a versatile material: it is easy to work with, only simple tools are required to reach a satisfactory standard, and it's relatively cheap. Card is certainly not difficult to come to terms with and anyone new to railway modelling will have had some experience of it at school. If you haven't, or schooldays are way back, card is easy to have a go with, if you get it wrong just try again until you get it right; it's all part of the great experience.

Above
E Rankine Gray's book expounds the qualities of card suggesting few limitations in its use and even for locomotive building. Despite its age there are many hints that span the test of time into modern day usage. Many varieties of kit are available today; they capture the spirit of the much earlier examples and can easily be superdetailed.

BASIC SKILLS FOR CONSTRUCTION

Cutting

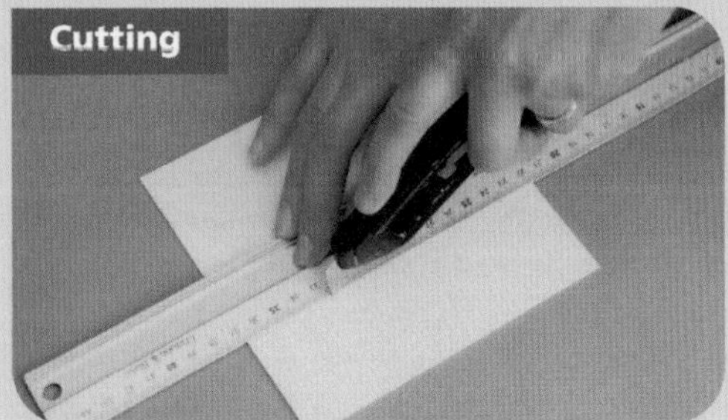

Mark out the correct measurements in soft pencil to show the cutting line. Use a steel rule or straight edge to cut against, and keep the blade upright, at 90° to the card. Make a light cut first followed by subsequent heavier cuts. Protect the required card part with the rule so that any knife slippage occurs into the waste area. Change the blade when it starts to blunt and strokes become harder.

Making corners

A thin thread of PVA, or other similar adhesive such as UHU, along the edges to be joined usually suffices. The parts are pressed together, wiping off any spillage that squeezes out with a damp cloth. Prop the assembly up against small blocks to hold the joint in place until the glue hardens. A triangular brace can be fitted for reinforcement along the inside of the joint as shown here.

Folding

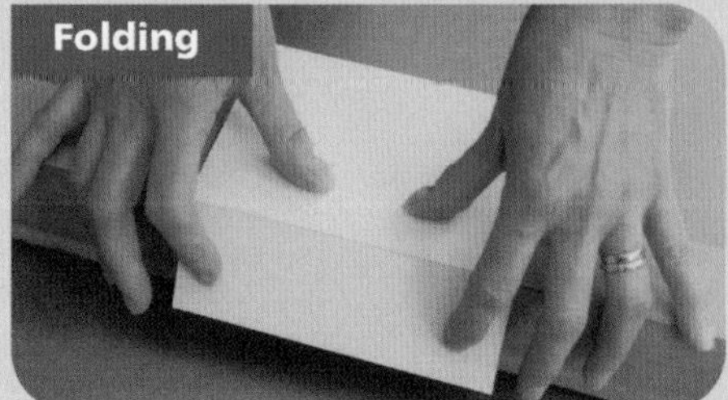

An angular fold will create a corner piece without having to glue. Mark up the position of the fold and evenly cut about halfway through; too little, and it won't fold easily, creasing on the inside, but too much, and pieces separate. Line the cut along the edge of a right-angle former, such as a piece of timber, and fold, making sure that the card does not slip from its desired position.

Edge colouring

Folding exposes two thin edges of card at the corner. If a light coloured base card is used with a darker coloured finish, the fold will leave two noticeable edges. I use good quality coloured pencils for colouring the gap, as cheap ones, in my experience, can skip and the colour does not adhere as one might hope. This method is suitable for colouring the exposed edges on card kits as well.

Advanced curves

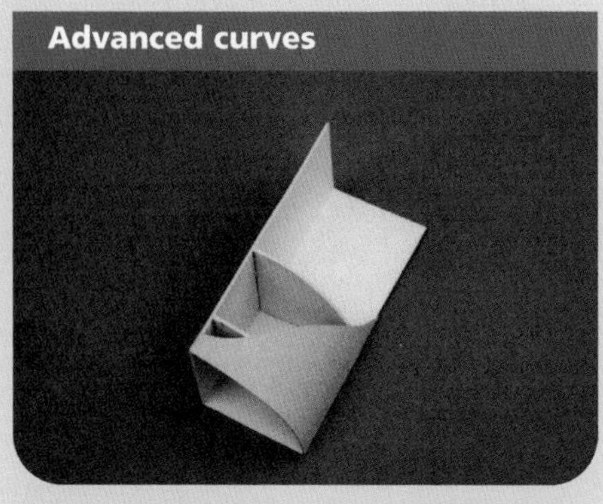

Curved corners can be made by fixing a number of formers at regular intervals out of thicker board and gently bending and gluing thinner card to form the curve as shown. To cut the curved formers, I think you can still buy a special blade from some art and craft shops which fits a drawing compass – the type with centre threaded rod and knurled nut which effectively locks it at the required radii.

Laminating

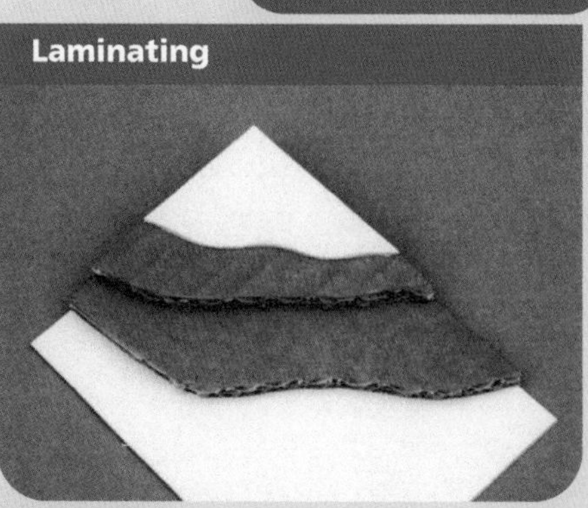

Laminating is a great way of strengthening card. You could laminate up to almost any reasonable thickness depending on what you want to achieve. The basic process is shown; white mounting board on both outside surfaces to give a quality finish and a corrugated card core, with the 'grain' alternating in between. Useful for building shells – cereal packets can be used in this way.

Cutting mitres

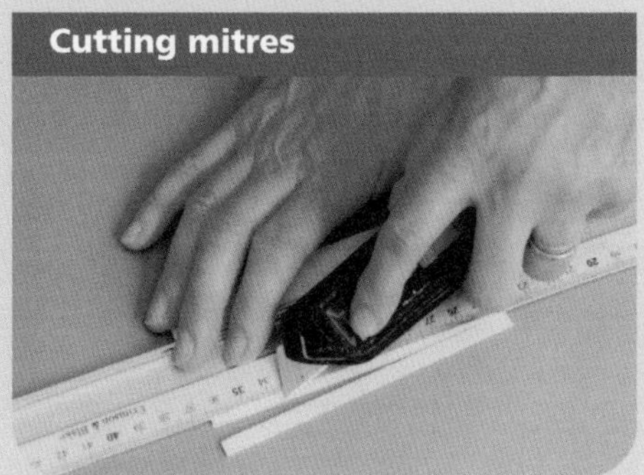

A mitred corner combines the structural quality of thick card with the visual appearance of a very thin edge. Cutting mitres takes practice, as you will need to keep the whole knife at a consistent angle throughout the entire process. An angled safety rule may help, but if you plan to cut many, a special mitre cutter (as used for cutting picture mounts) can be obtained from art shops.

Gluing aids

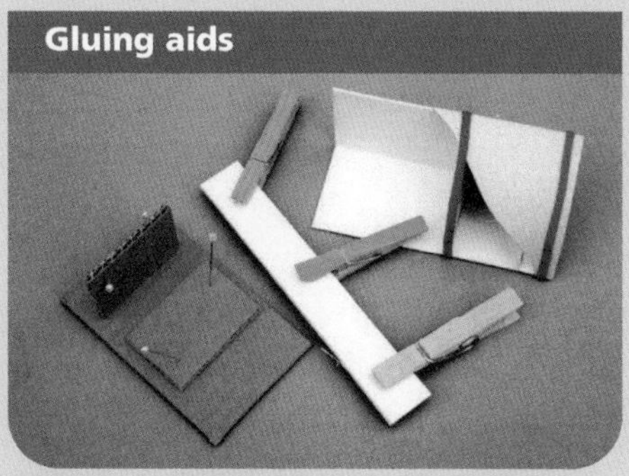

Whatever glue you use, they all take time to dry depending on; amount used, area involved, temperature within the room and the glue type (PVA, impact, UHU etc). Sometimes the pieces can be held in position with both hands but often various aides have to be called upon. Elastic bands, clothes pegs, pins and of course a good pile of books where large flat areas are involved.

Finishes

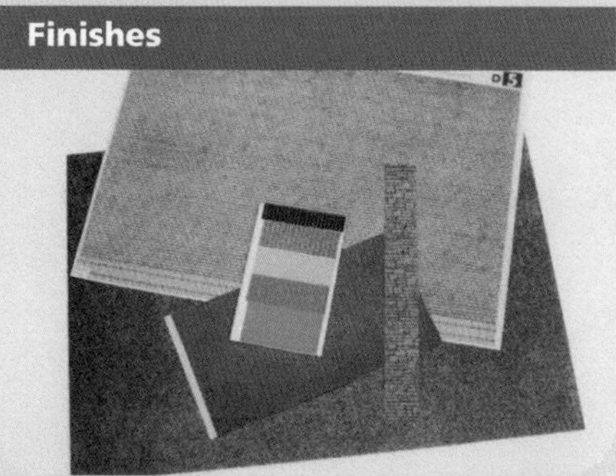

Here's a selection of paper finishes to aid modelling; slate, stone and brick sheets from Superquick are shown with Metcalfe tarmac sheet (rear), together with a sample board of five brick colours from the Exactoscale range. Fixogum by Marabu, wallpaper paste or thinned PVA can be used to fix building papers. For large flat areas consider a spray adhesive such as 3M Photo Mount.

Spray adhesive

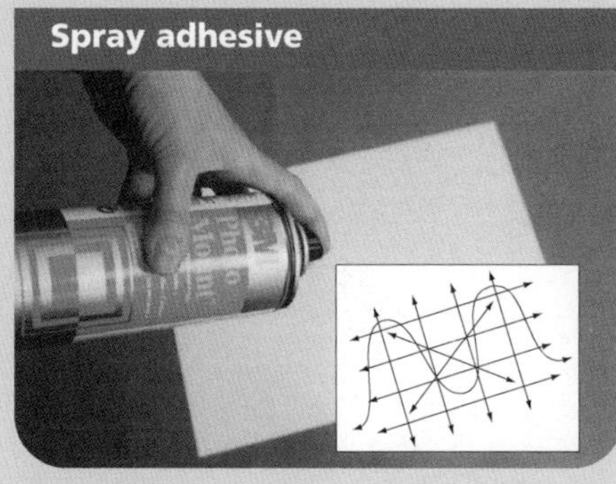

When using Photo Mount, wear a spray mask and work in a well-ventilated area. Firstly spray top to bottom horizontally, then side to side vertically, top left to bottom right diagonally, followed by top right to bottom left, also diagonally, finishing with one last shot around the outer edge. Repeat the whole process for the other surface, making sure that every 'fly-past' consists of a light spray.

Attaching brickpaper

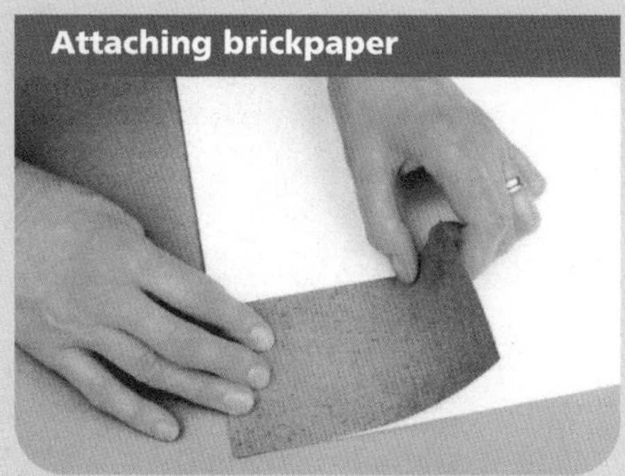

Leave the spray mount to go tacky for a few minutes then press the paper onto the card ensuring that you create no air bubbles. I usually start from a top corner, holding the bulk of the sheet away from contact, line up the top edge and then lower the sheet onto the card gently pressing down from the centre outwards in both directions. Retaining walls can be produced very quickly in this way.

Tools of the trade

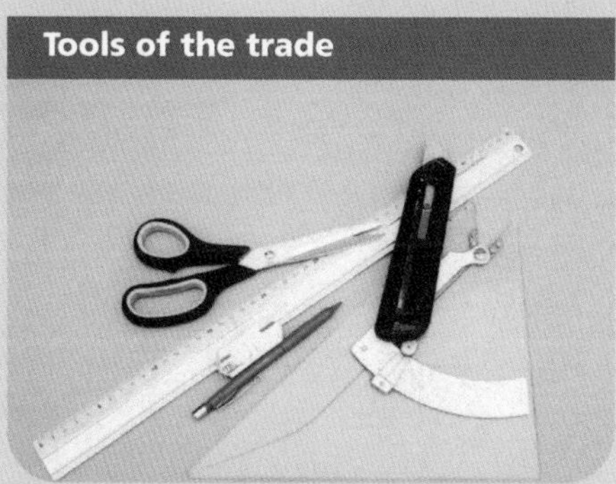

The cardboard model maker's toolbox need not be extravagant. Although I use an adjustable plastic square, a basic fixed one is equally suitable. It goes without saying that sharp blades should be used with care, and if necessary, supervision will be necessary when minors are involved. Concentrate at the moment of cutting and don't allow yourself to be distracted by anyone or anything.

Modelling with card and brick papers

Long before the advent of plastic sheet with relief detail, brick, slate and stone effect papers were the only medium modellers used to reproduce these prototype building materials. If there is one criticism of these papers, it is the lack of relief in the mortar courses, and between slates, that led to the development of the plastic sheet alternatives.

In reality, the relief on plastic is actually too deep, but both the eye and the mind expect it to be there. Well-maintained mortar courses in real brick walls will only be a matter of about 5mm deep; in 4mm scale that is just 0.065mm – hardly noticeable in fact. Stone and tile courses will be deeper, generally, and the difference will be imperceptible at normal viewing distances. Today, it is just the expectation of relief that causes modellers to question the use of these papers.

On the other hand, there are numerous advantages with brick papers; they are very easy to use, inexpensive and are ready-coloured. The use of brick papers is thus down to personal preference, so whilst they might not be right for one modeller, they may be right for you.

The S C Jenkins drawing of Bampton station appeared in the October 1977 issue and is reproduced on page 84 at 2mm/ft for anyone wishing to have a go at building it. It can be scanned or photocopied at 200% to produce a 4mm scale drawing.

You will need nothing more than a good modelling knife with a new blade, a pencil, straight edge and ruler, a medium brush to use as a paste brush, and a fine paint-brush together with paints of your choice. A materials list is provided in the panel opposite.

Evo-Stik impact adhesive was used for gluing the parts together and ordinary wallpaper paste secured the brick paper in place: this dries much more quickly than diluted PVA, and is just as strong. To help prevent warping, paste a piece of paper to the back of the card.

The prototype

Bampton station was known as Bampton (Oxon) in order to differentiate it from the station of the same name on the Exe Valley line in Devon. In 1940 it became Brize Norton & Bampton, to recognise the creation of the adjacent RAF airfield. The station was situated 15 miles from Oxford on the Fairford branch, and shared the architectural style of other station buildings along the line, which was promoted by the East Gloucestershire Railway. It opened in 1873, and closed in June 1962.

As with any scratchbuilding project, the first task is to mark out the cutting lines on the source material. Here the dimensions are being measured off the scale drawing and the 2mm thick card marked up using a 2H pencil.

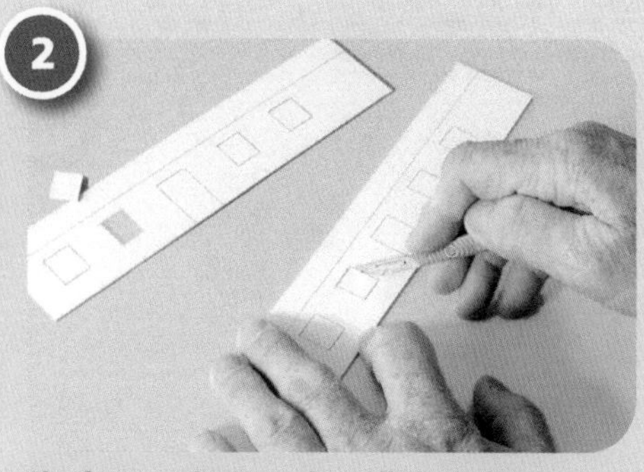

The front and rear main walls have been separated from the sheet and the door and window openings are seen being cut out with a scalpel. A straight edge can be used as a blade guide to help if preferred.

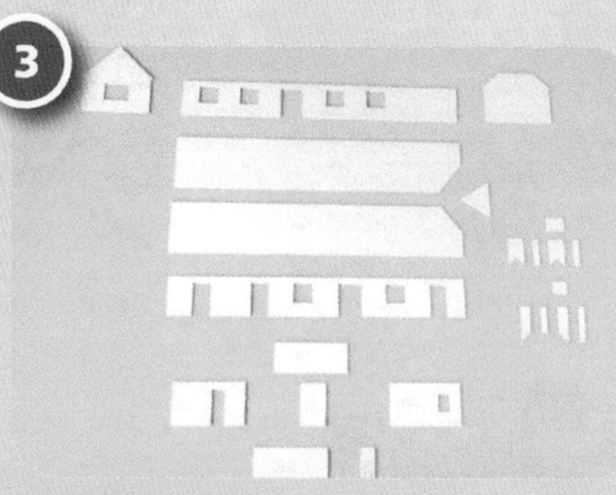

After about an hour or so all the main parts have been cut out from the card sheet. The model now looks just like a kit of parts. To get this far only one brand new blade was needed in the scalpel handle.

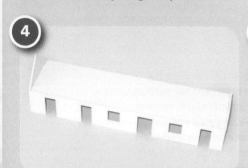

Using Evo-Stik impact adhesive, the shell of the main building was assembled and a further piece of board was measured and cut to act as both a ceiling and a structural reinforcement.

Assembling the two roof sections was also straightforward. Again, as with the wall sections, the joint was not mitred, so the card pieces were measured and cut to allow for the necessary overlap at the ridge.

The small hipped section of the roof was the trickiest part. A degree of trimming was necessary to ensure close-fitting edges. A little at a time was removed, in a slight mitre, and checked until the best fit was achieved.

All the wall and roof parts were assembled so as to create a set of sub-shells in readiness for attaching the stone effect paper covering. This way makes the alignment of the stone course at corners a lot easier.

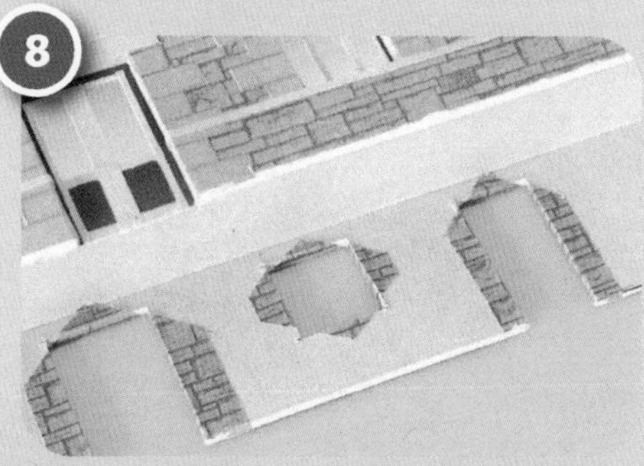

The stone finish paper sections were cut to fit over each wall face. Each section was glued on with wallpaper paste. When dry, the window and door openings were cut diagonally, and the tabs folded back on the inside and pasted down.

The main shell is seen here with the stone finish in place. Corner quoins were cut from the Superquick sheet and attached as seen. The long lintels are overlays made from self-adhesive label paper.

The self-adhesive overlays show up in this close-up. The corner quoins from the Superquick sheet are somewhat oversize; if preferred, custom ones could be cut from the self-adhesive paper and coloured accordingly.

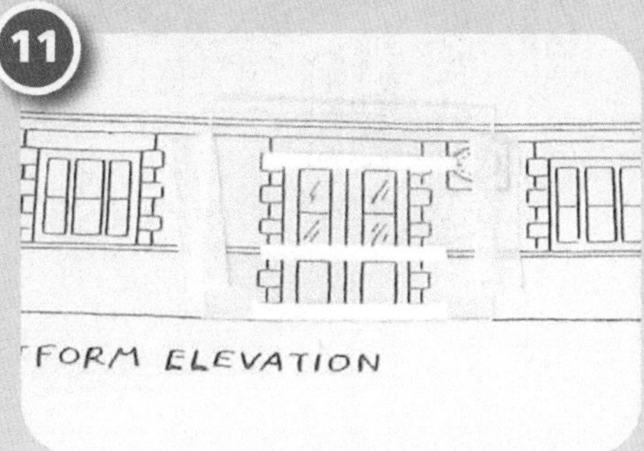

The door and window items are pieces of 10thou Plastiglaze covered with strips cut from the self-adhesive label paper. Each glazing piece was taped over the drawing and the adhesive strips cut and stuck in position.

A completed door section removed from the drawing. Masking tape was used to hold the Plastiglaze in place over the drawing whilst the panel sections were cut and stuck down in position.

13

Trimmed to size: the finished door and window sections were made slightly larger than the openings in the walls. This provided just enough mating surface to glue the item on the inside face of the wall and to create a robust joint.

14

Door panels were painted using Humbrol matt enamel paints. The overlaps on the self-adhesive strips are much less apparent once the 'frames' are painted, and especially so at normal viewing distances.

15

A thin bead of impact adhesive applied around the perimeters of the door and window sections was more than sufficient to provide a strong bond. Care was taken to ensure they were each fitted square to the openings.

Using self-adhesive label strips for window glazing bars

There are numerous methods of producing window glazing bars. One way is to mask the glazing piece carefully with tape and paint the bars on. Another is by gluing fine plastic, card or even wood strip to the front surface of the glazing. Both methods can leave traces of glue or paint on the clear sections, even with care.

This method uses self-adhesive label paper, such as that made by Avery. The glazing is cut from a sheet of Plastiglaze, or similar, and about 1mm oversize all round. Using a straight edge and fine blade, strips of label are cut to the required width, peeled from the backing paper and stuck down on the front face of the glazing. The glazing frame is made in exactly the same way, but stuck around the edge with a small overlap. The window is then turned face down, the bars are trimmed slightly oversize so the resultant overlaps can be folded down the sides. These overlaps are invisible from normal viewing distances.

Being paper, the strips can be painted with water-based paints, thus avoiding smears on the clear parts.

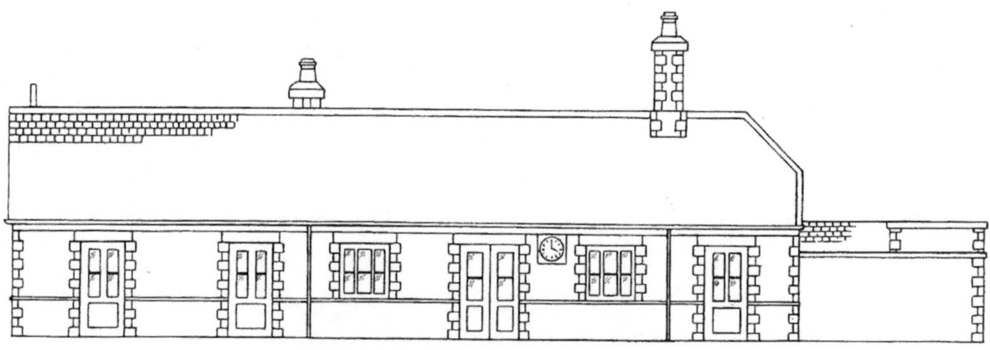

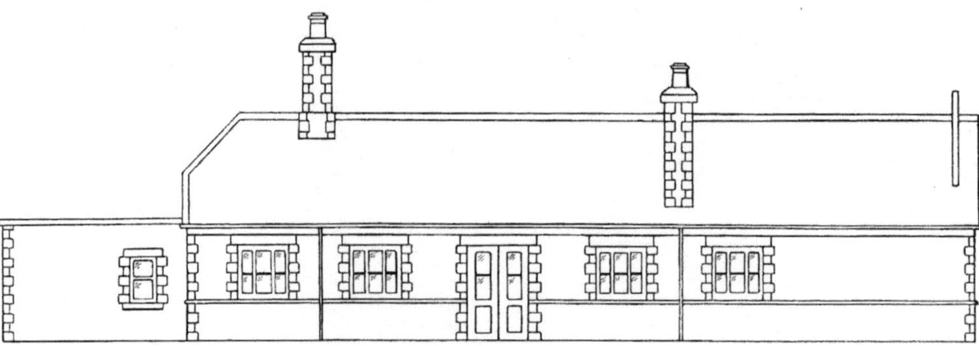

Scale 2mm = 1ft. From an original drawing by S C Jenkins, first published in RM October 1977.

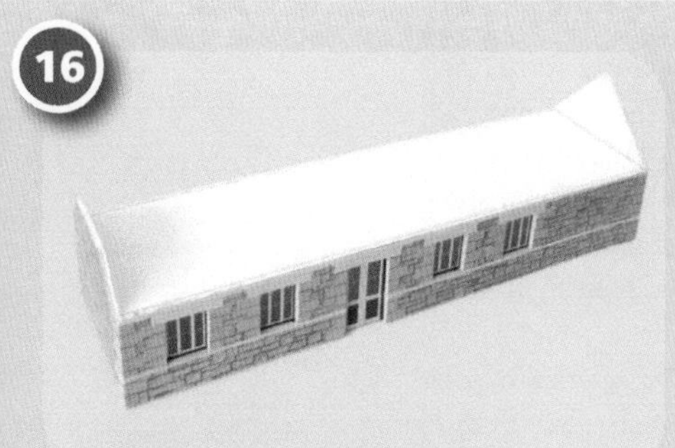

The main section of the building is now virtually complete. The toilet annex sections are treated similarly and attached to the main shell with impact adhesive. The lintels were painted to match the stone paper tint.

The chimney stacks were covered with stone effect paper as well, although the quoin stones were not used as they were too big. As seen on the finished model, flaunching around chimney pots was made with double thickness card.

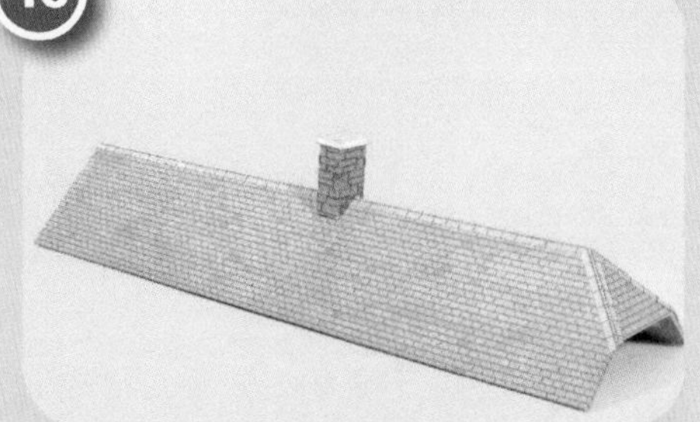

Superquick slate effect paper was used to cover the roof, ridge tiles from the same sheet were applied to finish. The roof was then glued in place and small detail items; gutters, fall pipes, etc, were added as described.

Self-adhesive label paper (the type used in desktop printers for producing mailing labels) was made use of for window glazing bars and some overlays on the stonework (to represent lintels). Windows and doors are very easy to make in this way, and the process is explained in more detail in the panel on the opposite page.

The step-by-step sequence begins on the previous page and continues above. Small detail items such as gutters, fallpipes and chimney pots are plastic items that all came from the bits box. Suitable alternatives are available in the Wills builder pack range, but if you wanted to remain totally loyal to card, they could be made up from postcard and rolled paper!

Some final dry brush weathering was applied to create subtle highlights on corners as seen below. The gate was made by scoring a piece of self-adhesive label to represent the timber planks. Chimney pot flaunching was made up from two pieces of mounting board laminated together, the top piece shaped to produce the slope.

This model took only a few hours to build and, with the detail parts coming from the bits box, cost less than five pounds.

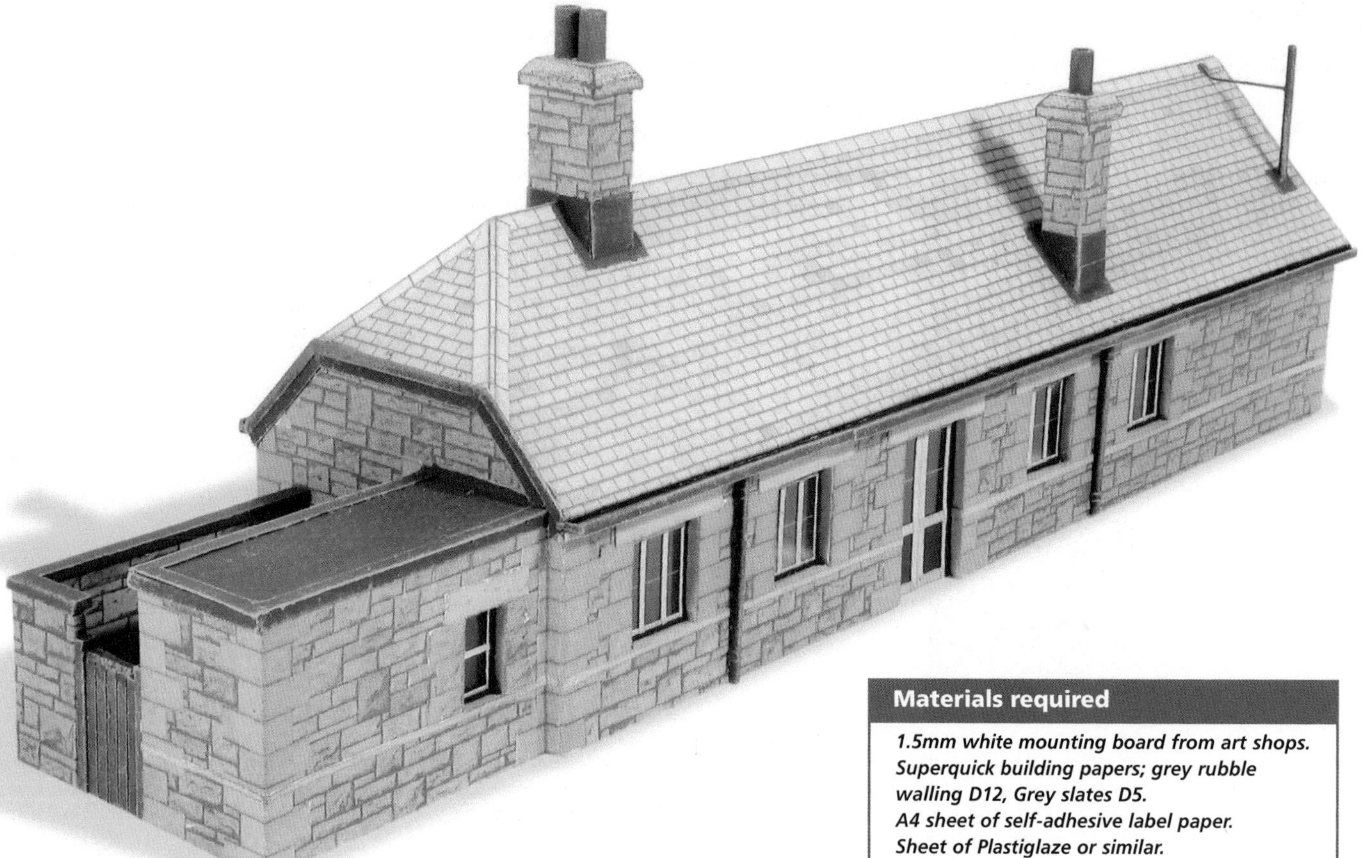

Materials required

1.5mm white mounting board from art shops.
Superquick building papers; grey rubble walling D12, Grey slates D5.
A4 sheet of self-adhesive label paper.
Sheet of Plastiglaze or similar.
Ordinary wallpaper paste.
Impact adhesive.
Paints of preference.

Building plastic kits

Above
The finished result: the Peco LK-16 shelter and hut. The parts are moulded in colours that represent the Southern, but any livery will do.

The range of models available as kits is huge and diverse, and encompasses structures as well as rolling stock items. The best place to start is with a simple structure kit such as the Peco LK-16 Platform Shelter and Hut illustrated here; it is moulded in pre-coloured plastic, so does not need painting to complete. A basic tool kit will be required including: craft/modelling knife, such as the X-acto type as seen in our sequence, or the equally useful Swann-Morton No.3 scalpel with a 10A blade; a small flat file to clean up the edges where parts have been cut from the moulding sprue, These are widely available, often as part of a set of needle files; an engineers' square to check that sub-assemblies are true before they are set aside as the joints harden; as a temporary measure you could cut a square former out of stiff card (not ideal, but much better than trying to manage with nothing at all). A small brush for applying liquid cement, the ideal size is probably an O or OO and should be able to form a decent point; and finally some liquid polystyrene cement for gluing the parts together

Plastic kit assembly is very straightforward, though as with any new activity – start slowly. Two old adages spring to mind; you must learn to walk before you can run, and practice makes perfect! As your skills grow, so can the complexity of the kits you tackle. Remember to read the instructions that come with the kit and be sure that you understand them before starting work, ignoring any experienced modellers who might be inclined to boast that they never bother to read the instructions!

There you have it, a finished OO gauge Station Shelter and Hut, ready for placing on the platforms.

1 Cutting the parts from the sprues

To minimise the amount of clean-up required, cut as close as possible to the component. By ensuring that the craft knife blade stays parallel you will avoid damaging the part.

2 Dressing the parts with a file

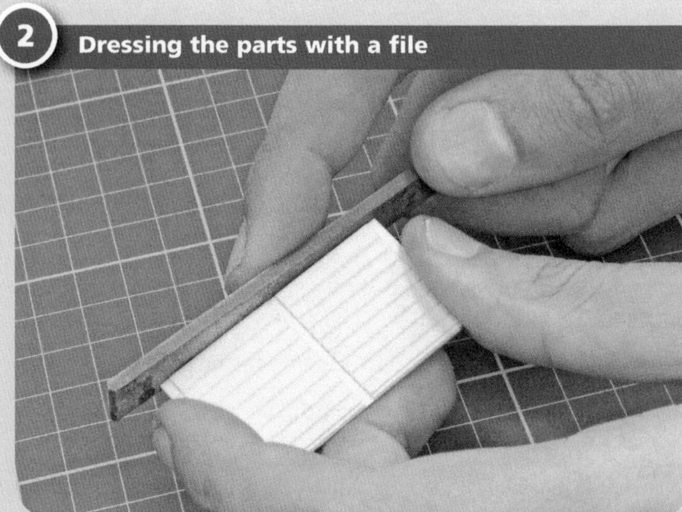

Keep the file absolutely parallel to the edge being cleaned up to avoid causing damage by accidentally filing the component out of shape. Work carefully, applying only gentle pressure and stop as soon the edge is smooth with no trace of the pip left by the craft knife.

3 Applying the solvent

When parts are cleaned up, run a small amount of solvent onto the surfaces to be joined. Bring the two edges together and apply a further run of solvent along the back of the joint. Capillary action will draw the solvent into the joint. Hold together for a few seconds.

4 Setting aside to allow the cement to harden

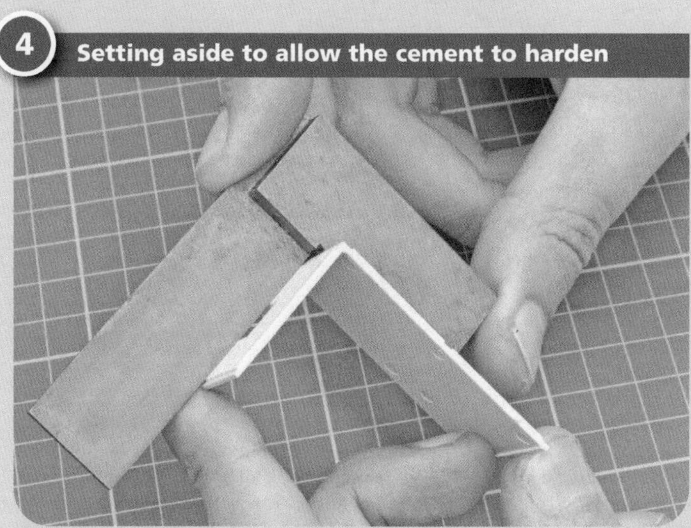

Take care not to allow excess solvent to run through the the joint to the front surface as your fingers will leave an impression in the softened plastic. While the joint is still pliable, use a square to ensure all is correct. Put carefully to one side to allow joint to harden.

5 Glazing the windows

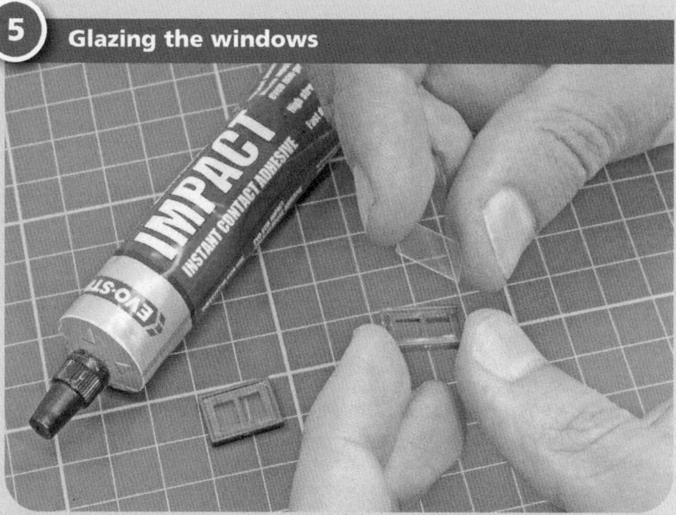

While the walls are setting hard, cut out the window glazing material and fix into place on the rear surface of the window frames with small amounts of contact adhesive. Take care not to get any adhesive on the front surface of the windows.

6 Fitting the windows into the walls

Apply the solvent to the inside surface of the wall around the edges of the window openings. Fit window in place and run solvent around the joint. Press gently to ensure window is seated correctly. Allow to set.

7 Adding frame timbers to corners

Apply a little solvent to the underside of corner frames and to the area of the walls where they will go. Press gently into place to locate. Take care, excessive solvent might ooze out and spoil the final appearance.

Building plastic rolling stock kits

Although the range of ready-to-run wagon types has increased immensely over the last few years, thanks to the major manufacturers, there are still numerous gaps in their ranges. These gaps can often be filled by kit manufacturers, some of which have been trading for many years and have countless examples in their ranges. This is especially the case if you plan to model one of the 'big four' or pre-Grouping railways. Often kits of older wagon and coach types for these earlier railways are only available in etched brass or nickel silver, but firms such as Ratio, Parkside Dundas, Slater's and Cooper Craft, still offer wagon and coach kits in plastic.

Just as with structure kits, these are relatively straightforward to put together, the major difference of course, is that they have moving parts – wheels and axles, bogies, etc. – so they are a little more involved. Nevertheless by starting out with a simple wagon kit as a test piece, you can gain some experience of building models which have to be mobile when finished.

We have chosen a Parkside Dundas 16T mineral wagon kit to illustrate how a simple rolling stock kit goes together. Although similar types of this wagon are available ready-to-run, this particular kit was chosen to demonstrate the simplicity of the task. Most plastic kits require painting and lettering to finish; more information on this can be found in the relevant section on page 110.

Above
The Parkside Dundas kit for the ubiquitous BR 16T mineral wagon presents a very straightforward kit-building exercise, ideal as a first rolling stock construction project for a newcomer to the hobby. This example had been finished with transfers from the Modelmaster Decals range and weathered using acrylic paints and Humbrol weathering powders.

Below
A selection of popular 4mm scale coach and wagon kits. With care and a lot of patience, these can be assembled and finished in even complex liveries, such as the deceptively simple GWR livery as here.

1 Kit contents

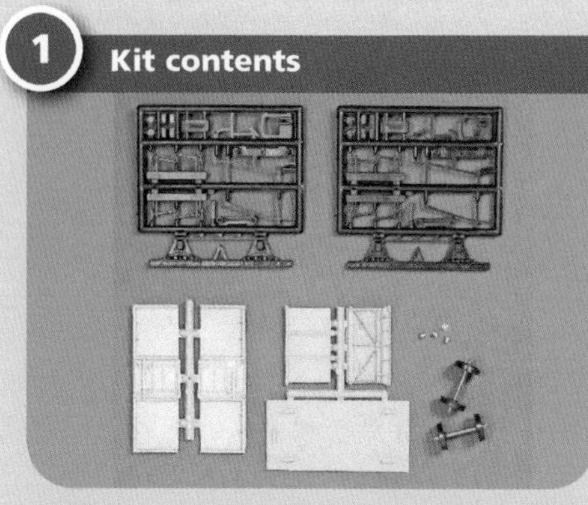

This kit (Parkside Dundas ref.PC21) contains all the parts needed to construct a complete wagon; the only additional items required are solvent, paint, transfers and a handful of basic modelling tools.

2 Cutting parts from the sprue

The kit comprises moulded plastic parts, all attached to a sprue. The parts need to be removed from the sprue as illustrated. To minimise the amount of cleaning up required, cut as close as possible to the component. By ensuring that the craft knife blade stays parallel you will avoid damaging the part.

3 Cleaning the parts

Before the parts can be joined together, any pips and traces of flash need to be removed. A set of needle files is ideal for this purpose. Work carefully and with only gentle pressure on the file, to ensure the part is not damaged.

4 Joining the parts

The assembly of this kit begins with one of the ends being joined to a side, with these then attached to the floor. First, check the fit of the two parts to be joined, and then hold in position whilst running solvent along the inside of the join with a fine brush. Capillary action will draw the solvent into the joint. Hold together for a few seconds and check the join is true using an engineers' square.

5 Adding the bearings

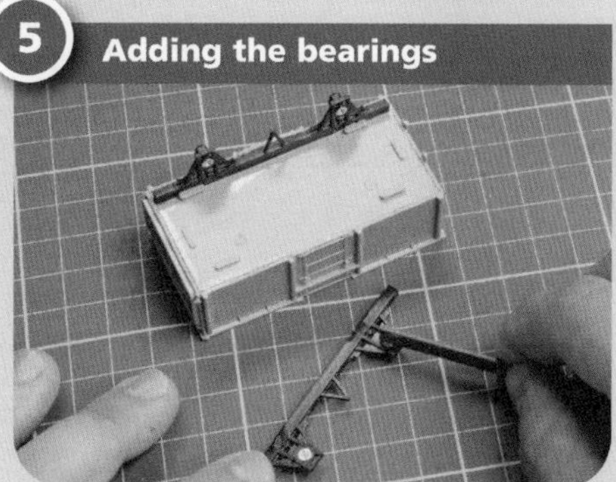

The chassis sideframes are the next items to be fitted. Brass bearings need to be pressed into the backs of the axleboxes so that the rims sit almost flush; the edge of a flat needle file is ideal for this. Attach one of the sideframes against the lugs on the underside of the floor as illustrated, and allow the joint to harden completely. Check that the sideframe is set exactly vertical.

6 Inserting the wheelsets

Hold the second sideframe in position against the lugs on the floor, and then insert the wheelsets. Keep the wheelsets in place by holding the axleboxes firmly together and then run solvent along the inside edge of the second sideframe. Continue to hold in position until the solvent has hardened. Check that both sideframes are set vertical and that the axles are parallel to the floor and ends. Next add the buffer beams, hooks and buffer heads as illustrated.

7 Fitting the chassis detail

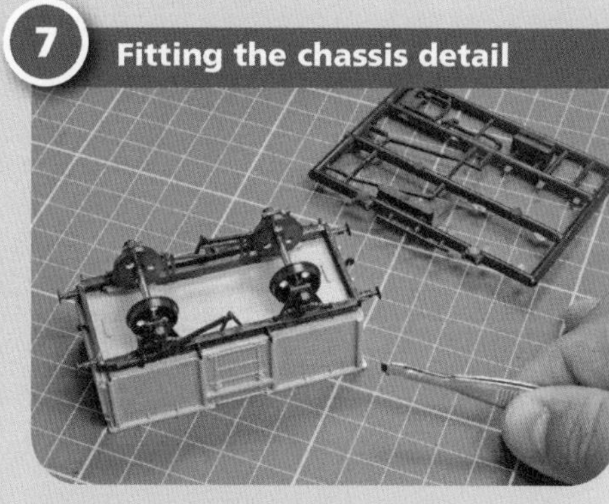

Brake gear and chassis details vary between prototypes, but there are usually instructions and diagrams supplied with the kit to guide the modeller. Note that this wagon has the brake shoes on one side only. Here, the gusset plates are being fixed in place along the underside of the body using tweezers.

8 Final details and couplings

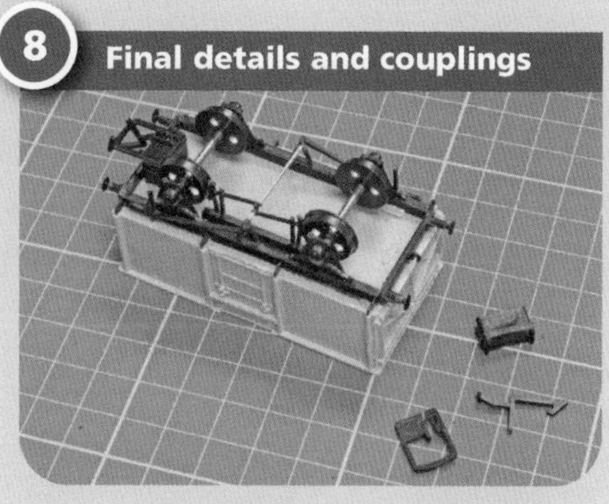

The kit includes a part for the rod that runs between the two V-hangers. However, it has been substituted here for a section of brass rod. The last items to fit are the couplings; components for tension lock couplings are included in the kit, assembled and fitted as illustrated.

9 The completed wagon

The completed wagon can be test run, if desired, prior to painting, lettering and weathering to suit. By their nature, plastic wagons tend to be quite light and benefit from additional weight. Open wagons such as this one can have extra weight fitted in two ways; under the floor between the sideframes if running 'empty', or in the wagon underneath a suitable load if running 'full'.

Skills Workshop

Modelling with plasticard

Although plastic has had applications in railway modelling for about 70 years, polystyrene sheet materials for scratchbuilding first appeared about 50 years ago, Slater's being one of the first companies to market it under the brand name of Plastikard, which has since become a generic name for the material. Today it comes in many forms, most usually as plain A4-sized sheets, in thicknesses ranging from 5thou (0.125mm) to 80thou (2mm) for general modelling use, but also in a huge variety of moulded, milled or embossed sheets with relief representing brick and stonework, planking, corrugated iron, slates, tiles and so on, and often referred to colloquially as embossed plasticard. In addition there are countless moulded styrene rods, strips, tubes and beams which can be worked and used in conjunction with sheet styrene.

The real virtue of plasticard is its versatility and ease of working. It is very easily cut, joined, filed, shaped, textured and painted, and all sorts of shapes and objects can be made from it, be they items of rolling stock, buildings, lineside details and components. It can be covered with building papers in the same way as cardboard or laminated, to make heavier items such as steel castings or the compound curves of coach roofs.

A few basic tools are all that is needed to work with plasticard and these are listed in the attached panel.

Joints

Anyone who ever assembled an Airfix plastic kit probably used a tube of polystyrene cement: a gel-like clear solvent that was applied straight from the nozzle. Generally this is unsuitable for normal use with plasticard and it is usual to use a liquid solvent applied with a fine brush (see step 4). Brands such as MekPak, Butanone and Plastic Weld are all suitable.

Being inflammable, with hydrocarbon solvents it is important to follow the safety advice printed on the labels; use in well-ventilated spaces, keep away from sources of ignition, no smoking, etc.

Sharp blades

As with cardboard, a sharp blade is paramount for cutting styrene sheet. However, it can be so tempting to continue using a blade that has become partly blunted, but in so doing the risk of the blade 'jamming' as the cut is made, or worse, skidding off at an angle, increases, and in proportion to potential injury. So keep a good supply of fresh blades to hand, and take care when changing them. Swann-Morton blades are razor sharp and changing them with small long-nosed pliers is advised.

Above
Sheets of plain and embossed plasticard, and some of the tools needed to get the best out of them. These include a razor saw (top) and an engineers' square (above left).

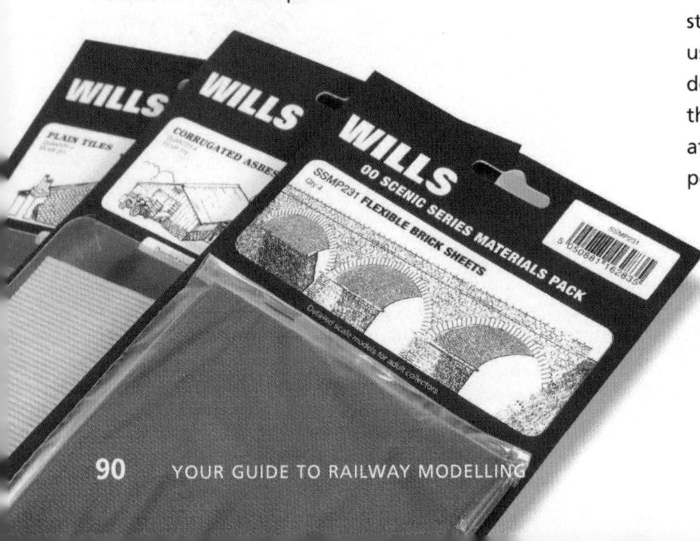

Below left
Wills sheets of embossed plasticard for 4mm scale are supplied four to a pack; they are quite small in size (130mm x 75mm) and are approx. 2mm thick.

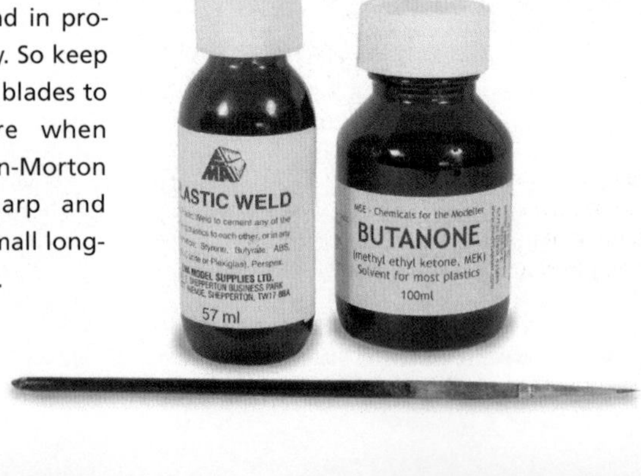

Below
Liquid polystyrene cement is supplied by a variety of manufacturers.

1 Cutting

To make a straight cut in plasticard, use a metal straight edge and make two or three strokes with the blade, slightly increasing the pressure each time. This process scores the plasticard sufficiently to snap the part off from the main sheet using your fingers. If the piece being cut away is a sliver that is too narrow to hold, keep stroking the blade along the cut several times, until the sliver parts.

2 Deburring

When each cut is made, the plastic deforms slightly, as with some metals, and creates a slight raised burr along the length of the cut on both sides. This has to be removed before joining and is most easily done by carefully paring (scraping) the burr away with the knife blade. Heavier burrs, such as occur with thicker sheets, may need sanding and/or filing to create a good clean edge.

3 Rounded corners

These are made by clipping small slivers off with the knife to form a rough curve made up of short chords with jagged corners. The flat side of a medium-sized file with fine teeth is then used to round off the jagged corners into a smooth radius. This is much easier than it looks as the soft properties of the plastic allow the excess to be removed very quickly. It is much faster than with wood or metal.

4 Joints

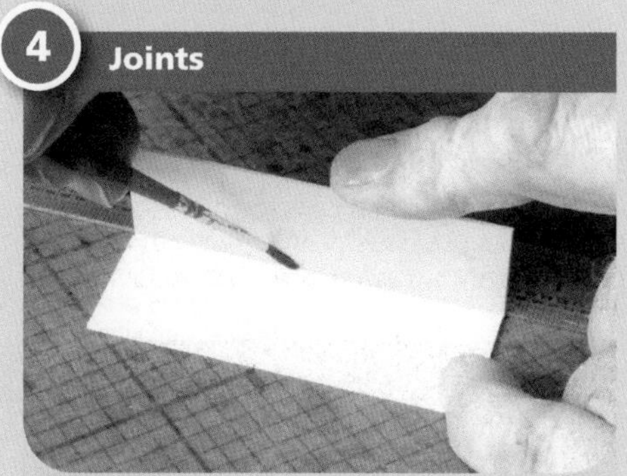

Joining plasticard parts is accomplished with liquid solvent applied with a brush. The most difficult aspect is knowing exactly how much solvent to use: too little and the joint is brittle; too much and the plastic deforms. Essentially though, the thicker the sheet, the more solvent is used: being aware of exactly how much solvent to use is knowledge that comes with experience, so some perseverance is called for.

5 Forming

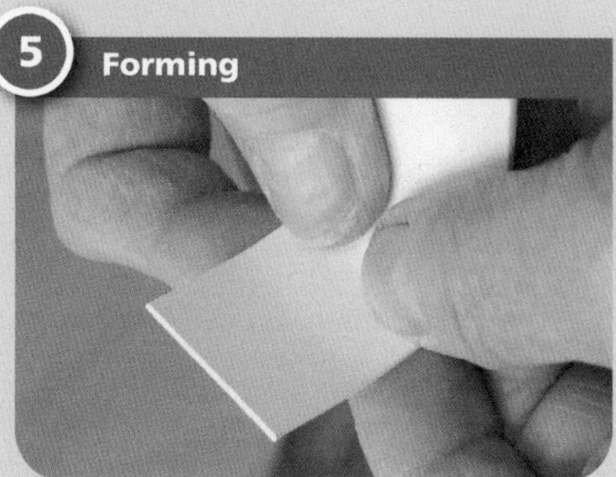

There are several ways to form plasticard. Because it has malleable properties, thin plasticard can be shaped to a degree by rolling between the fingers. Forming thicker gauge sheets or larger workpieces may require the sheet to be taped down to a former made from timber or similar. Boiling water from a kettle is poured over to soften the plastic which is then plunged into cold water to 'fix' the curve.

6 Marking out

A normal HB pencil is probably the best item to use to mark out cutting lines on the non-porous surface of plasticard, though it does have a tendency to smudge away to nothing very easily. Fine indelible fibre tip markers can be used, but the width of the resultant line may prove to be an issue when cutting. Ballpoint pens are best used only in an emergency.

Tools

- **Craft knife.** *Any proprietary brand will suffice but a traditional Swann-Morton scalpel with interchangeable blades is a firm favourite.*
- **A heavy duty knife** *such as a Stanley retractable one is also suitable but too heavy for all but the thickest of sheets.*
- **Fine-tooth razor saw.** *Some modellers prefer to cut thicker sheet with a razor saw, but it can also come into its own when cutting out awkward shapes.*
- **A fret saw.** *Not entirely necessary, but again useful for cutting out awkward shapes.*
- **A few files.** *Medium flat files with fine teeth, needle files of various profiles.*
- **Fine sandpaper** *and emery paper.*
- **Steel straight edge** *for cutting and measuring.*
- **Fine brushes** *for solvent application.*
- **Pencil** *for marking out.*
- **Engineers' square.**

Heavy gauge sheets

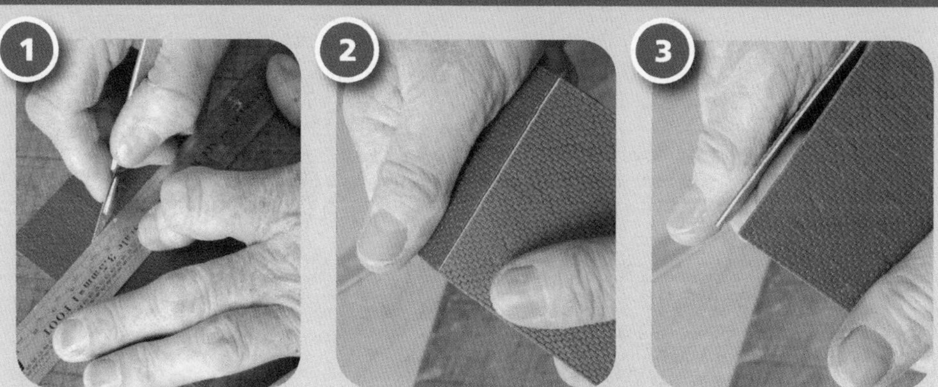

Thicker sheets with a moulded relief of brick or stonework, such as in the Wills series, can be cut in exactly the same way as plain sheets. Using the straight edge and a sharp blade, line up the knife with a mortar course and run along two or three times with a slight increase in pressure each time (1). As with the plain sheet, the moulded sheets can be held between the fingers (2) and the parts snapped cleanly away (3). Remember to deburr the parts by paring away with the knife blade. Some modellers like to cut these heavier gauge sheets with a razor saw – this is also possible, but can leave a much heavier burr that requires a lot of work to remove.

Advanced techniques with plasticard

Above
This lineside crane was constructed from plasticard using the techniquees described here to make identical components.

Plasticard is ideal for making a quantity of identical shapes, such as the canopy brackets and steel castings and parts for a lineside crane, as shown here.

In essence, plastic sheet is rather like very soft and easily workable sheet metal. It can be cut, drilled and filed like metal, only more easily, and it is cold 'welded' using solvent, rather than solder or brazing rods. Thin strips behave just like thin metal strips, in that they can be bent to form any profile, and thicker sheets will resist buckling equally well as equivalent metal sheets.

Identical shapes are made by temporarily laminating together several sheets of plasticard, with the top laminate being used as the cutting template. The process is shown in the accompanying step-by step sections.

The canopy brackets were made for use on a London & North Western Railway station building constructed from the Grand Junction station wall modules available from Parkside Dundas.

Furthermore, it can be laminated and shaped into solid curved profiles to make very strong and lightweight forms, the sort of shapes that replicate complex sheet metal work and pressings.

Gear teeth

To create the teeth effect on the wheels use a junior hacksaw blade and gently saw through to the desired depth. The leading edges of the teeth should be rounded using a small file.

Pulley wheel and gears

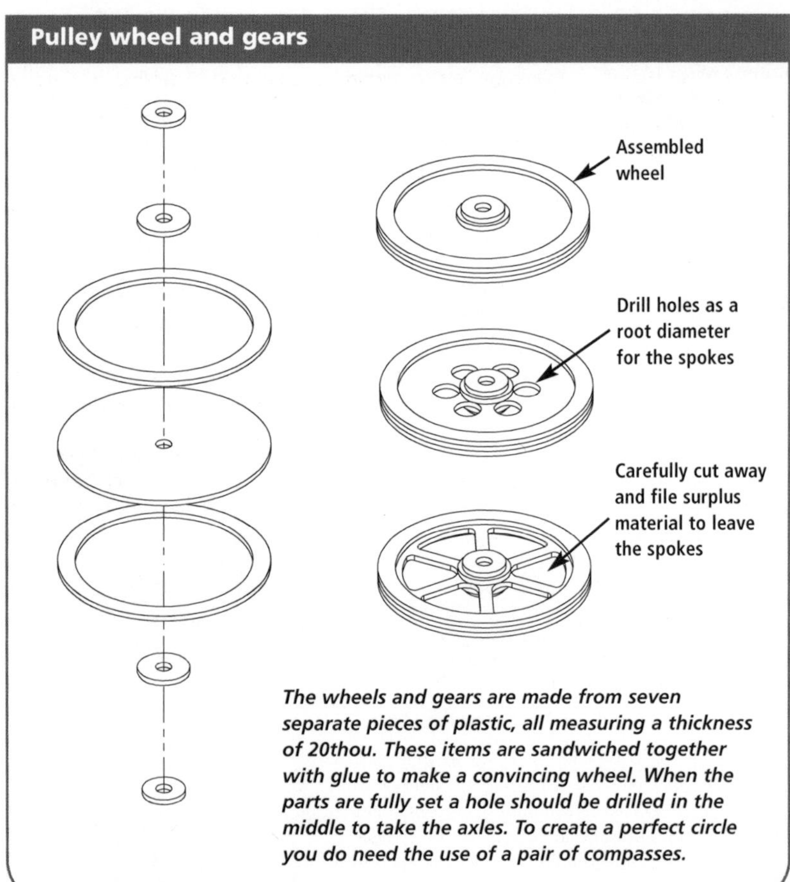
Assembled wheel
Drill holes as a root diameter for the spokes
Carefully cut away and file surplus material to leave the spokes

The wheels and gears are made from seven separate pieces of plastic, all measuring a thickness of 20thou. These items are sandwiched together with glue to make a convincing wheel. When the parts are fully set a hole should be drilled in the middle to take the axles. To create a perfect circle you do need the use of a pair of compasses.

IDENTICAL SHAPES - frame castings and pressings

1

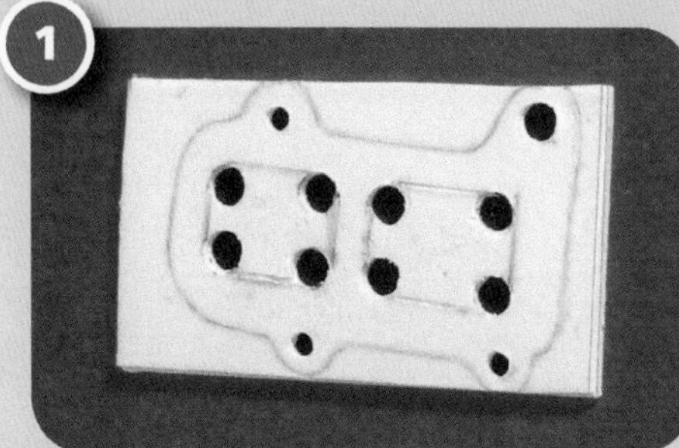

The method of producing identical brackets, described opposite, can also be used to make frame parts for machines, such as the yard crane. Such frames were either cast in iron, or riveted to shape from sheet metal. To make two frame halfs, tack two identical pieces of plasticard together and mark the desired shape on the top piece. Drill the corners as shown, then cut and file both halves to the required shape.

2

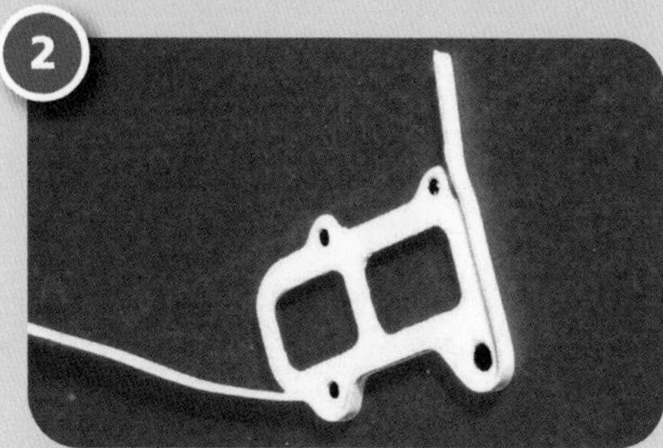

Separate the two halves by sliding your scalpel blade carefully between them (in similar manner to that shown in step 4 below) and clean up the faces with some gentle rubbing with fine sandpaper. To attach the edge flanges, cut a thin strip of 10thou plasticard and glue it in place at one end. Once the joint has hardened, glue the strip length by length around the perimeter of the shape.

3

The completed pair of frames with the edge flanges in place. The two halves can be assembled into a frame using lengths of rod threaded between the small holes. The larger hole might be used as axle bearing for a rotating spindle, such as a chain bobbin on a crane. All sorts of castings and pressings can be made this way, which is especially useful for making lots of identical parts.

IDENTICAL SHAPES – station canopy brackets

The canopy brackets seen here were made specially for the model of the station building at Mossley Hill in Liverpool. See the June 2009 issue of RM for the full article.

1

Firstly, determine the number of brackets required and cut that number of identically-shaped pieces of 20thou plasticard to the overall dimensions of the bracket. In batches of about 10 maximum, and using a small amount of solvent each time, tack them together in a column as shown, with a larger extra piece at the bottom to use as a handle. Tack on a template of the bracket on the top piece.

2

Using ordinary drill bits in a hand-held chuck, drill out the circular holes using bits of the appropriate diameter. It is imperative here that the drill goes through absolutely perpendicular to the column, otherwise the individual items won't be identical. The best tools here are a well-trained eye and hand, watching the drill going through from all sides. A pillar drill may help but isn't essential.

3

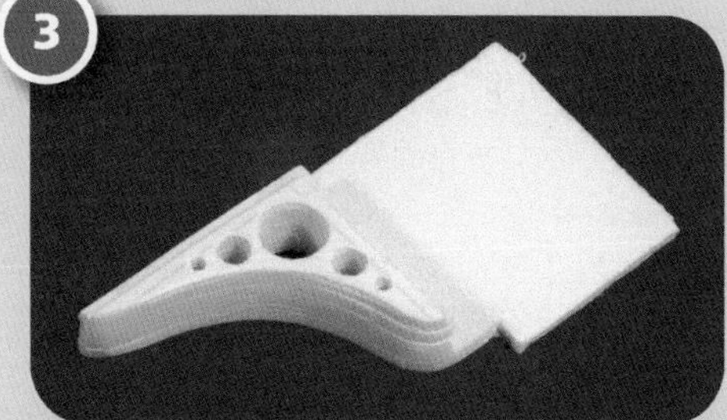

The next task is to trim away the unwanted material. Use a scalpel and half-round file to pare and file away the unwanted plastic: it is a slow process, but as the plastic is soft, not an arduous one. Again, the best gauge is the human eye, perhaps used with the aid of an engineers' square, but don't forget the previously drilled holes on the underside, they can act as your guide too.

4

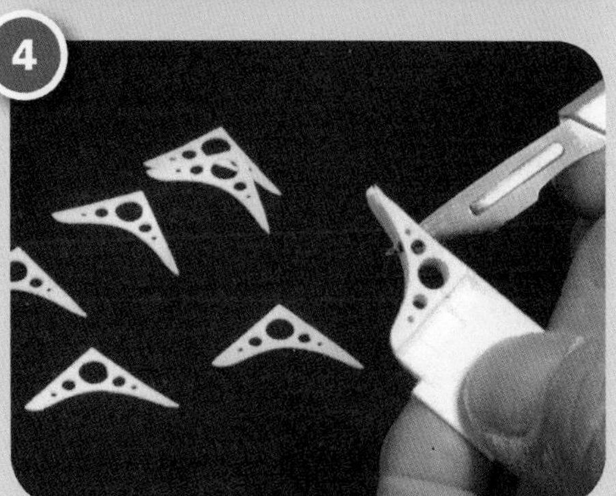

Once the shape of the bracket has been achieved, it is now time to un-pick the individual sections from the column. This is where you find out if you used too much solvent to tack them together in the first place! If all was well, the pieces will come apart by carefully sliding the scalpel blade between them. The surface of each piece is then smoothed down by rubbing gently on fine sandpaper.

5

The final step is to fit the edge flange. As with the previous sequence, a thin strip of 10thou plasticard is cut to 2mm-3mm wide to suit and one end is tacked in place with solvent. The joint is allowed to harden completely, then length by length, the strip progressively attached around the edge with solvent, trimming off the excess. The brackets are now ready for fixing in place.

A station building in plasticard

Above
A prototype view showing the building at St. Cyrus station, taken on 16 June 1960. Arriving from the north is an RCTS/SLS joint Scottish railtour.
Photo: W A Camwell/ Stephenson Locomotive Society (SLS ref. 27325)

The subject of this model is of the former Montrose & Bervie Railway Co station building at St Cyrus in Kincardineshire. The line, which opened on 1 November 1865, eventually came under the ownership of the North British Railway and became known as the Bervie branch. St Cyrus was roughly a third of the way along the branch, and its timber station building was typical of those found on the route.

Dimensions of the building were obtained from a drawing published in The North British Railway Study Group Journal No.73. These were photocopied and resized to 4mm scale.

The construction of the walls uses a basic shell of 40thou plain plasticard, covered with laminates of Slater's 10thou textured Plastikard. The design sports timber planked walls and a perimeter brick plinth around the base of the building. The 40thou base layer is butt joined at the corners whilst the brick layer has ends feathered to enable a perfect mitred corner to be made, as shown in the sequence on the opposite page.

For the roof I again wanted to use textured plasticard – this time moulded slate sections, but being a long building, I had to find some long moulded roof sections. Longer sections are available in the Peco LK-79 builder parts kit,

MAIN STRUCTURE

1

The walls and ends of the station building were prepared by scaling off the dimensions on the drawings and cutting out the parts from 40thou plasticard. Door and window apertures were cut out carefully with a sharp blade and filed smooth.

2

Once all the parts had been prepared they were cemented together around a floor piece, which was also cut from 40thou plasticard. The assembly was left to dry thoroughly, during which time the other components required were prepared, such as the planked outer walls.

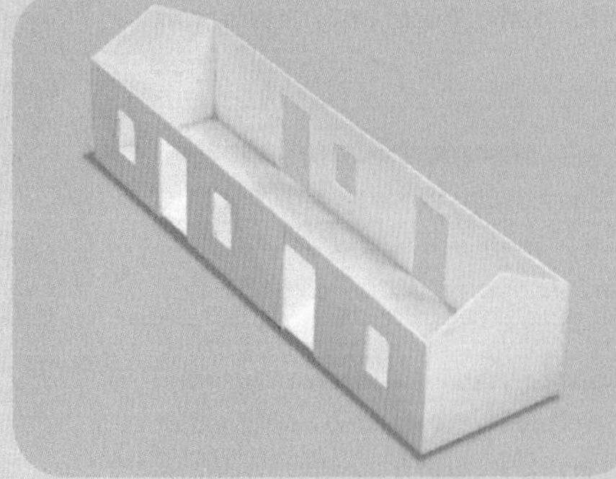

3

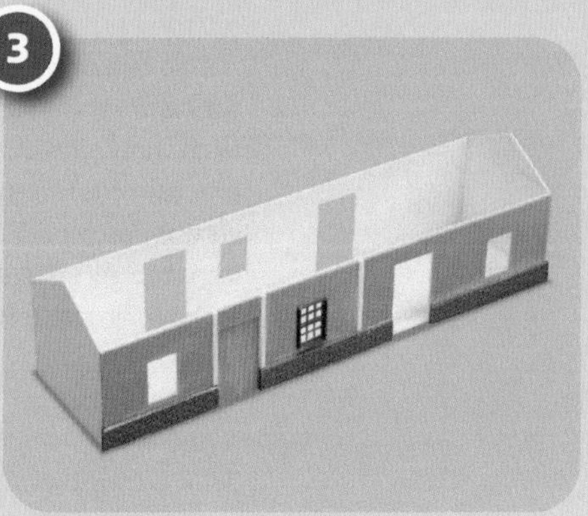

This view shows the building with these components in place. The planked outer walls were cut from 10thou embossed sheet; note in the view of the finished model that there is a mixture of planking, vertical and horizontal. Microstrip and Peco windows were also used.

MITRED CORNERS

The plinth is made of a base layer of plain 40thou plasticard, butt joined at the corners, and covered with an overlay of 10thou embossed brick plasticard, the ends of which are feathered at 45°.

The overlays are secured to the base layer with solvent, pushing the feathered edges gently together. When dry, clean out the mortar courses with flour paper.

When dry, chamfer the top edges to create flaunching and apply brick base colour. Fit to the model, adding mortar courses at the final weathering stage.

ROOF BUTT JOINTS

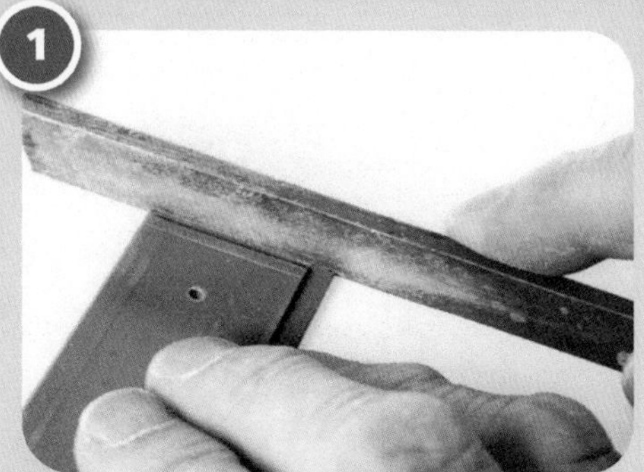

A slight chamfer, to leave a feather edge on the detail faces, is filed onto the ends of the sections being joined.

With a reinforcing piece cemented on the rear face of one section, solvent is then brushed into the joint and onto the ends of the roof sections.

The two halves are then pushed together firmly; the solvent softens the feather edges so they weld together smoothly.

Tilt the two halves upward as shown and hold in place for a minute or so; this pushes the softened plastic at the edge further together.

Before the joint hardens fully, turn the piece over and press both halves flat again. Add a further reinforcing piece across the back and trim to fit.

After the joint has set hard, smooth the slate face gently with flour paper until any remaining gaps disappear. A final coat of paint hides the joint completely.

but even these were too short, and had to be butt joined to obtain the correct length. Matching the sections up is not as difficult as it might seem and is described in the sequence, above. Because the roof sections are opposite-handed, two LK-79 kits are required. The sections are joined on the workbench making a long strip which is then trimmed to length before fitting.

To finish the model, chimneys were made up in a similar manner to the plinths, and chimney pots fabricated from oddments of plastic sprue.

For the windows, I opted to use those supplied in the Peco LK-78 kit, along with guttering and fall pipes.

Modelling with Wills plastic sheets

Wills moulded plastic sheets are available in a large variety of textured finishes and ideal for aspects of architectural modelling. In this section Paul Marshall-Potter builds this simple cottage from Limewashed Stone sheets for the walling, and Pantiles sheets for the roof, together with Peco builder pack LK-78 parts for the details, such as doors and windows. The Wills building sheets, which typically are 1.5mm-2mm thick, require a heavy duty craft knife – such as a Stanley – to cut, which is preferable to a scalpel or light modelling knife. Paul has used one here, although it's often a matter of personal preference if you get the results you expect.

The idea is to capture a typical cottage common across areas of the UK where both pantiles and limewashed brick or stone are typical. From observations Paul designed a simple building which captures the feel of that type of dwelling. In the east Midlands village where he lives; plenty of the houses have a single storey store/provisions shed attached to the house. He also wanted quite a low roof height.

With no actual prototype from which to obtain measurements, the design was evaluated by eye, using a 4mm model figure to get the proportions right for the walls of the house and internal ceiling heights. The dimensions were jotted down on a simple sketch for reference as Paul went along. However we have included a scale template which can be used to assist in cutting out the parts, doors and windows.

To cut the material, work from the reverse side of the sheet and use the knife fitted with a heavy duty blade. Paul finds he can get an accurate, clean, deep cut, which when the workpiece is flexed, shows through on the front face of the material. He then scores the front face of the material gently so that there's a clean break when the material is cut right through. He always uses a steel ruler, rather than an aluminium one which can easily get damaged along the straight edge. Windows, doors and detail items are all secured with liquid solvent. The end result was a very pleasing building that exceeded Paul's expectations – there's no reason why others shouldn't try it too!

Components

Peco LK78 Building Components – Doors, Windows, Gutters
Wills SSMP206 Pantiles
Wills SSMP215 Limewashed Stone
Wills SS46 Building Pack A
Wills SS86 Windows, Doors, Gates & Porch
Revell plastic filler for ridge tile cement
Halfords white plastic primer for my undercoat

Below
The completed model, surrounded by outbuildings which can also be constructed using the same methods and materials.

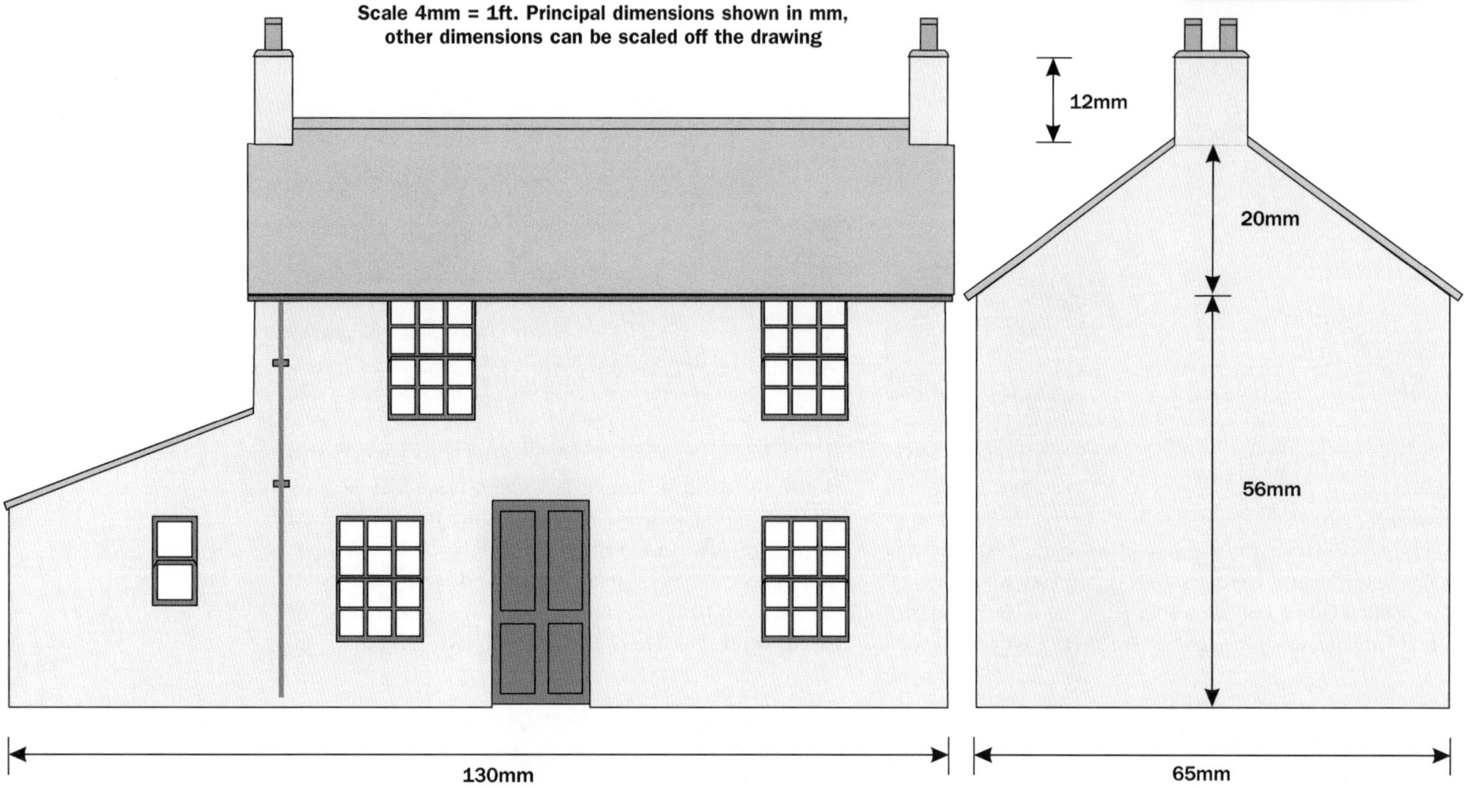

Scale 4mm = 1ft. Principal dimensions shown in mm, other dimensions can be scaled off the drawing

12mm

20mm

56mm

130mm

65mm

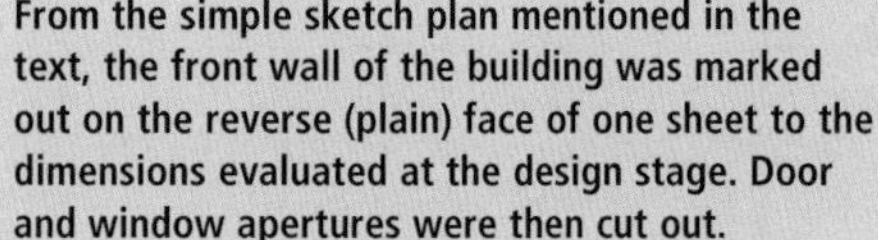

From the simple sketch plan mentioned in the text, the front wall of the building was marked out on the reverse (plain) face of one sheet to the dimensions evaluated at the design stage. Door and window apertures were then cut out.

The shape of the rear wall of the building was now marked on the reverse of another sheet using the front wall as a back-to-back template. This ensures that both front and rear walls are to the same size, making for an easy assembly.

Marking in pencil the cutting lines for door and window openings on the rear wall. These are sized to accommodate the relevant Peco or Wills doors and window frames. I varied the positions of them a little, leaving out one window.

Using a steel edge and heavy duty blade, score the first few cuts gently. Then as the cuts get deeper you can place more pressure on the cutting edge. I turned the sheet over and scored the other side before cutting right through.

This shows the rear wall complete with doors and windows in position. The window and door lintels are from the Wills SS86 pack and are examples of those easy to add details which make such a difference to the appearance.

With the front and rear walls completed, the end walls were cut to size and attached in readiness for assembly into the basic shell. I used some square offcuts of the moulded sheet as corner strengthening pieces.

The basic building shell assembled. Note that all the corner joints were mitred so as to achieve a good fit. Any unsightly gaps that result at this stage can be filled with the Revell plastic filler and carefully smoothed over.

The chimney stacks are added to the gable ends; they were made a little overlength so they fall below the roof line. There are strengthening pieces fitted into the core of the stack which also double as locating tags.

Instead of inner walls I used some scrap plastic sprue to make a strenthening joist which prevents the sides from bowing in or out. The chimney stack tops have been added from the Wills building materials pack 'A'.

Moving on to the roof sections, I made card templates for them first, to check that they would be square and fit properly. The templates were used to mark up the reverse of the pantile sheets prior to cutting.

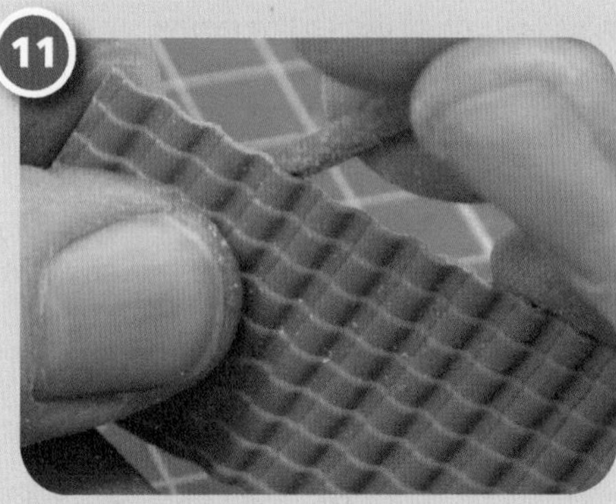

The lower edges of the pantile roof sections were thinned with a half-round needle file to replicate the thin curved edge of the pantiles at the eaves. This also facilitates the fixing of gutters underneath.

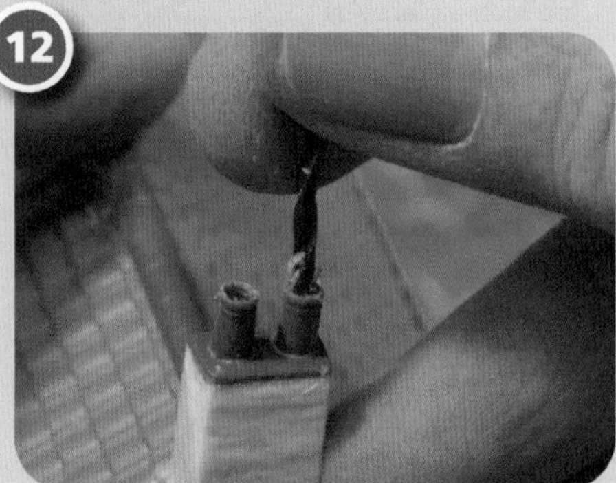

Chimney pots from the Wills SS46 pack were made up from two halves and glued in position on the model. When thoroughly dry they can be hollowed out with a suitably-sized drill bit held between thumb and forefinger.

Guttering, downpipes and ridge tiles are added from the various Peco and Wills builder packs. I cemented them in place prior to painting which is my preferred construction method, but others may wish to paint the parts first.

The ridge tile moulding from the Wills SS46 pack is solid and leaves a small gap underneath when fitted in place. This can be improved by applying model filler to represent the sand and cement mixture that would be applied in reality. I press this in underneath the ridge tile and then flood it with liquid cement until it becomes a thick paste; further smoothing helps to get it into all the small apertures.

The finished assembly is prepared for painting. The walls are first given a white undercoat with acrylic paint, then finished off with a 'dirty' wash of grey. Pantiles will be painted with varying shades of terracotta colour to give subtle variations.

Wills Craftsman series kits

If you don't fancy designing a building from scratch yourself, there are several building kits in the Wills Craftsman range which use the method of construction shown in the previous pages. They include pre-printed cutting templates and full instructions. Illustrated here is the village Post Office, an ideal building for any rural based model railway layout.

Also available
In addition to the Post Office, the range includes stone and brick country stations; single and double engine sheds; brick and stone goods sheds; a water mill; shops; cottages; semi-detached houses; and a country inn.

Above
The Wills Craftsman kits include sufficient plastic sheets to build the structure, and can be customised if desired.

Skills Workshop

Modelling with metal

In this section we will look at the methods for marking, cutting and joining different metals, together with the essential tools required. Whether you aspire to building your own track using nickel silver rail and copper-clad sleepers, or constructing an etched brass locomotive kit, this introduction to working with metal aims to steer you in the right direction.

Etched brass and nickel silver

Brass and nickel silver are versatile materials that have become widely used for etched kits of locomotives, rolling stock and even structures. The etching process is well suited to the production of small detail items such as grilles, valve gear, panelling and rivets. As well as etched brass kits, plain, flat sheets of brass and nickel silver can also be used as a raw material to fabricate assemblies from scratch; both materials are available in a large selection of sizes and thicknesses. The material can be marked for cutting using a skrawker and cut with tin snips (or a Stanley knife for sheets less than 10thou thick). The cut edges sometimes have sharp burrs, so cleaning up all edges with files and emery paper is good practice, even if the cut appears to be clean and accurate. Folds can be achieved using a vice or specialist folding jigs (such as folding bars). A pillar drill is useful for making precise holes in heavier thickness of sheet.

Brass wire and rod is commonly used for locomotive handrails and other detailing applications; the material is very forgiving and can withstand a lot of bending and shaping before becoming weak or breaking.

Small brass detailing accessories can be fixed to larger assemblies made of different materials (such as a plastic structure or rolling stock kit) using impact adhesive or superglue (i.e, cyanoacrylate). However, soldering is the most appropriate method for assembling complete etched kits.

Etched kits are generally supplied as 'flat-pack' frets of parts. Some manufacturers do, however, provide large curved items (such as locomotive boilers, fireboxes and carriage/wagon roofs) pre-rolled to assist the modeller. Parts are removed from frets using a craft knife, or tin snips if the brass tabs are of a heavier gauge. Tabs and burred edges can be cleaned up using needle files and emery paper. Assembly often makes use of a 'slot and tab' arrangement, which assists with the accurate alignment of parts whilst increasing the strength of the joints. Because parts are etched flat with only shallow detail, three dimen-

Above
This Lynton & Barnstaple 2-6-2T in 009 was built from an etched kit produced by Backwoods Miniatures. Although a highly complex example of modelling in metal, the principal construction methods are relatively straightforward.

Left
Etched kits usually come as 'flat-pack' sheets of components, which are pre-cut but attached to the fret by small tabs. This is how the Connoisseur Models kit for an O gauge 0-4-0T was supplied, the completed model being illustrated alongside.

Opposite
Another Backwoods Miniatures etched kit, this time for the L&B Baldwin 2-4-2T. Note how some of the major components are whitemetal castings.

BASIC SKILLS FOR BRASS AND NICKEL SILVER WORK

Marking out

A scriber and an engineers' square are used to score a line across the section. Because the section is shiny, the scored line can prove quite difficult to see so, if preferred, the metal can be coated with a thin layer of engineers' blue paint before marking out. The paint is removed where the marks are made, making them much easier to see. The paint will, however, need to be cleaned off completely prior to soldering the brass components.

Cutting

To cut, if the material is quite thin then a heavy duty knife will suffice, but otherwise a pair of sharp tin snips can be used, as illustrated here. The blades need to be sharp so that a clean cut can be achieved, with as little distortion to the metal as possible. It is preferable to try and make one long cut with the snips, rather than lots of little cuts.

Deburring

The action of cutting through the metal tends to create slightly curled or distorted edges, especially if the blades of the tin snips are not as sharp as they should be. However, if any distortion does occur then it can be pressed out using a pair of smooth jawed pliers, with any remaining burred edges cleaned off using files and emery paper.

Butt joints

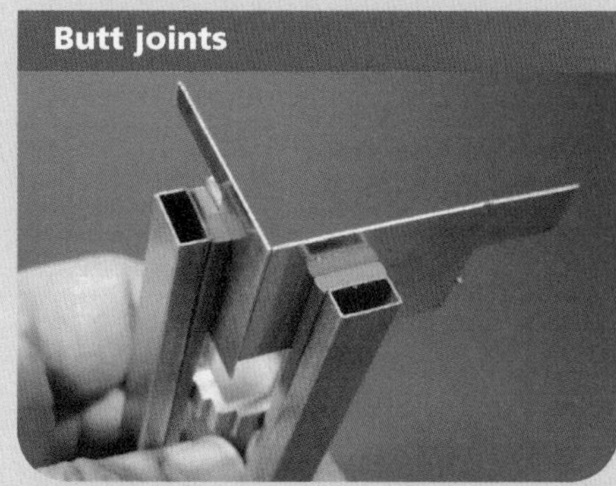

Butt joints are often used in etched kits, where the edge of one part is placed against another, with a soldered joint created inside the resultant angle. The Combo Right Clamp illustrated here is one of many useful workshop tools available to assist with the holding and accurate alignment of parts for soldering together.

Tab and slot joints

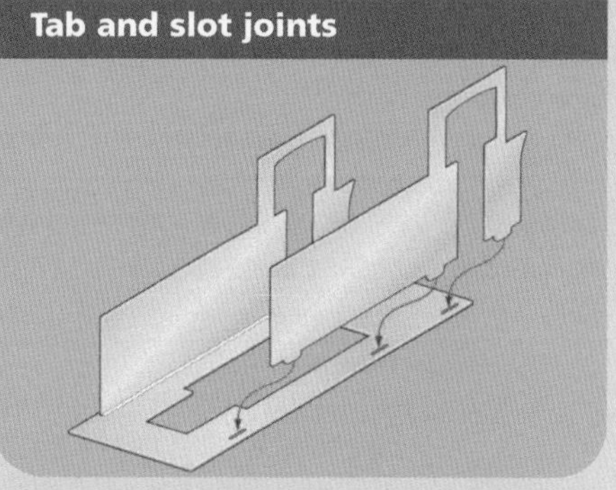

Many etched kits make use of a 'tab and slot' arrangement for assembly, whereby tabs along the edge of components slot into cut-outs in adjoining parts. This aids both their alignment and fit. On this kit (see also photo of the kit fret on the opposite page), tabs along the lower edge of the sidetanks engage with corresponding slots in the running plate.

Laminations

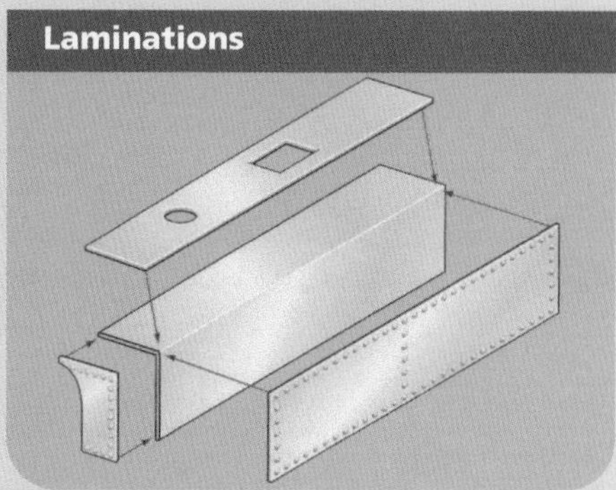

Sections of etched brass or nickel silver can be laminated together, either to increase the thickness and rigidity of a component or to add surface detail. Here, the shell of the right-hand sidetank from an L&B Baldwin 2-4-2T model (illustrated below) has riveted overlays laminated on top.

TOOLS FOR WORKING WITH METAL

- **Skrawker or metal scriber** *for marking out sheet metal.*
- **Engineers' square** *for ensuring true right angle joints.*
- **Steel straight edge** *for cutting against and measuring.*
- **A heavy duty knife** *such as a Stanley retractable one suitable for cutting through thin sheet and fretwork tags.*
- **Various saws; fine-tooth razor saw, junior hacksaw, fret saw, large hacksaw for bigger jobs** *choose the saw to match the size and thickness of material being cut.*
- **Tin snips** *large and small versions for different size jobs.*
- **A few files** *medium flat files with fine teeth, needle files of various profiles.*
- **Metal bending jigs and rolling bars** *not always essential for simple jobs, but useful when tackling metal loco kits etc.*
- **Small metalworking vice and/or Combo right clamp** *for holding workpieces.*
- **Emery paper** *for final smoothing and finishing.*

Above
This O gauge locomotive kit (a DJH product for an LNER G5 0-4-4T) is a composite of etched brass and nickel silver parts together with castings for the body.

sional items (such as angle iron and coupling rods) often require folding or laminating together from a series of parts to build up the required thickness. As a result, etched kits contain more parts than a comparative item produced as a plastic or whitemetal kit.

One particular advantage of thin brass and nickel sheet is with representing rivet detail; etched kits often have rivets part-etched, with the rivets themselves being individually punched out using a centre-punch.

Whitemetal

Whitemetal is a low melting point alloy, often used for casting small batches of components which are soft and easily worked. It is a heavy alloy and is therefore an ideal medium for locomotive kits where the resultant weight is useful for improving the adhesion of the model. Many wagon kits have been produced over the years using whitemetal, but the material is too heavy for coaching stock.

In the past, many kits comprised entirely whitemetal components, but over the years kits have evolved to include a composite of materials, such as whitemetal locomotive kits with smaller brass parts and details.

Cutting and cleaning of whitemetal parts is, broadly speaking, identical to that of plastic kits; a modelling knife together with a selection of needle files and emery paper will suffice. To cut thick castings, a heavy duty blade, such as a Stanley knife, is best. Whitemetal items are cast, so there are usually pips and traces of flash that need to be cleaned off. Being a soft material, castings are sometimes subject to distortion, for which pliers are useful for easing items back to the desired shape. Care is required, however,

Below
The Peco body kit for this O-16.5 Quarry Hunlset contains entirely whitemetal castings, supplemented with a small number of brass detail fittings.

because whitemetal is quite brittle and will break very easily.

Soldering is not essential for joining whitemetal parts; an impact adhesive or two-part epoxy can be used if preferred. Because of its low melting point, a low melt solder and suitable flux, together with a temperature controlled iron, will be needed.

The drawback of whitemetal is that components (particularly larger ones such as those for the superstructure of a locomotive) are quite thick, with the result that any exposed edges often appear quite coarse.

Soldering techniques

Soldering is the method of joining two pieces of metal together using an alloy. The alloy (known as solder) has a melting point significantly lower than the metal being joined so that, when heated, it flows and adheres to the metal surfaces. Once cooled, a very strong bond is achieved. A liquid or paste flux is added to the joining surfaces, before adding the solder, to encourage the solder (by capillary action) to flow and form a strong joint. (Some solders that are available are 'self-fluxing' and contain flux within the compound.)

Many types of solder and fluxes are available, designed for different tasks and metals. In railway modelling there are two main applications for soldering; electronics and model construction. Although the basic principles are common to both applications, soldering iron sizes, solder types and fluxes do vary depending upon the job in hand.

Soldering is often perceived as something of a 'black art' and many are hesitant to attempt it for the first time. However, the basic techniques can be easily learnt and, with practice, this valuable skill can be mastered and applied to a large array of railway modelling applications.

Solders

Solder is a low melting point alloy of different base metals, usually comprising mainly tin. The most common solder for modelling applications is obtainable from DIY electrical suppliers; these have a melting point of 224° celcius and are suitable for use with standard 240V irons.

Most solder comes in wire form and can be either multi-core (i.e with a flux core), or plain. Multi-core solders are ideal for use where the surfaces to be joined are clean and pre-tinned, such as with layout wiring, but can also be used for small scale modelling work. Plain solder is preferred for etched kits or track construction, and the use of a separate flux is essential.

Right
A typical selection of solders, each suited to different tasks and applications, including 70 degree low melt solder (for whitemetal) and 180 degree solder for brass and nickel silver.

Far right
A whole host of different liquid fluxes are available, as illustrated here, from suppliers including Gaugemaster and Carr's.

JOINING WHITEMETAL PARTS

Whitemetal castings can be soldered together, but an alternative is to use an impact adhesive or two-part epoxy. Here a Peco whitemetal kit has been assembled using impact adhesive; a quantity of the adhesive was squeezed onto an off-cut of styrene sheet and applied sparingly using a piece of scrap plastic.

Fluxes

Available in liquid or paste form, fluxes can be resin (also known as rosin) or acid based. Resin fluxes are 'passive' and only react at high temperature, wheras the acid ones are 'active' and continue to react after a joint has cooled. The flux in multicored solders are all resin based and are particularly useful for delicate electronic applications where cleaning off residual flux may be impractical. However, on models, residual resin flux needs to be removed with turpentine or white spirit before painting.

Liquid fluxes are a solution of zinc chloride or phosphoric acid (the latter most commonly used for soldering whitemetal), and therefore must be handled with caution. Resin fluxes are also available in liquid form, usually dissolved in a solvent solution.

Paste fluxes (such as Fluxite) are chemical based acid fluxes and intended for plumbing work, but are suitable

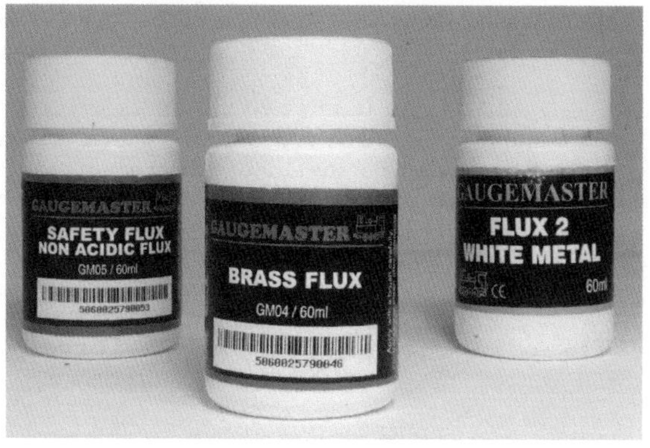

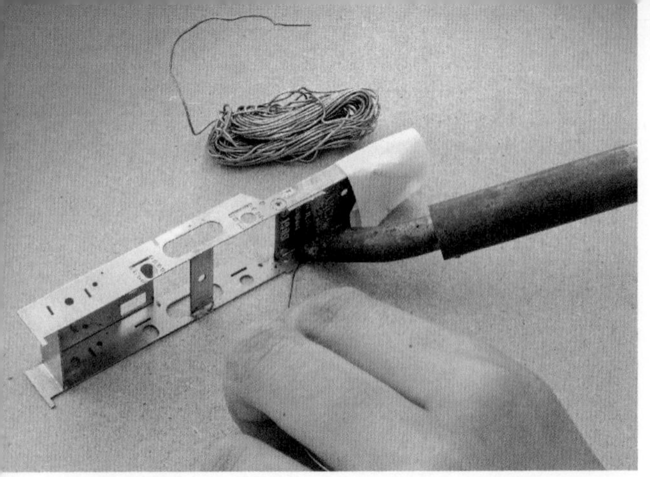

for most model railway soldering applications (i.e brass, nickel silver and steel etc). Most paste fluxes are soluble and can be washed off with warm soapy water. Thorough cleaning afterwards is vitally important as the acidity will continue to 'eat away' at soldered joints. It should also be noted that any residual flux on the surfaces of models will impair the paintwork finish.

Choosing your flux

Electrical work

For most electrical wiring tasks and the joining of feed and return wires to rails and terminal connections, resin flux incorporated into multicored solder is ideal. However, use of a separate flux is useful for tinning wires and keeping the iron tip clean.

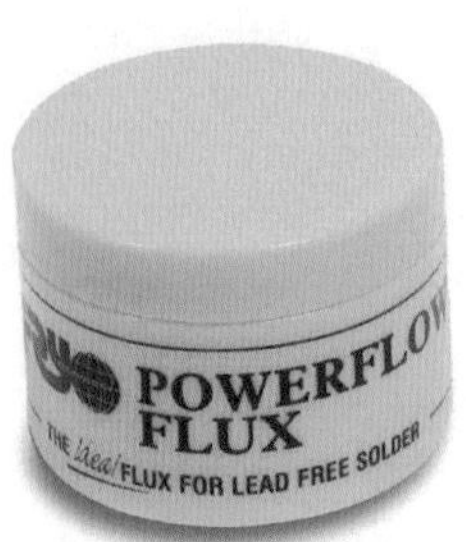

Kit building

A range of liquid fluxes (such as Carr's) are available from specialist suppliers, with fluxes to suit the job in hand. Alternatively, a good quality modern paste flux (such as Fry's Powerflow) can be used.

Soldering irons

Using a soldering iron which is appropriate for the job is important for ensuring joints are soldered successfully. The heating capacity and electrical rating of a soldering iron is measured in Watts; the higher the wattage the quicker it will dispense heat into the joint. Generally speaking, small etched components require less heat to assemble, but larger etched components act as a heat sink, and therefore require a more powerful iron to solder together.

Most standard soldering irons operate between 200 degrees celcius and 240 degrees celcius and are easily obtainable through the model railway trade, and from DIY/electrical suppliers.

Choosing your iron

15 – 18 Watt Suitable for fine, delicate construction and electronic assembly. Appropriate for situations where too much heat would be likely to damage or dismantle adjacent components.

25 Watt A small general purpose iron for wiring and trackbuilding in the smaller scales.

40 Watt A more powerful general purpose iron which is suitable for small kit construction and trackbuilding in the larger scales.

65 – 75 Watt Suitable for kitbuilding applications such as soldering etched locomotive frames.

120 – 175 Watt These types are best for large scale (7mm and upwards) etched kit construction.

Further reading

Modelling with metal is a vast subject for which a full exploration is beyond the realms of this publication. However, for readers who wish to further their knowledge of the subject, there are many publications available through the model railway trade which deal with specific topics related to modelling with metal.

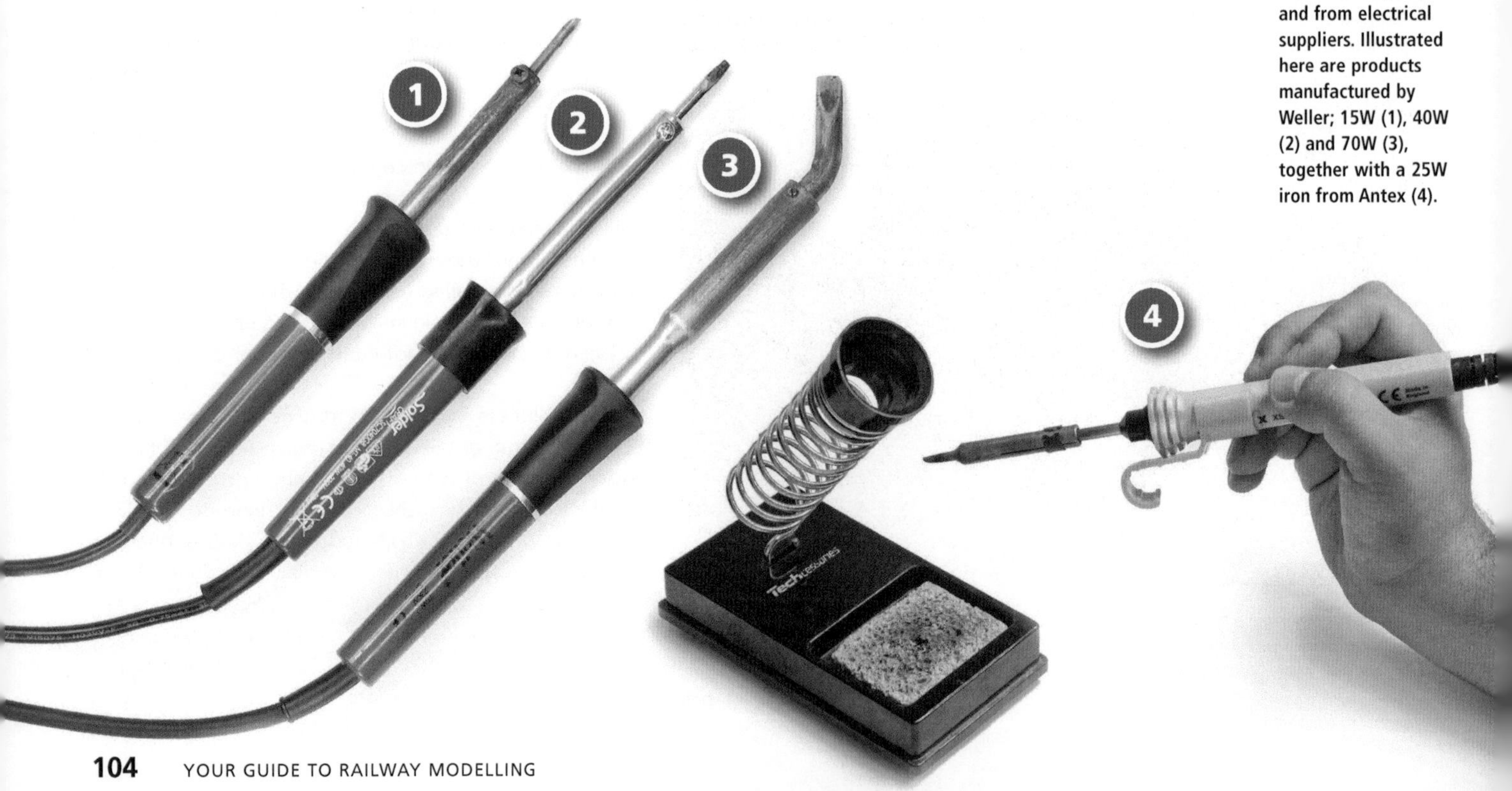

Far left
This etched chassis kit (a Branchlines product for a Peco O-16.5 Quarry Hunslet body kit) is seen in the process of construction using a 70 watt soldering iron.

Below
There are numerous soldering irons available through the model railway trade and from electrical suppliers. Illustrated here are products manufactured by Weller; 15W (1), 40W (2) and 70W (3), together with a 25W iron from Antex (4).

MAKING A SOLDERED JOINT WITH BRASS STRIP

1

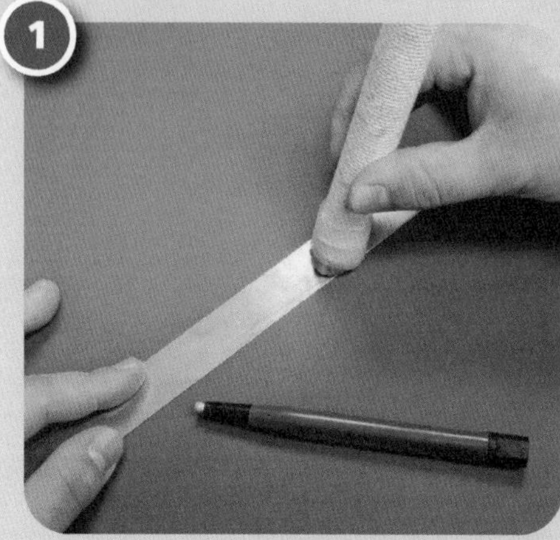

Starting with two pieces of brass section (in this case 17thou/0.45mm), the first job is to clean the surfaces of dirt, grease or metal oxide which could impair the ability of the solder to key to the metal. A fibreglass stick is ideal (as illustrated), but be careful of the glass fibre fragments that will accumulate on the workbench. Emery paper and files can also be used if appropriate. A glass fibre pencil (also illustrated here) is useful for smaller pieces.

2

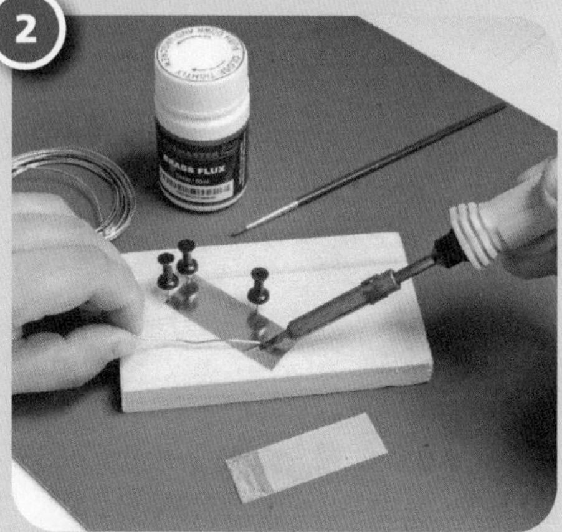

To join two pieces together, both joining surfaces need to be cleaned again and then 'tinned'; the process of applying a thin coat of solder to each piece. To assist with tinning, a flux is first applied to the cleaned surfaces. This prevents further oxidisation and encourages the solder to flow smoothly and evenly. The tip of the iron is placed onto each of the surfaces in turn. After a second or two, introduce the solder to the tip of the iron and, if the material is hot enough, the solder will flow evenly across the surface. The process of cleaning and tinning also applies to the tip of the iron; simply melt a small amount of solder on the tip of the iron before applying it to the material.

3

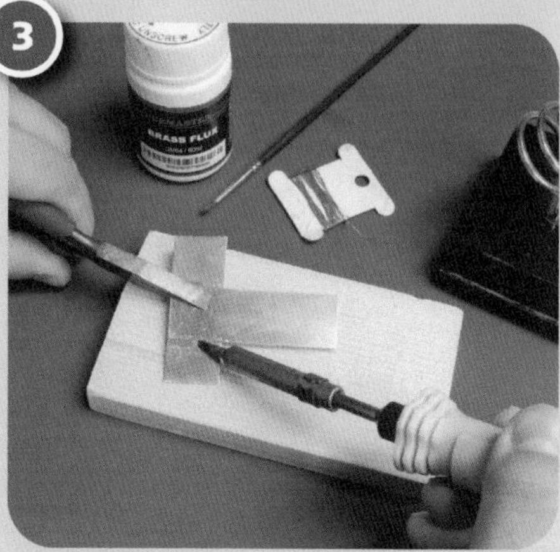

The next step is to bring the two tinned pieces together. Small items can be held in position with a pair of pliers; they will become too hot to hold by hand. Apply a little flux to the join, melt a small amount of solder onto the iron and then place it onto the join. Hold the iron against the join for just enough time to allow the molten solder to run into the join, and hold the pieces steady whilst removing the iron. Don't linger too long with the iron otherwise the pieces (or any connected to them) may become damaged. A few seconds after the iron is removed, the solder will change from a shiny molten appearance to solid dull silver. This indicates that the solder has cooled and solidified, and that the joint has been made.

4

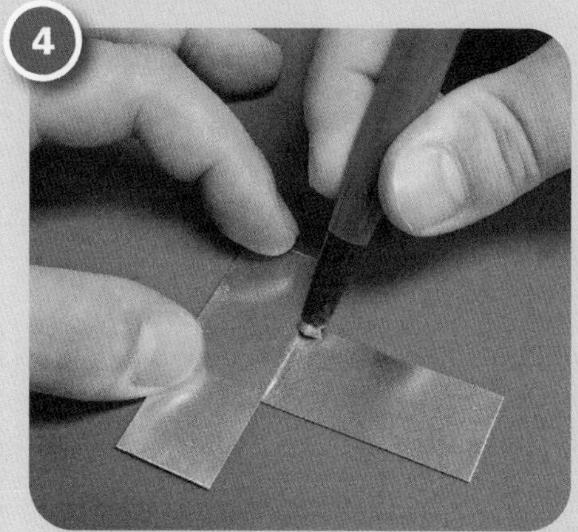

A good soldered joint will exhibit a smooth appearance without any pitting or rough parts. The real test is to pull the two parts gently in opposite directions to confirm that the joint is sound. Once satisfied, remove any residual flux with a rag, followed by a burnishing brush. Cleaning off all traces of flux is essential because if left, the active components in the flux can corrode the joint over time.

TROUBLESHOOTING FOR SOLDERING

Problems can occur at all stages of soldering and almost always this is because the solder either will not flow properly or will not key to surfaces. Here are some common problems:

Surfaces will not tin

If the solder is molten on the soldering iron, but will not run onto the surface of the material;

- *Check that the material is one that can be soldered, Most non-ferrous metals used in modelling (such as brass and nickel silver) as well as soft iron and mild steel, can, but mazak and aluminium cannot.*
- *Check the joining surfaces are clean and shiny and that flux has been correctly applied. If necessary, re-clean thoroughly and re-flux.*

How large are the items being joined?

If the pieces being joined together are quite large, they will conduct heat away from the joint area and the solder may not tin or flow properly, and a weak joint will result. In this instance a more powerful iron is required.

Parts will not join

If the solder flows, but quickly becomes dull and pitted upon cooling leaving the parts separate. This generally occurs because insufficient heat has been applied to the joint;

- *Check that the iron has reached the correct temperature.*
- *Was the iron placed on the joint for a sufficient amount of time?*
- *If the items being joined are quite large then a more powerul iron may be required.*

Parts join but break easily after cooling

This is known as a 'dry joint'. This can also be a result of insufficient heat being applied to the joint, or one of the joining surfaces not being tinned correctly. Clean the parts thoroughly and start again.

A good joint fails after a period of time

If this happens it is usually because the solder has crystalised and lost its strength. A likely cause of this is corrosion by active flux residues. This can be prevented by ensuring that all traces of flux are cleaned off the parts after making the joint.

Building metal kits

Metal kit construction is one aspect of the hobby that modellers find both challenging and fulfilling. The variety and complexity of kits is huge and knowing where to start can be daunting. However, getting to grips with metal kit construction (particularly for locomotive models) opens up all sorts of possibilities in terms of the prototypes that can be considered; there are many unusual, rare or short-lived locomotive classes that would be uneconomical to be manufactured in ready-to-run form and this is where kits come in to their own, filling these gaps for modellers.

Starter kits

For the beginner, the best route into kitbuilding is probably by tackling one of the simpler designs, or a 'starter kit' as demonstrated here. The subject of this article is an etched kit for O gauge from the Connoisseur Models range, although starter kits are available for 4mm scale from manufacturers including DJH (of an Andrew Barclay 0-4-0ST and BR Class 02 diesel shunter). These kits are specifically aimed at someone new to locomotive kit construction. With the skills and experience acquired from building one of these, the modeller can then progress to kits of increased complexity.

The Connoisseur kit

The kit (ref.CL-Polly) is not based on a specific prototype, but is inspired by the LSWR C14 0-4-0T locomotives and is of similar outline to the old Tri-ang OO gauge 'Nellie' starter model. The main body and chassis components are etched in brass, with a pre-rolled boiler and cast fittings (see photos 1 and 2). Etched nameplates reading *Polly* and *Nellie* are also included; those for *Nellie* were chosen for this model.

The comprehensive instructions (which are fully illustrated and run to 24 pages) are intended to guide the modeller through the build, step by step, from opening the box, right through to a finished, working model. Those considering building this kit themselves can download a set of sample instructions via the manufacturer's website (see contact details).

Required to complete are: two sets of 3'6" 10-spoke coupled wheels (Slater's ref.7842W), plunger pick-ups (Slater's ref.7157), Mashima 1833 motor and 40/1 gearset.

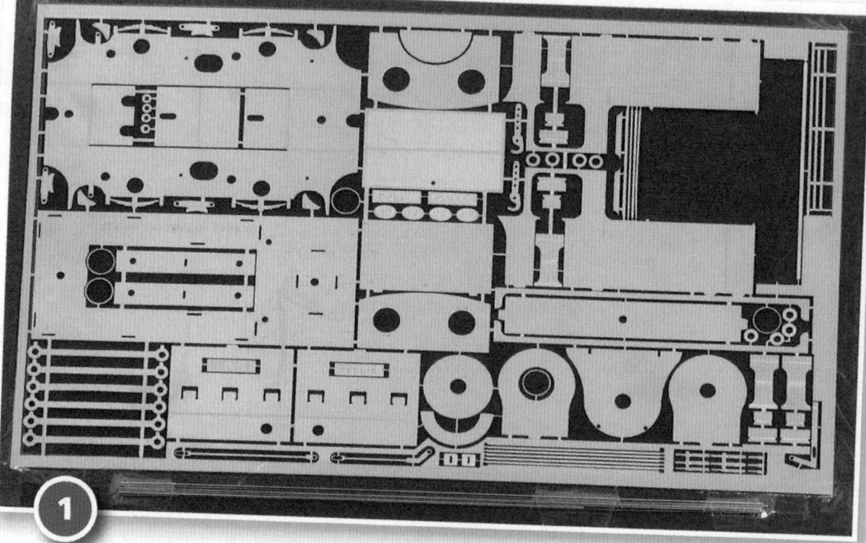

1

The main fret from the kit; note the the fold-up chassis, laminations for the coupling rods and use of 'tab and slot' joints to accurately position the tanks and bunker on the running plate.

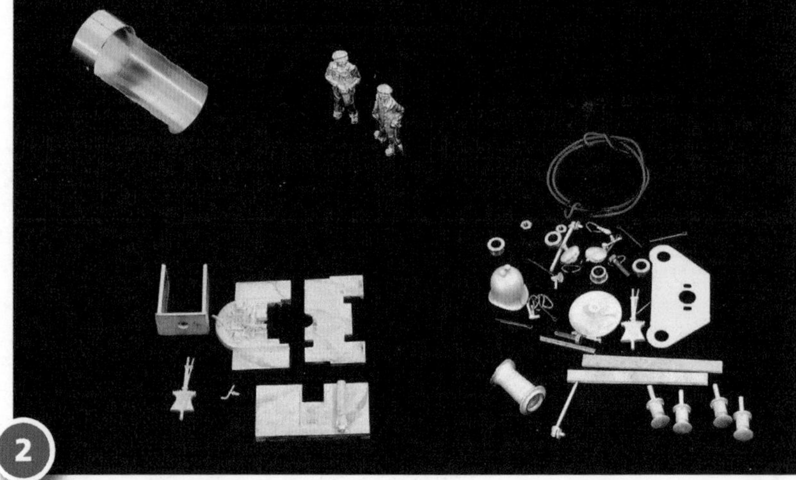

2

The main etch is accompanied by a host of castings and other parts including a motor mounting plate, buffers, cab backhead, printed circuit board and electrical wire for pickups, three link couplings and boiler fittings. There are also 6BA brass bolts and nuts provided for fixing the body to the chassis.

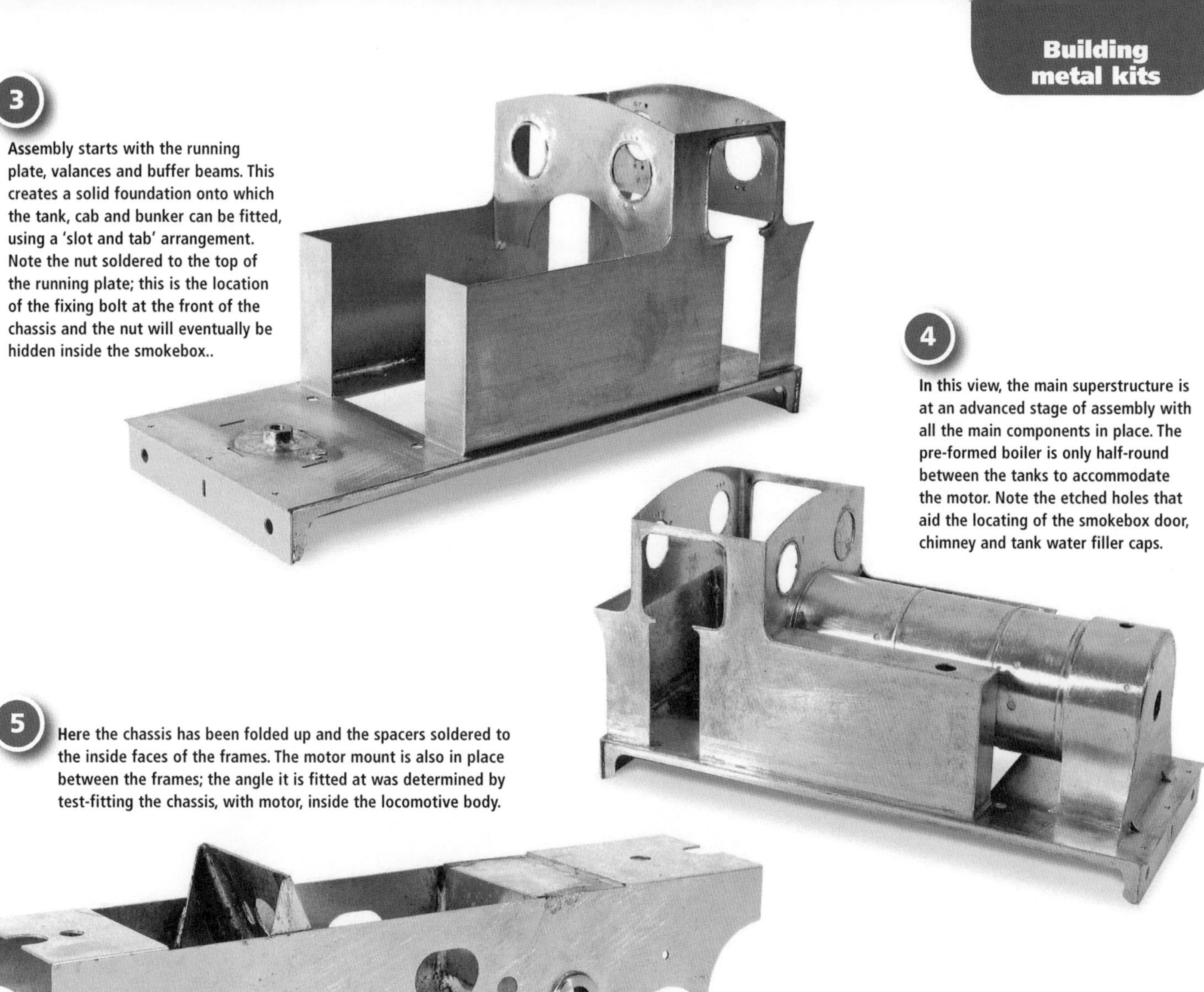

3

Assembly starts with the running plate, valances and buffer beams. This creates a solid foundation onto which the tank, cab and bunker can be fitted, using a 'slot and tab' arrangement. Note the nut soldered to the top of the running plate; this is the location of the fixing bolt at the front of the chassis and the nut will eventually be hidden inside the smokebox..

4

In this view, the main superstructure is at an advanced stage of assembly with all the main components in place. The pre-formed boiler is only half-round between the tanks to accommodate the motor. Note the etched holes that aid the locating of the smokebox door, chimney and tank water filler caps.

5

Here the chassis has been folded up and the spacers soldered to the inside faces of the frames. The motor mount is also in place between the frames; the angle it is fitted at was determined by test-fitting the chassis, with motor, inside the locomotive body.

Tools and materials

The manufacturer recommends a Weller 40 Watt soldering iron for the main assembly together with an Antex 25 Watt iron (with 3.2mm bit) for the smaller details. 145° solder is suggested for all joints (such as Carr's) and Carr's green label flux.

Miniature crocodile clips are useful for clamping parts together whilst soldering. Specific to locomotive chassis construction are tools for opening out holes in the chassis for the axles; holes are etched undersize and so need to be opened out using a reamer. These are precision tools (available in varying sizes from suppliers including Squires) that are used to open up holes gently to the correct size without them becoming mis-aligned or oval in shape.

Construction overview

The assembly starts slightly unusually with the bodywork, then alternates later on with the chassis before returning to the bodywork and then back to the chassis. The main stages were followed with only minor deviations and adaptations along the way.

Starting with the main bodywork, the footplate, cab, bufferbeams and valances were soldered together first (photo 3). The side tanks/cab sides are a tab and slot fit in the footplate, an arrangement which assists greatly with getting everything square and in the correct position. Care taken in getting this part of the assembly correct also helps to ensure that the boiler will be positioned accurately at a later stage.

The boiler is a sub-assembly which has alignment marks on it and the smokebox, which when lined up will ensure that the boiler will sit correctly on the inner side tank tabs with the smokebox sitting level on the footplate. The boiler bands also have etched locating lines on the boiler to assist with placing them in the correct position (photo 4).

It is best to assemble the basic chassis at this point to check it fits the bodywork. As the gearbox is soldered in place in the chassis, we fitted the motor that we would be using in order to check that the angle at which the gearbox was to be positioned would allow clearance in the bodywork. When we were satisfied, the gearbox was soldered in place (photo 5). This allowed the cab interior to be soldered in position using low-melt solder (photo 6). Assembly continued with fitting all the detailing parts to complete the bodywork. We made the cab roof removable (as suggested in the instructions) to facilitate painting of the cab interior (photo 7).

The kit is supplied with nameplates for *Nellie* and *Polly*, which would usually be glued in place after the painting stage, but we decided to deviate slightly here by soldering the *Nellie* plates in position.

Completion of the chassis involves fitting the brakegear and the sprung pick-up housings (Slater's part number 7157).

Finishing details and painting

The bodywork and dismantled chassis were thoroughly washed and left to dry and then spray-painted using aerosol grey primer followed by satin black aerosol (photos 8 and 9). Doing this obscured the *Nellie* nameplates, so a mask was fabricated from a scrap piece of plastic sheet and the nameplate surface was then polished with very fine wet-and-dry paper to reveal the name and border (photo 10).

The buffer beams and nameplates received a coat of cream primer applied by brush followed by a red topcoat, before the nameplates were given a final polish, again

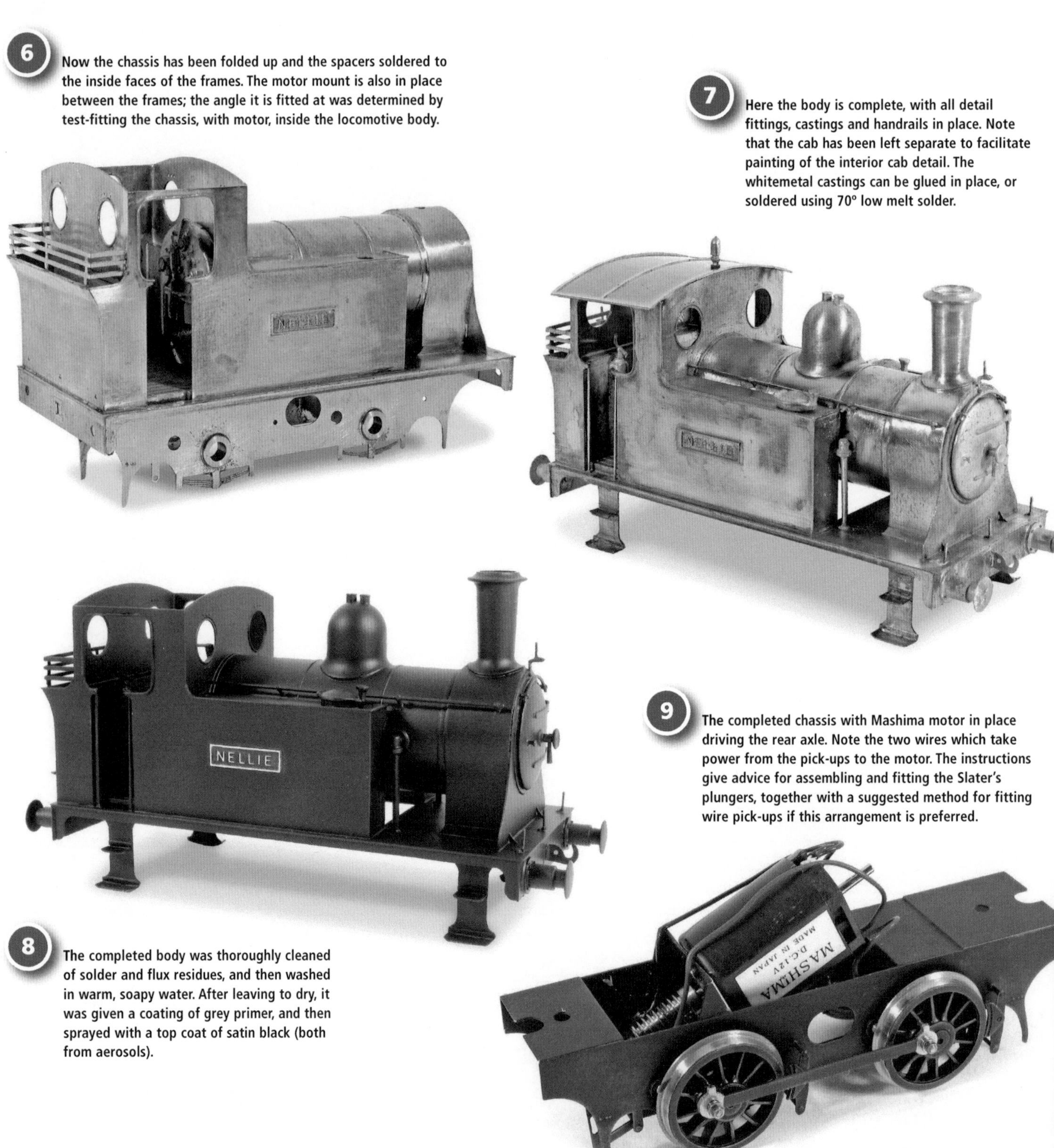

6 Now the chassis has been folded up and the spacers soldered to the inside faces of the frames. The motor mount is also in place between the frames; the angle it is fitted at was determined by test-fitting the chassis, with motor, inside the locomotive body.

7 Here the body is complete, with all detail fittings, castings and handrails in place. Note that the cab has been left separate to facilitate painting of the interior cab detail. The whitemetal castings can be glued in place, or soldered using 70° low melt solder.

8 The completed body was thoroughly cleaned of solder and flux residues, and then washed in warm, soapy water. After leaving to dry, it was given a coating of grey primer, and then sprayed with a top coat of satin black (both from aerosols).

9 The completed chassis with Mashima motor in place driving the rear axle. Note the two wires which take power from the pick-ups to the motor. The instructions give advice for assembling and fitting the Slater's plungers, together with a suggested method for fitting wire pick-ups if this arrangement is preferred.

10 Because the nameplates had been soldered to the tanks, these were covered with the primer and top coat. The raised surfaces of the plates were therefore burnished using emery paper, with a styrene mask used to prevent the tank sides from being damaged. The same mask was used when the background of the plates were painted red, with the letters then burnished again.

using the plastic mask to protect the paintwork. Cab detail was also brush-painted (photo 11), with handrails and buffer heads being picked out in Humbrol Metalcote which can be polished when dry. Finally, the kit is supplied with a footplate crew, which were painted and then glued in position.

The completed kit (photo 12) results with a rugged, characterful locomotive that is ideal for a modeller starting out in O gauge. It is perfectly suited to the Peco range of O gauge Setrack and could even provide the starting point for a small industrial layout.

Available from

Connoisseur Models
1 Newton Cottages, Nr Weobley, Herefordshire
HR4 8QX
Tel: 01544 318263
www.jimmcgeown.com

11 The insides of the cab were painted cream, with backhead fittings picked out as appropriate. Red enamel paint was used for these and also the buffer beams. The loco crew (supplied as whitemetal castings) have been painted to suit and glued in position on the cab floor; a further reason for leaving the roof as a separate item.

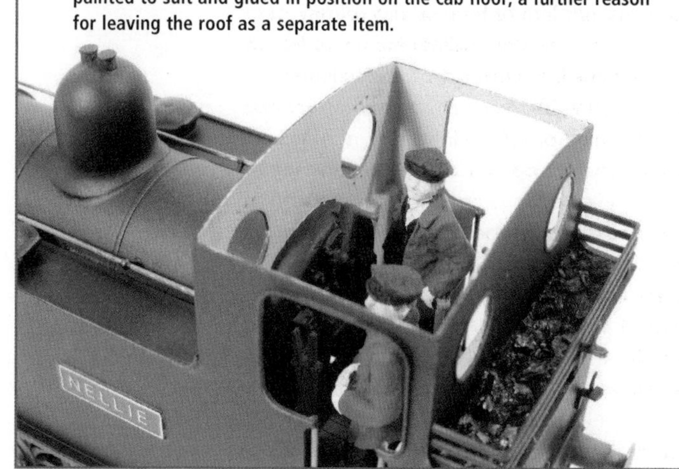

12 The finished model, ready for service. There is something very satisfying about watching a locomotive running on a layout that is the result of all your own work and, flushed with the success of this first attempt at locomotive construction, you could be inspired to assemble a collection of kit-built models for your railway.

All shapes and sizes...

Metal locomotive and rolling stock kits are available in virtually every scale and gauge in the hobby. For those wanting to try their hand at building a more authentic locomotive than a freelance *Nellie*, Connoisseur Models also has within its 7mm range an etched kit for the NER Y7 0-4-0T; the larger of the three models seen in this line-up. Phil Parker described the construction of it in the December 2008 RAILWAY MODELLER, which also included his 3mm scale model (built from a Finney & Smith kit) and his 4mm version constructed from a Stephen Barnfield kit.

Painting and finishing models

Above
This O gauge brake van (built from a Parkside Dundas plastic kit) was painted, lettered and weathered using materials and techniques described in this section.

Painting and finishing is the important final stage of model construction, whether it be an item of rolling stock or lineside structure. The aim is always to achieve a correctly coloured and blemish free result; poor finishing can spoil an otherwise excellent model. In this section we explore different approaches to painting; together with a look at using transfers for the lettering and numbering for rolling stock; and various weathering techniques to give your finished models a work-a-day appearance.

Preparation for painting

Before attempting to paint the model, it is critical that it has been prepared so that it is ready to take paint. This means ensuring that any blemishes are filled and smoothed (using Humbrol model filler for example), and any stray glue, solder or excess filler is removed. With plastic kits it is important that all filings have been cleaned.

The model also needs degreasing (including fingerprints!) as any grease on the surface will impair the ability of the paint to key to it. A simple way of doing this is to wash the item using a soft brush in luke warm water and dilute detergent. Once rinsed and thoroughly dry, the model should then be stored in a dust free place, such as in a plastic food container.

It is also important, prior to painting, to consider how the model is to be handled whilst this is carried out; if you are brush-painting a coach, for example, then it could be possible to handle the underframe whilst painting the sides and roof, and vice versa. However, if using spray techniques then some form of paint stand is almost essential. Stands can be fabricated using cardboard packaging and tubes.

Different models will require slightly different procedures for painting; as a general rule, any parts or areas which will be hard to reach with a brush should be paint-

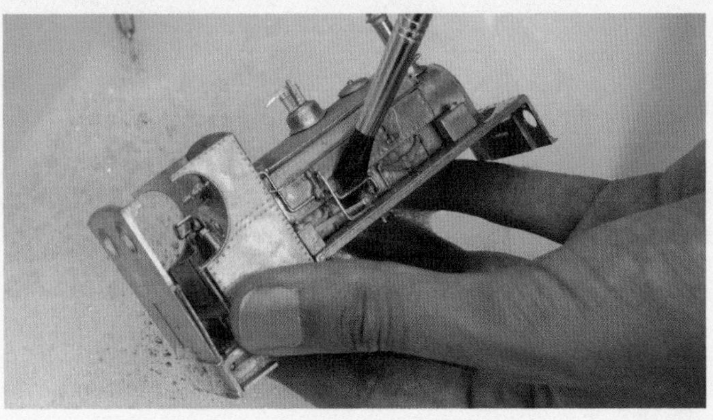

Far left
This whitemetal locomotive body (a Peco Quarry Hunslet for O-16.5) is being prepared for painting by first washing thoroughly in warm, soapy water.

Left
The view shows the same model after it has been given a coat of grey primer from an aerosol. This shows up any blemishes on the model that require further work, and also provides a key to which the topcoat can adhere.

ed before final assembly. If there is clearly visible interior detail (such as in a signal box for example), this can be built and painted as a separate sub-assembly and added later at the final assembly stage.

Priming

Certain materials (particularly metals) benefit from some form of undercoat or coat of primer, particularly brass. Car primers are a popular choice (available in white, grey and red oxide) and are suitable for use on plastics and metals. A benefit of the priming process is that it highlights any flaws which have been missed at the preparation stage, which can be rectified before it's too late. Leave plenty of time after priming before attempting to apply a top coat; although the surface may appear dry quite quickly, the paint could still be 'soft' underneath and the model should be left for at least 24 hours to harden thoroughly.

Types of paint

There are numerous different types of paint available to the modeller, each suited to different applications, most available in matt, satin (or semi-gloss) and gloss finishes. Matt or satin finishes usually look best for small-scale models, although transfers tend to adhere better to gloss finishes. Therefore, if a gloss top-coat is applied, a suitable matt varnish can be used to dull the shine of the finished model to a more realistic appearance.

Enamel paints (such as Humbrol and Precision Paints) are solvent based and matched authentic railway colours are available in small tinlets. These paints are best used on metal and plastic kits for locomotives, rolling stock and structures.

Water based paints include emulsions, acrylics, poster, powder, gouache and water colour. The latter types are available from suppliers of art materials and are generally better suited to scenic, structure and backscene applications. However, ranges of modellers' acrylic paints (such as those under the Humbrol label) are suitable for use on locomotive and rolling stock models.

Car aerosol paints, which are acrylic based, are often used as top-coats for models (by choosing a colour that closely matches the railway colour required) and are suited to models of plastic and metal construction.

Household undercoat and gloss paints, and varnishes, are appropriate for painting baseboard timbers, framework and fascias.

Painting methods

There are three basic methods of applying paint; brushes, aerosols and air-brushing, all of which have their particular advantages and disadvantages.

Brush painting

This is arguably the easiest and least expensive method of applying paint. The key to success is using good quality brushes (such as sable bristle brushes from artist suppliers, or range of dedicated brushes from Humbrol) and ensuring the paints are mixed properly, particularly if enamels are being used. Use brush sizes appropriate to the task in hand; Nos.2 – 6 for covering larger areas and sizes 00 – 000 for fine detail work. Look after your brushes; brushes can be damaged if they are not cleaned thoroughly after use. Use thinners to clean brushes of enamel paints and water for water-based mediums.

Optimum results are achieved by applying several thin coats, rather than one thick one. To do this, decant a quantity of the paint into a separate container and dilute with one or two drops of thinner. Allow each coat to dry thoroughly before applying the next. Try to work relatively quickly and methodically from one end of the model to the other, and never be tempted to go back over areas where the paint is partially dry. With practice, a good, brush-mark free finish will be obtained.

Paint can also be applied 'dry' with brushes, the bristles of which are only partially coated with paint. This is known as 'dry-brushing' and the technique is most usually used for weathering models (see page 118).

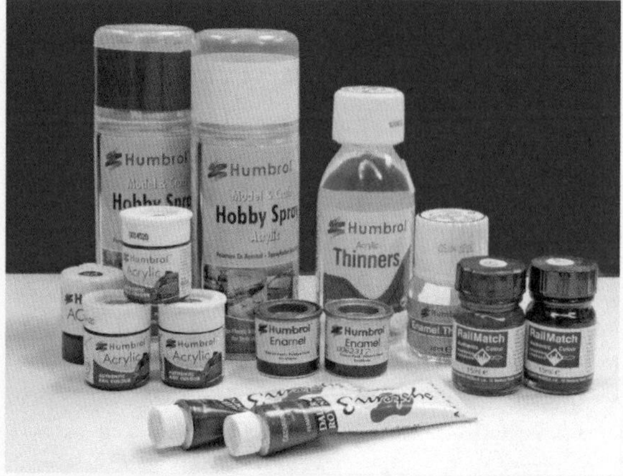

Top right
A representative selection of different painting materials and media available to the modeller, including enamel and acrylic paints and thinners. A range of enamels, suited to railway modelling, is also available from Precision Paints.

Above right
The Quarry Hunslet receives its first coat of Humbrol enamel paint, applied using a suitably-sized brush. Two thin coats are better than one thick one, which might obscure fine detail.

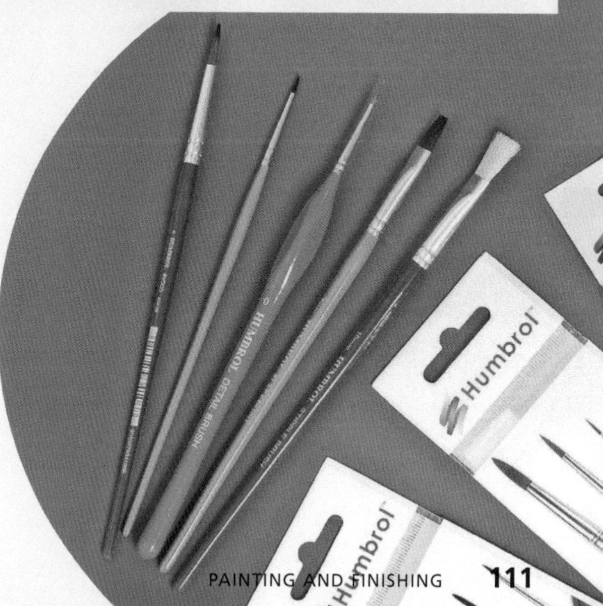

Right
A good selection of brush types is essential for brush painting. Small, fine tipped sable brushes are ideal for detail work, whilst slightly larger, flat brushes are suited to achieving a smooth, even finish over the surfaces of a model.

Aerosols

Aerosol spray paints can be useful when a smooth, even finish is required, or when a large area needs covering. Enamel-based aerosols are available from model railway paint suppliers (such as Humbrol), as well as acrylic-based car aerosol paints which are equally suitable.

Before use, aerosols need to be shaken well for two or three minutes to ensure the pigments and thinners are properly mixed. It may be worth testing the aerosol on an old model or piece of scrap material first before attempting to spray the actual model.

Spray the model by making a series of gentle sweeping passes along its length, with the nozzle held at a distance of around 4" – 6". Apply several thin coats and allow each to dry before applying the next. Avoid applying too much paint in one go because this will cause it to clog and run. Also avoid holding the nozzle too far away as this will give a speckled, gritty finish. Another effect, known as 'orange peel' (because the paint has the appearance of orange peel when dry) is the result of spraying with paint that has been improperly mixed.

The mist that is created by aerosols (and air-brushing) is harmful if inhaled, and therefore the manufacturer's guidelines should be followed when using these products. Always work in a well-ventilated area (preferably outdoors) and use a dedicated 'spray booth' (even if this is just a large cardboard box) to ensure that any stray paint does not damage surrounding objects or furniture.

HOW TO PAINT A PLASTIC KIT

Here we demonstrate how the Ratio Pump Boiler House kit in OO (ref.508) can be painted using Humbrol acrylic paints. It represents the typical type of plastic structure kit that is commonplace on many model railways, in all scales, and is used here to illustrate priming with an aerosol and basic brush-painting techniques. The kit has been fully assembled (aside from windows, see below) and is ready for painting. However, before applying any paint, all surfaces need to be clean and free from any oil or grease. The model should also be washed in warm soapy water, rinsed and left to dry thoroughly.

1 Spray with primer

This is optional (the parts in the kit are moulded in suitable 'base' colours) but it does give you the chance to create a plain canvas on which to base subsequent operations. Shown here working outdoors, the old cardboard box catches the overspray and helps prevent dust from blowing onto the paint surface while it's still wet.

2 Painting brickwork

Brick colours vary with both region and era so choose or mix one which matches your prototype. Individual bricks can be picked out in subtly different shades but don't overdo the differences, or an unrealistic 'patchwork quilt' effect will result.

3 Adding the mortar courses

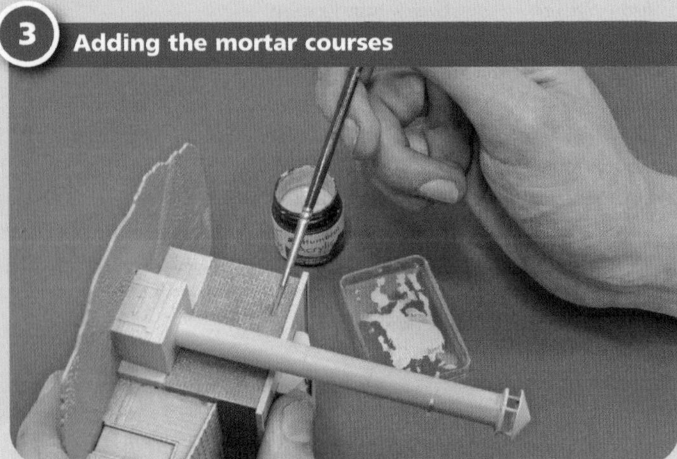

When the brick colour is fully dry, wash diluted mortar colour across the brickwork. It will settle into the mortar courses. As the paint dries, carefully dab the surface with a tissue, removing paint from the bricks, but leaving it in the grooves of the mortar courses.

Airbrushing

A step up from using aerosols is airbrushing. This basically involves paint being expelled through an air gun, operated using compressed air. A vast range of different airbrushes is available from manufacturers such as Iwata, and the equipment you choose will be dependent upon the type and frequency of work it will be used for; basic types have simple on/off valves to control airflow, whilst precision airbrushes have variable airflow control. The more specialist tools also allow fine detail work to be carried out with very little masking. When starting out, a propellant canister of compressed air will probably be sufficient, but if a lot of air-brushing is to be undertaken then a small compressor could be considered.

With airbrushes, the spraying technique is similar to aerosols, but allows for a much finer and controlled paint application. Whereas, in an aerosol, the paint is already mixed to correct consistency, with airbrushing the paint needs to be thinned accordingly. The amount of thinning required will be dependent upon a number of variables including room temperature and paint viscosity, so there will be an element of trial and error required. As a rule of thumb, start with a ratio of 80–85% paint to 15–20% thinners, and vary accordingly. As with aerosols, it is worth experimenting on old item from the scrap box first to test the paint application before working on the actual model.

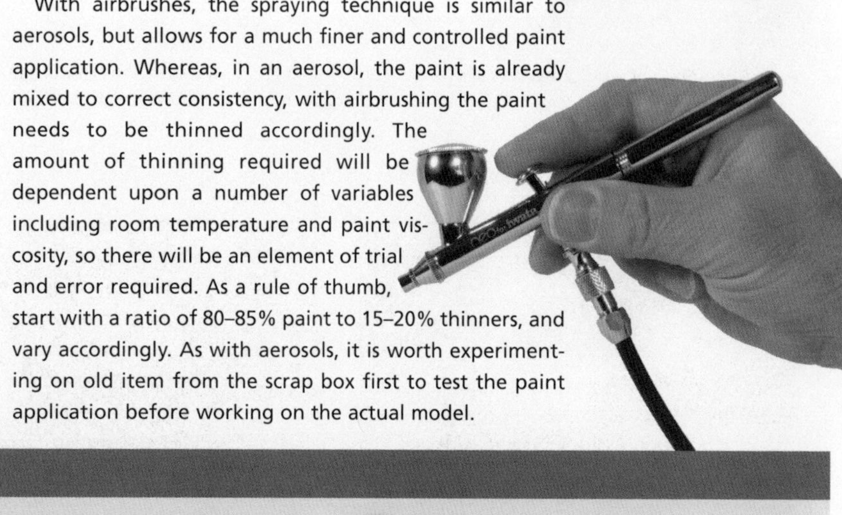

4 Painting the stonework base

Using the appropriate colour for the type of stone being modelled, paint the stonework. If you use horizontal strokes to match the surface detail, it will disguise any brush marks. Add mortar courses, using the same method as for the brickwork.

5 Dry brushing the stonework

Stone can be difficult to represent with just one colour. With a 'highlight' shade and a flat brush, first remove most of the paint from the brush on a tissue and then lightly skim just the tip over the relief detail. Each pass will deposit very little paint, so repeat as necessary.

6 Painting the woodwork

With a medium sized sable, paint the woodwork. If, as is the case on this model, the planks and wood grain run vertically, then use vertical strokes; again this will help to camouflage any brushstrokes you may leave.

7 Painting the chimney

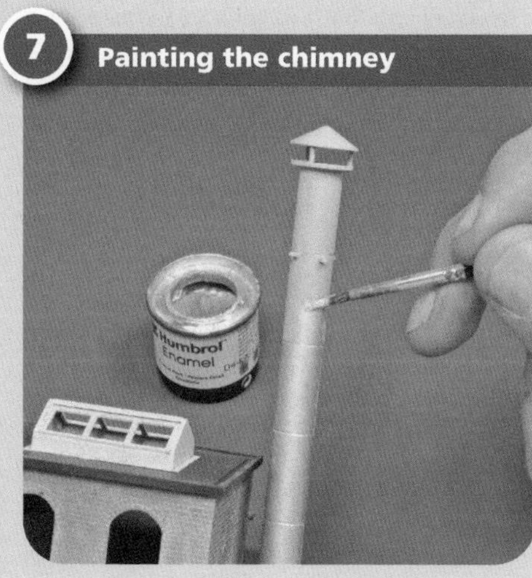

Here we are modelling a silver painted prototype. If you want to represent a bare metallic surface instead, there are some interesting specialist products available, some of which involve gently buffing the surface after drying.

8 Painting the details

The model is really coming to life now. Weathering is beyond the scope of this brief introduction, but if you do want to give it a try, have some colour photos of the real thing to hand as you work, to inspire and guide you.

9 Add glazing and final details

When painting is complete and all is fully hardened, add glazing to the windows along with any other final details which would have got in the way of painting. The plastic base included in this kit has been enhanced with the application of a static grass product.

Left
Wagon kits produced by Parkside Dundas in its O gauge range are supplied with waterslide transfers. Ranges of transfers are available from firms including Modelmaster Decals and Fox Transfers.

A critical aspect of airbrushing is ensuring all the equipment is thoroughly cleaned after each use. The full topic of airbrushing is beyond the realms of this publication, and modellers interested in pursuing this method further should consult one of the many dedicated books which are available on the subject.

Masking

Whether using an aerosol or an airbrush, base colours will require masking off when additional colours are applied on top. For small areas, a masking fluid (such as Humbrol Maskol) can be painted on and peeled off afterwards. Larger areas, such as coach sides, need to be masked off with tape, for which a proprietary modelling masking tape (such as Tamiya lo-tack) is ideal.

Lettering, numbering and lining models using transfers

Nearly all locomotives and items of rolling stock will require some form of numbering, lettering and lining. It is possible to letter items by hand (using a very fine brush) or add lining using a bow pen, but these are highly skilled methods. Far more appropriate for the beginner is the vast range of transfers which are available from a number of suppliers within the hobby. Covering all manner of prototypes, and available for all the popular scales including 2mm, 4mm and 7mm, transfers provide the means for even the most inexperienced modeller to apply high quality finishing touches to their models. Fox Transfers, Modelmaster Decals and HMRS are amongst the specialist suppliers from which transfers can be obtained. There are four basic types of transfer, each with a different method of application. All types benefit from sealing with a coat of varnish (such as Humbrol Decal Fix) to protect them from subsequent damage when the model is handled.

Waterslide transfers

Essentially these consist of the lettering, insignia design or lining element printed onto a transparent carrier film, which is attached to a pre-gummed absorbent backing paper. The element required is carefully cut out from the full sheet (using scissors or a sharp knife) and soaked in water for about 30 seconds. Once released from its backing paper the transfer element can be removed from the water and positioned on the model. Excess water can be lightly blotted away using tissue, with care taken not to accidentally move the transfer. Waterslide transfers are best applied to a gloss paint finish, which helps to disguise the sheen of the carrier film.

Dry print transfers

These are basically self-adhesive items which are supplied on a thin plastic carrier film. To apply, the sheet is positioned with the required element over its intended position and the back of the carrier film is gently rubbed with a soft pencil. They can be applied to matt, satin or gloss paint finishes, although care is required during application to ensure adjacent transfers are not inadvertently rubbed onto the model.

Below
A sharp scalpel, metal cutting edge and tweezers are essential for the application of most transfer types. Transfers can be sealed in place using a product such as Humbrol DecalFix.

USING WATERSLIDE TRANSFERS

Transfers are used primarily as a means of adding lining, numbering or lettering to an item of rolling stock or locomotive. Here we will demonstrate the process of applying waterslide transfers to add lining to a kit-built steam locomotive, in this case a narrow gauge Quarry Hunslet built from the Peco whitemetal body kit (also featured at the start of this section).

1 The transfers

The transfers used here are from the Fox range of waterslide transfers and comprise a pack of corners of varying radii (ref.FG 1283) and straight lengths (ref.FG 1281). The pack is complete with comprehensive guidelines printed on the inside, and it is advisable to refer to these before starting.

2 Preparing the model

Before adding the transfers the painted model is prepared by coating with Humbrol Gloss Cote varnish. This is to provide a suitable gloss finish to which the transfers can adhere. Make sure the surfaces of the model are also clean and free from dust and grease.

3 Cutting from the sheet

Use a sharp knife to cut the required transfer(s) from the rest of the sheet. Allow a margin around the transfer and do not cut into it unless you intend to (such as cutting a section from a length of lining).

4 Soaking the transfer

Immerse the transfer in warm water (Fox suggests adding a small amount of washing-up liquid) until the transfer becomes detached from its backing sheet. You can test whether it has separated by using gentle finger pressure.

5 Placing the transfer

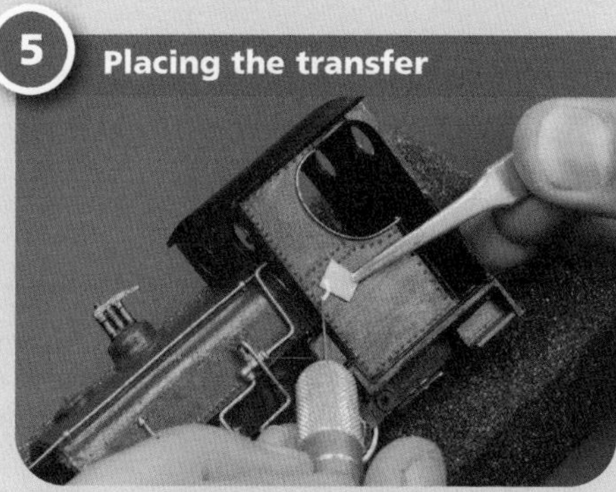

When the transfer and backing paper have separated, remove them together using tweezers and place in position on the model. Use the point of the knife blade to hold the transfer in place whilst using the end of the tweezers to pull the backing sheet out from underneath.

6 Fixing the transfer in place

Adjust the final position of the transfer (adding a drop of water if required to keep it mobile). Once satisfied with the placement of the transfer, carefully blot the excess water using tissue. Ensure there is no water or air bubbles trapped underneath. The three other corners for the cabside lining can now be added, as illustrated.

7 Adding the straight lengths

With the corners in place, the intermediate straight lengths can be added next, as illustrated. When assembling composites of transfers (such as here, or when placing individual digits to form running numbers), care needs to be taken to avoid disturbing the adjacent transfers already *in situ*.

8 The completed model

The lining was added to the other parts of the locomotive as required and then the model was left for a couple of days for the transfer adhesive to harden completely. The whole model was treated to a protective layer of satin varnish to seal the transfers in place and protect them from damage during handling of the model.

Below
Varnishes are available for different finishes, in both jar and aerosol form. Illustrated here are items from the Humbrol range, which can be applied to protect paint and transfers, whilst adjusting the surface finish to suit the model and individual tastes; generally, a matt finish is effective on models.

Below
A selection of the weathering powders available from Humbrol. If brushed on 'dry', weathering powders offer a relatively 'quick fix' for giving items of stock a working appearance; with practice, wagons can be treated thus in a matter of minutes (see overleaf).

Pressfix and Methfix Types
Transfers of both these types – which require different application methods but are closely related – are available from the Historical Model Railway Society. The details are printed onto a thin, gummed carrier sheet, which is itself on a thicker backing paper. With both types, the required item is selected and the thin carrier sheet is scored through to the backing paper. The item and its carrier sheet are then eased off the backing sheet and positioned face down on the model.

With the Pressfix variety, the transfers are self adhesive and just require pressing into place. However, Methfix transfers have an adhesive which needs to be activated using methylated spirits. Once in position on the model, the transfer is wetted with a 3:1 mix of methylated spirits and water, and left for 10 minutes to set.

With both types, the final phase is to remove the carrier sheet. This is wetted slightly with water and gently peeled off once it has softened. The advantage of Methfix over Pressfix is that they can be finely adjusted using a brush or cocktail stick; Pressfix transfers cannot be adjusted after placement on the model.

Varnishes

The use of varnish as a final coat to protect the model has long been a matter of personal preference; some prefer it, others don't like the all over sheen which a varnish gives. Varnishes can be applied by brush or aerosol in the same way as paint, and there are some situations where varnish is best applied (such as with powder weathering).

Weathering techniques

It is generally accepted in the railway modelling hobby that the term 'weathering' refers to the process of giving a realistically 'used' or 'working' appearance to a model. The topic is very subjective – many modellers elect not to weather their models – but the practice has become much more commonplace within the hobby in recent years. The major model manufacturers now offer 'weathered' versions of proprietary locomotives and items of rolling stock within their ranges as standard; a significant shift that has occurred within the last 10 years.

In reality, the physical appearance of every object will be affected by exposure to sunlight, atmospheric and environmental conditions. As well as the effects of sun and rain, which the term suggests, weathering can incorporate other factors such as corrosion, notably of metalwork and the frequency (or infrequency) something is cleaned. Therefore, every item on a model railway, whether it be the buildings, track or scenic items, should be finished with some consideration of weathering.

Weathering is often regarded as an aspect of modelling that requires an artistic temperament. Whilst there is an element of truth in this (weathering is as much about observation as it is application), it does not mean that the task is beyond the abilities of the beginner. Virtually all weathering effects can be developed from simple basic techniques which can be mastered through continued experimentation and practice.

Weathering using powders

Some modellers may be reluctant to attempt weathering with paint, particularly valuable items of stock for fear of causing permanent damage. This is where specialist weathering powders come in: These can be applied 'dry' using a soft brush, and if the result is unsatisfactory then it is possible to clean the powders off the surface of the model. Results can be improved with practice and, once content with the finish, the powders can be fixed with a suitable spray varnish (such as Humbrol 49 Spray Matt Varnish). Lightly weathered models can in fact be left un-varnished, but handling will cause disturbance and result with traces of powder on hands and fingers.

WEATHERING USING PAINTS

Paint can be applied as a series of light mists using an airbrush, but for the outright beginner, hand-weathering methods using brushes and cotton buds are perhaps more suitable.

1 Block colouring

This is essentially the blocking in of areas of a model with a 'base coat' of a weathered colour (such as a dark grey or brown) upon which further weathering work can be applied. On rolling stock, the principal applications of this would be on roofs and underframes, both of which quickly acquired a patina of brake dust and track dirt in service. Block colours are applied using well-stirred paint straight from the tin. Enamels or acrylics are both generally suitable. Here dark grey and brown acrylics have been mixed to provide a base coat for the wagon chassis and roof.

2 Washes

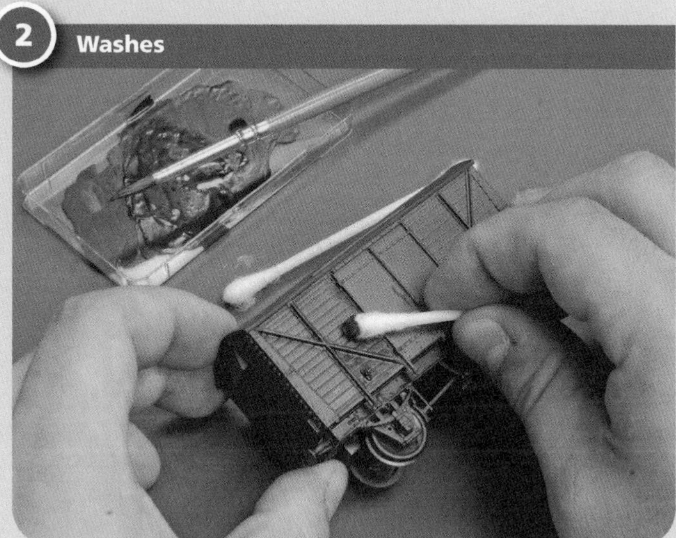

Paints can be thinned to varying degrees to create a range of effects. A very thin wash (lots of thinners with only a little paint) can be used to slightly tone down a basic livery or gleaming white transfers. Acrylics are perhaps more suited to this, as enamel thinners can be damaging to factory-applied transfers. A different effect can be achieved by creating a thicker wash to paint a whole panel or section of a model, and then partly removing the paint with a cloth or cotton bud (as demonstrated here). This leaves a residue of the paint in gaps, corners and around detail. It is best to work on small areas at a time so that the paint does not start to dry before you have chance to wipe if off.

3 Dry-brushing

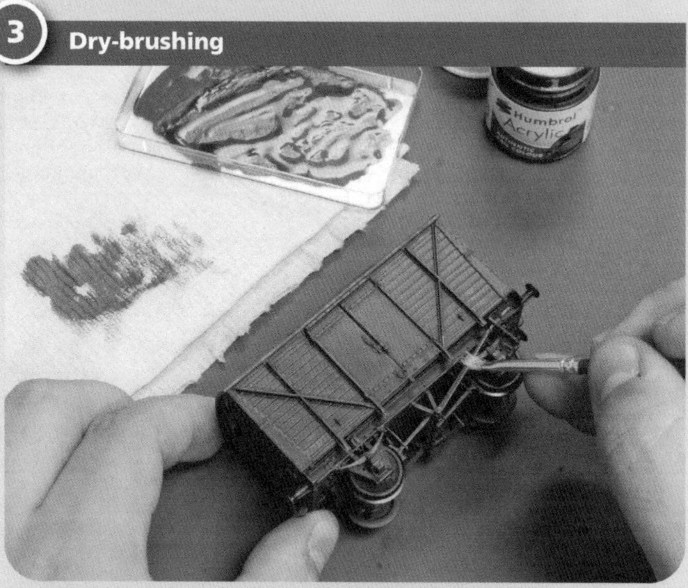

Dry-brushing, as the term suggests, refers to the technique of picking up paint on a brush, cleaning the majority of it off (using tissue) so that the brush is almost dry, and then lightly brushing the surface of a model with the residual paint that remains on the bristles. It is a very subtle effect which highlights details and has been used for many years by military modellers. It is particularly suited to highlighting chassis detail on wagons (as per this example), coaches and locomotives.

The finished model

WEATHERING USING POWDERS

Here we demonstrate the use of Humbrol weathering powders on a Bachmann Class 37 diesel model. The basic techniques described here are adaptable for a range of different models, including steam locomotive, coach and rolling stock models, together with road vehicles, buildings and other lineside structures.

1 Weathering the bogie sideframes

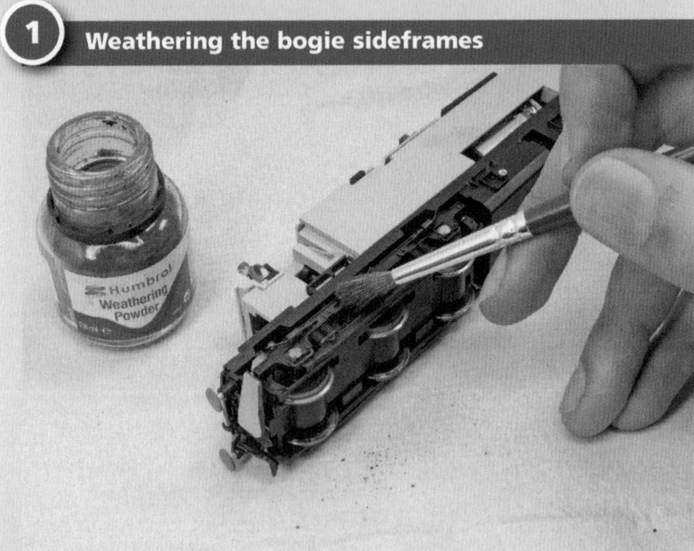

Before starting, the work surface was covered with tissue to contain excess weathering powder. The locomotive was dismantled and, dealing with the chassis first, small amounts of the Dark Earth colour were brushed into the bogie sideframes and chassis boxes. Excess powder was removed by gently tapping the model on the work surface.

2 Using a watery paste

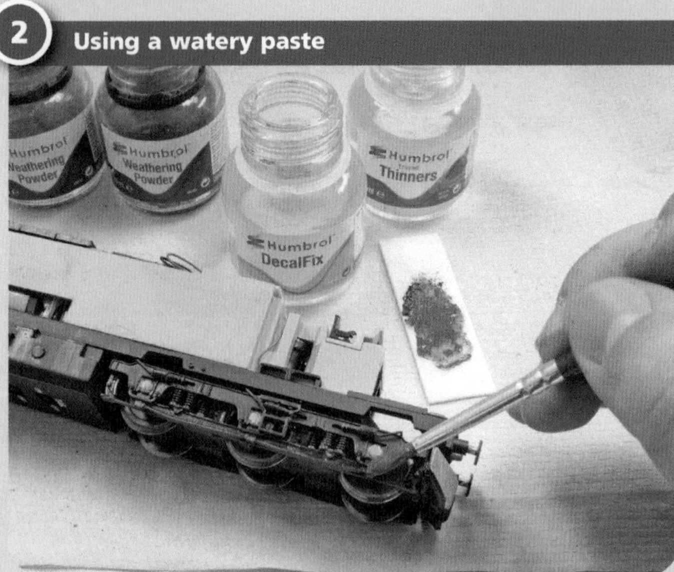

For the brake dust deposits, Rust was combined with a small amount of Dark Earth. Thinners were added to create a watery paste, to which Decal Fix was added (to fix it in place on the model). Small quantities were then brushed on the brake shoes and surrounding bogie details as illustrated.

3 Creating vertical streaks

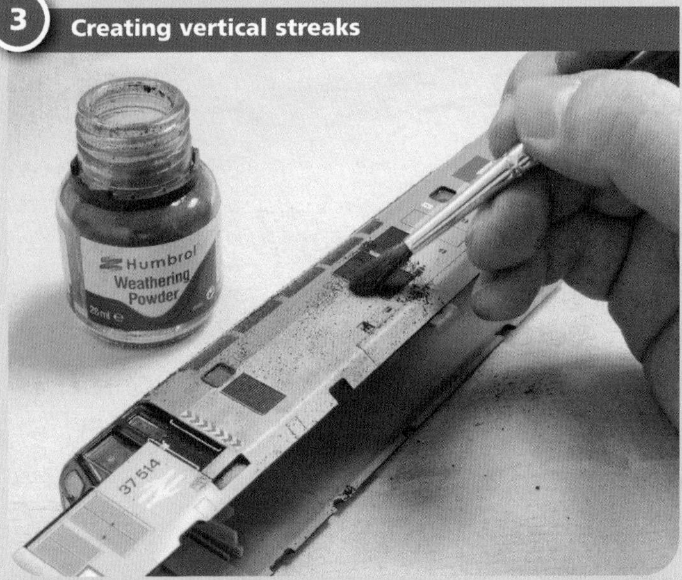

Attention now turned to the body and creating vertical streaks of dirt; Firstly, Dark Earth powder was brushed loosely over the body as illustrated, working to achieve an even coverage. Some powder was also stippled into and around the areas of moulded detail (such as window frames and grilles).

4 Using finger pressure

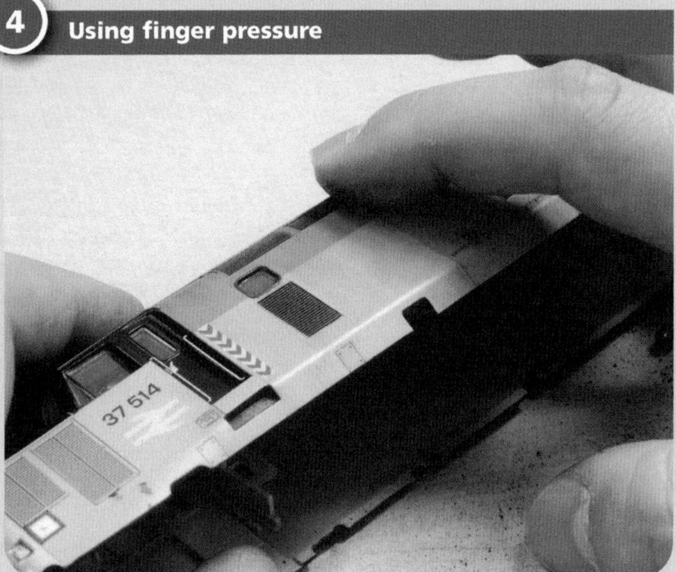

Then, by drawing a finger down the bodyside from top to bottom, and gradually working from left to right, the majority of the powder was removed. What was left settled into the crevices and moulded detail, and also created an uneven pattern of vertical streaks along the bodyside. Avoid leaving fingerprints on the model.

Practice makes perfect

We have illustrated the basic methods of painting and finishing models. The topic, of course, is very large and there are numerous other methods and techniques which have been used over the years. However, the methods described in this section will provide you with advice for most modelling projects that you will encounter. The golden rule with painting and finishing is to take your time and learn from your mistakes. Like most other things in this hobby, practice makes perfect.

5 Using cotton buds

The pattern was accentuated by using a damp cotton bud – at a few intervals along the bodyside – to create clean lines within the heavier areas of dirt.

6 The finished bodysides

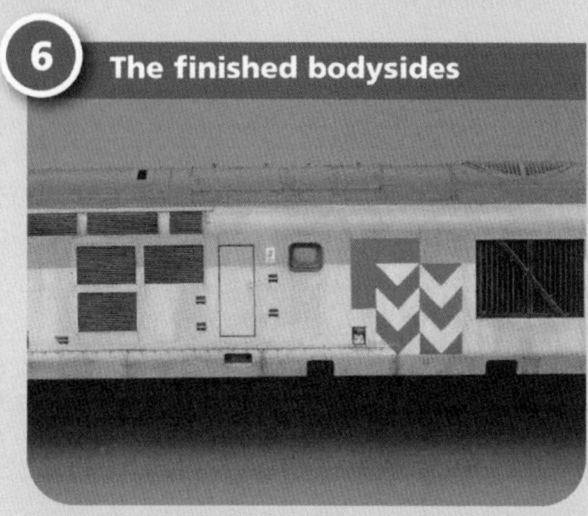

The resultant bodyside displays many variations of dirt build-up and depth. Note how the moulded detail has been enhanced with the addition of the weathering powder.

7 Weathering the roof

For the roof – which would be typically filthy with sooty exhaust deposits – some Smoke was mixed with small amounts of Rust and brushed 'dry' over the roof detail.

8 Bonnet-side grilles

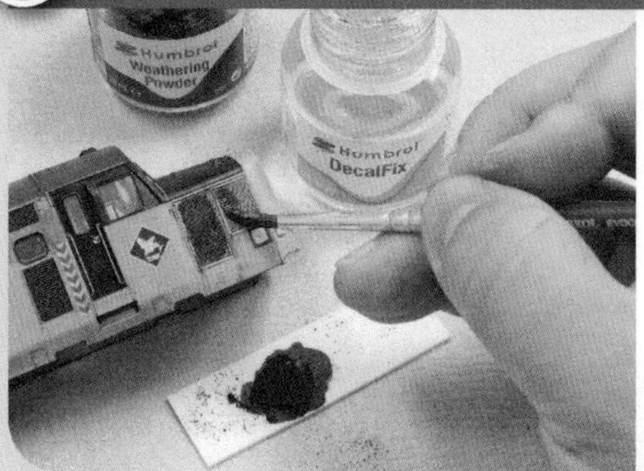

For the bonnet-side grilles at each end, Smoke was mixed with Decal Fix to create a paste. This was then painted onto the grilles (working on only one corner of the model at a time), ensuring that the mix was worked in between the louvres.

9 Wiping off to leave a residue

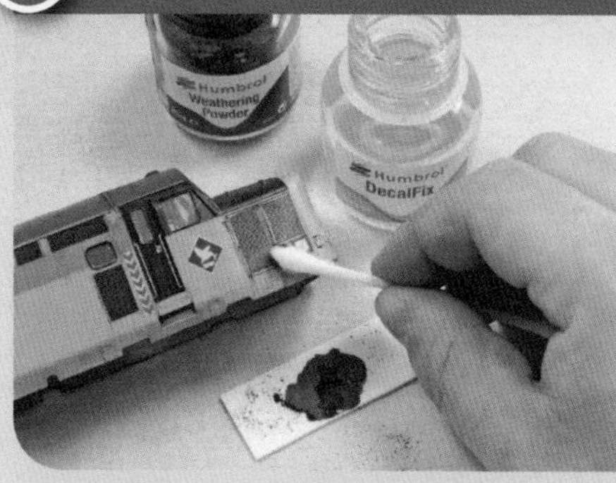

Almost immediately after application, a cotton bud was wiped across the grilles (using only light pressure) to leave a residue of the paste between the louvres.

10 Finishing touches

The model was reassembled and treated to a light pass with matt varnish from an aerosol to seal all the 'dry' powder in place. Additional embellishments included picking out the buffer shanks with metallic silver enamel paint and using tiny spots of gloss varnish to simulate oil and grease deposits on the fuel tank, spring detail and buffer heads.

Index

Acknowledgements

We are grateful to the following modellers, who contributed articles and/or created the layouts featured in this book: Simon Addelsee, Ian Allcroft, Clive Anscott, Andrew Beard, Ken Ballantine, members of Bentley Model Railway Group, John Bottomley, John Brewer, Tony Buckland, Ron Curling, David Dobbs, Ken Gibbons, Peter Goss, Ian Graham, Paul Jones, Dean Knights, Richard Lane, Steve & Ann Lewis, Paul Lunn, David Malton, Paul Marshall-Potter, Richard Morris, Alan Munday, Roger Nicholls, Dave Oliver, Cliff Parsons and team, Mike Pearson, Bob Petch, Andy Peters, Ian Pethers, Bob Phelps, members of Redruth Model Railway Club, Gareth Rowlands, Willy Smith, members of Soar Valley Model Railway Club, Mike Thomas, Craig Tiley, Tim Tincknell, Bill Tock and Len Weal.

Printed by
William Gibbons & Sons Ltd., P.O.Box 103,
26 Planetary Road, Willenhall, West Midlands WV13 3XT.

Peco Publications & Publicity Ltd,
Beer, Seaton, Devon, EX12 3NA, England.
Telephone: 01297 20580 Fax 01297 20229
Website: www.pecopublications.co.uk
Email: railway-modeller@btconnect.com

Glossary of terms

Big Four
Colloquial term describing the four big railway companies which existed after the Grouping in 1923, namely the Great Western; London, Midland & Scottish; London & North Eastern; and Southern railways.

Capacitor Discharge Unit (CDU)
An optional electrical device used to provide power for operating solenoid type point motors. It produces a short, intense burst of electrical power which gives an intial boost to the motor and ensures the blades of a point are moved positively from one side to the other.

Crossover
Two points laid together to allow trains to cross over from one line to the next. There are facing and trailing types. On the prototype, facing points were avoided as much as possible, but are more common today.

Diamond Crossing
Special piece of trackwork where one track crosses the other at an angle.

Double Junction
A junction of two tracks where one track crosses the other via a diamond crossing.

Double Slip
A diamond crossing with two pairs of blades. It is in fact the equivalent of two points placed toe-to-toe, but takes up much less space. It is used especially at station approaches and in goods sidings.

Electrofrog
Peco trade name for its turnouts with electrically live frogs.

Feed
The exact place where electric current is fed to the rails. The feed is regarded as the positive terminal in the control circuit. In a train set, power clips provide both the feed and the return connections. With a more advanced model railway, the feed and return connections are usually soldered wire droppers.

Fiddle Yard
Hidden area of a layout containing sidings in which trains are rearranged or changed before returning to the scenic area. Also called hidden sidings or off-stage sidings, they effectively represent the rest of the distant railway. A simple fiddle yard consists of a fan of sidings or loops. To save space in a fiddle yard, and eliminate the need for points, sector plates and traversers can be used.

Frog
Part of a point where the two diverging rails meet in a V. In the prototype they tend to be called 'crossing noses'. In model form there are dead frogs, which mean the frogs are electrically insulated (and usually made of plastic), and there are live frogs, where the whole frog is metal and electrically live to the tip.

Insulfrog
Peco trade name for its turnouts with insulated (ie electrically dead) frogs.

Loop
A long siding connected to the running line via a point at either end. There are crossing loops, which allow trains running in opposite directions to pass each other on a single track railway; passing loops where a slow train can lay-by to be overtaken by a faster train; and run-round loops which enable a locomotive to run from one end of its train to the other.

Nationalisation
The merging of all UK railways into one state-owned company. This occurred on 1 January 1948 with the birth of British Railways.

Operating Area
Space where the layout operator can sit or stand to control train movements.

Point
Commonly referred to these days as turnouts – especially throughout the Peco range – or switches. A special piece of track that allows a train to move from one line to the next.

Point Blades
Sometimes known as 'switch rails', these are finely tapered rails which make up the moving part of a point and divert the train or vehicle from one line to the next.

Pre-Grouping
The term used to describe the era of railways prior to the Grouping in 1923.

Privatisation
The dissolution of the nationalised railway system, which broke it up into individual privately owned companies. The official date of privatisation was 1 April 1994.

Rail Joiner
Used with model track for joining two rails together. There are metal ones (for conducting electricity) and plastic ones (for use when a track joint must be electrically isolated).

Return
The exact place where electric current returns from the rails and back to the controller. The return is conventionally regarded as the negative terminal in the control circuit.

Scenic Break
The part of a layout where the trains disappear from view into a hidden section. Scenic breaks can be devised in a number of ways but use of an overbridge or tunnel mouth is especially popular. Sometimes just a simple hole in the backscene is sufficient.

Sector Plate
A length of board with a series of sidings on it which is pivoted at one end. They are almost exclusively used in fiddle yards. By rotating the sector plate the running line can be aligned with any of the hidden sidings in turn, allowing the storage of locomotives and complete trains without the need to use points. Some sector plates are pivoted centrally and are known as 'train turntables'. They allow the reversal of complete trains without the need to lift any of the stock off the track.

Self Isolating
This term is used to describe a point which is wired so that electrical continuity is only directed to the route to which the point is set. In general, proprietary points are self-isolating, allowing a locomotive or train to be held stationary on the line to which the point is not set.

Solenoid
An electro-mechanical device consisting of a coil of very fine insulated wire wrapped around a hollow cylindrical core. When energised, the solenoid creates an electro-magnetic field which has sufficient energy to pull a soft iron rod through the hollow central core. The mechanical movement can be used to throw point blades or move signal arms. Two solenoids arranged inline can be used to make a twin-solenoid point motor such as those made by Peco.

Three-rail
System of layout wiring, such as the original Hornby Dublo equipment, which uses a central rail as the electrical feed with the return being through the two running rails. Though electrically sound, it was not at all prototypical and was eventually superseded by two-rail.

Tiebar
A metal rod in the prototype but in model form is usually made with plastic. A bar that joins the point blades together and moves them simultaneously from one side of the point to the other.

Traverser
Used in both prototype and model form. On the layout it is used more usually in the fiddle yard and consists of parallel tracks mounted on a deck which can be moved sideways. It enables the running rails to be aligned with any one of the traverser sidings, allowing locomotives and trains to change tracks without the need to instal points.

Turnout
See point.

Turntable
Often abbreviated to TT. A rotating bridge or circular plate of various sizes for turning locomotives or wagons. A locomotive turntable is an essential part of most steam depots, except perhaps on branch line engine sheds. Wagon turntables were usually found in cramped warehousing sites where it was impossible to lay curved track.

Two-rail
System of layout wiring using one running rail as the feed and the other running rail as the return, ie one rail is positive, the other negative.

Wire Dropper
Electrical connecting wires soldered to the side or underneath of the rail which pass through a hole in the baseboard surface, enabling layout wiring to be hidden from view.

Printed in Great Britain
by Amazon